The History of Qatari Architecture

In the Name of Allah, the Most Gracious, the Most Merciful.

Dedication

I dedicate this book to all the masons and builders who built the unique buildings illustrated in this book, whom we recognise as the true architects.

To our merchants and travellers who brought creative ideas from other cultures that made our architecture as wonderful as it is.

To my wife and children.

Ibrahim Jaidah

I also would like to dedicate this book to all the people whom have contributed to make this book a great illustration of traditional Qatari architecture.

Malika Bourennane

Ibrahim Mohamed Jaidah
Malika Bourennane

THE HISTORY OF QATARI ARCHITECTURE

from 1800 to 1950

SKIRA

Design
Marcello Francone

Editorial Coordination
Emma Cavazzini

Editing
Timothy Stroud

Layout
Antonio Carminati
Serena Parini

First published in Italy in 2009 by
Skira Editore S.p.A.
Palazzo Casati Stampa
via Torino 61
20123 Milano
Italy
www.skira.net

Printed and bound in Italy.
First edition

ISBN: 978-88-6130-793-3

Distributed in North America by
Rizzoli International Publications,
Inc., 300 Park Avenue South,
New York, NY 10010, USA.
Distributed elsewhere in the
world by Thames and Hudson
Ltd., 181A High Holborn,
London WC1V 7QX, United
Kingdom.

Acknowledgements

I would like to express my sincerest gratitude to all those who made it possible to complete this book.

Special thanks to H.H. The Emir Shaikh Hamad bin Khalifa Al Thani, for reviving our wonderful culture in all its aspects – from architecture, music and poetry to all the other arts – and preserving the rich local heritage of Qatar, not just to protect, understand and explore the country's past but to use it as a base in the building of a modern nation founded on solid roots and a strong identity. I will always cherish the collection of photographs taken by early travellers to Qatar that was given to me by H.H. when I was starting out; it opened my eyes to what is truly Qatari architecture and made me dedicate my career to researching and practising the Qatari vernacular.

To my mother, who is a father, sister and best friend, who taught me how to dream, imagine and create; without whom I would never be who I am.

To all those who are like a peaceful reef in the stormy ocean… my friends and colleagues.

To Dalal Farhat, for helping me produce the materials for this book over the past 11 years.

To Macario Cammanong, for his wonderful imagination, which made it possible to transfer surveys and photos into wonderful sketches.

Compiling this book seemed like a dream. For many years I was overwhelmed and surrounded by the results of my research until Malika Bourennane joined my firm. Through her work, all those piles of drawings, books and photos were turned into workable resources. Special thanks go to her for analysing and compiling the materials that have been incorporated in this book.

Ibrahim Jaidah

Contents

Preface

Traditionally, in the old architecture of Qatar the urban development of cities and villages was based on the creation of agglomerations of housing units. These agglomerations were the essence of traditional Qatari architecture, which can defined as an architecture of social values. Historically, Qatari architecture has developed from the requirement to satisfy different social factors such as religion, privacy and the extended family. In addition to these, the climate also played a major role, dictating the overall shape of the buildings, their facades and openings.

After the discovery of oil Qatar became a wealthy country and began to embark on the construction industry. This has led to a large expansion in the number of high-rise buildings and other modern types, and in consequence Qatar has seen the transformation of its vernacular architecture. The new modern architectural language was developed at a high social level that extended beyond mere details to take in the overall form of the house. It is argued here that the loss of local, vernacular traditions may have been due to a simultaneous weakening of the values attributed to traditional structures and style, which would have facilitated the spread of the new style by freeing it of its status associations. Moreover, with the introduction of modernity and modernisation, developments in architecture and the variation of building types in Qatar resulted in the construction of high-rise glass buildings that bear no relation to traditional Qatari architecture. This wave of exciting new architecture in the country should not, however, be allowed to divert attention from the heritage of traditional building forms. In Qatar, varied forms of traditional architecture exist that combine distinctive decorative features with forms that have developed in response to the region's demanding climate.

The rapid physical development of Qatar has resulted in numerous projects that have not employed the old Qatari architectural styles in their designs. In consequence, all those features that were part of the country's unique architectural character need to be analysed and documented. They merit preservation so that future generations will have the opportunity to appreciate and remember them. The purpose of this book is to record and demonstrate the history of Qatari architecture through the description of old cities and villages, public buildings and domestic spaces that have been declared part of the country's cultural heritage. The book also deals with the importance of the history of traditional Qatari architecture as a means to maintain the population's cultural identity.

Surviving traditional buildings give us a glimpse of the life of the people of Qatar before the discovery and exploitation of oil and gas sparked off the modernisation process. These buildings are endowed with elements that provide today's architects with lessons to guide contemporary design. Some architects in the Gulf region struggle to adapt to processes of rapid change and to revive traditional architecture, thus it is of importance to look at these old buildings and learn: about different spaces and their relationships, about why they were built and how they were used, and about their construction and materials. We are only just beginning to try and understand the relationships between spaces and openings – relationships that will give us a much better appreciation of such factors as house form, building design, privacy and gender. These relationships are the bearers of messages, which, if we succeed in reading them correctly, may take us into the minds of the past and enable us to create contemporary vernacular architecture using modern solutions and materials. Traditional architecture has the charm of creating strong links between buildings and their context, both physically and culturally. It has also long been a foundation of Qatari identity with regard to social interaction from the domestic to an urban scale. Its study and preservation promises to safeguard values and a character that not so long ago were at risk of vanishing.

I received my early exposure to architecture in the fascinating spaces that surrounded me as a young boy growing up in the old neighbourhood of Al Jasra. I used to walk around and observe the unique sense of space and elements of society reflected in Qatari architecture – the beautiful courtyards, and the roofs and arches that connect houses and link neighbours, families and society together. In my youth I was always interested in creating spaces, buildings and small houses out of pieces of wood, crafting artworks and visiting important, monumental buildings such as mosques, cathedrals and palaces. I realised that my innate creativity and passion for architecture had inspired me to learn more about the Arts. With this goal, I decided to travel to the United States and enrol in an architecture course at university.

Studying architecture stimulated my creativity, as reflected in the varied range of designs I sketched, but learning the history of architecture as seen in different places and civilisations was of equal inspiration, such as the Renaissance period, the Bauhaus and the many different movements of the past.

With its continuous evolution, architecture remains of constant interest, in the same way that the materials and engineering capabilities it makes use of also develop, greatly affecting general architectural practice – a consequence that has existed throughout history. As is happening in other Gulf countries, Qatar is at present undergoing huge expansion and changes brought about by rapid urbanisation. This is mainly the result of the discovery of oil and extensive international migration of many of its inhabitants. These factors have created opportunities for the construction industry to put up buildings and lay down infrastructures of modern design, mainly in the city of Doha, in new urban developments. However, the prototypes and urban design models of these new buildings do not reflect traditional Qatari architecture, and thus I felt that it was of great importance for a book to be written that illustrates the development of architecture in the country.

This book gives insights into and demonstrations of Qatari architecture. For us, the writers, we are hoping that it may give the new generations of architects an opportunity to work their way back towards the traditional architecture. We also intend to document Qatari vernacular architecture and make an exemplary patriotic contribution by exploring, researching and creating a unique history based on our own experiences and practices for future generations to remember. At present it is very important to revive the cultural heritage by keeping pace with research and ascertaining the key concepts of traditional Qatari architecture as it disappears, replaced by modern architecture. Our approach has twin prongs: the demonstration of traditional designs in various projects and the revival of local traditional architecture.

The primary aim of this book was to illustrate different Qatari buildings from the past. Some inaccuracy in the names of the owners and buildings, or the descriptions of the houses themselves can be assumed as our sources of information were survey-related studies and oral accounts. However, during our research we noticed that some changes and additions had affected, to different extents, most of the buildings described, which we assume were mainly carried out during the 1960s and '70s. In our drawings we have attempted to minimise certain elements added to the old buildings and to maintain others, for example, parapets and roofs. We are also hoping to translate the second edition of the book into Arabic, and intending to include buildings that not have been described in this edition as well as the names of the buildings' owners.

The Survey of Old Qatari Buildings conducted by GHD and the Building Engineering Department for the Supreme Council of Culture was used to describe the majority of Buildings in this book. In our opinion this survey is the most valuable resource in existence for the documentation of Qatari Architecture.

Introduction

The purpose of this chapter is to provide the reader with an introduction to Qatari vernacular design with its relation to Islamic architecture. A number of common aspects and values in the Islamic world – such as religion, tradition, privacy, extended family, and even climate, have played a major role in the innovation of space planning and the architectural design seen today in a number of old cities and towns.

It should be recognised that vernacular or traditional architecture all over the world, especially in the warmer climates, evolved ways of building to achieve acceptable levels of comfort. These ways of building meant that the building configuration and its fabric would largely resist hot or cold climatic conditions to provide thermal comfort. If additional devices were required to enhance comfort, they would be of a supplementary nature. When compared to modern building practices, this strategy was inherently more energy conserving.

Architecture is not only related to buildings but represents the identity of peoples and civilisations. It has also defined unique structures that have demonstrated the identity, the shape and the image of a city. The qualities and features of architecture in the Islamic world set it apart from all other architecture. Its most outstanding feature is the focus on interior space as opposed to on the outside or facade.

The most typical expression of this focus on inner space is in the traditional house. Rectangular dwelling units are typically organised around an inner courtyard. The facade of this house offers high windowless walls interrupted only by a single low door. Often these courtyard houses are clustered together in a walled complex to serve the needs of extended families. The courtyards are used for carrying out domestic activities as well as being the setting for social interaction. Entrance to the complex is through a single door that leads to a passageway from which the individual dwellings can be reached. It has been said that the traditional courtyard house is never a completed project. As family size increases, more rooms are built on the lot's unused land. Once the land around the courtyard has been covered, expansion occurs vertically.

The Arab house is never complete: as each extended family grows, so does the house, thereby reflecting the history, accumulated growth and family structure of a number of generations. The assertive nature of the individual Islamic dwelling can be clearly seen in the construction of modern houses. The open-air interior courtyard performs an important function as a modifier of climate in hot, arid areas. It allows for outdoor activities with protection from wind and sun, and also serves as an air-well into which the cool, night air can sink. And the plain, thick-walled street facade of the house – with few or no windows – is designed to resist severe elements like hot winds and sand. The roof is usually flat with high parapets. The most characteristic decorative feature of the courtyard house is the ornate roof line. The architecture of the courtyard house has been called the *architecture of the veil*. The introverted nature of this architectural typology expresses the need to exclude the outside environment while protecting that which is inside: the family and its private life. Because of the lack of emphasis on external appearance in Islamic architecture, a building –a mosque, for example – might be hidden from view by secondary, adjacent buildings. If the facade is visible, it is rare that this will give any indication of the building's size, shape or function.

In "What is Islamic architecture" (in *Architecture of the Islamic World,* Thames and Hudson, 1978) Ernst J. Grube writes that the dominant form of true Islamic architecture is its hidden interior. In other words, it is architecture that must be experienced by being entered and seen from within. Closely related to the idea of "hidden architecture", Grube notes, is the absence of specific architectural forms for specific functions. Most forms in Islamic architecture can be adapted to a variety of purposes: structures for a specific function might assume a variety of forms. Furthermore, Grube writes that generally Islamic architecture is given to hiding its principal features behind an unrevealing exterior; it is an architecture that does not change its forms easily (if at all) to accord with functional demands, but rather tends to adapt functions to preconceived forms that are basically the contained inner spaces.

The Gulf's architectural forms have to some extent been limited by two important factors, those of climate and the availability of building materials. The principal feature of Arabian residential architecture has always been the measures taken to protect the inhabitants from the heat of the Gulf summer. This requirement has led to houses being built with thick walls for insulation, with few windows, and with devices designed to take advantage of any potentially cooling breeze. Thick, well-insulated walls help to minimise heat gain by conduction, but this needs to be reinforced by reducing the effects of the heat. Consequently, a common feature of Arabian indigenous architecture is the absence of windows on the exterior walls of a house. Another characteristic of traditional Gulf townscapes was that the buildings tended to be very closely clustered together, separated only by narrow shaded alleyways. This meant that buildings offered each other mutual shading, but this may simply have been a by-product of clustering buildings closely together for greater security within a defensive perimeter or city walls.

Compared with other areas of the Islamic world, there appears to be very little written about the traditional architecture of the Gulf, and even less about Qatar. It can be argued that Qatar's architecture is not representative of the whole of the Gulf, but it is a reasonable place to look at if for no other reason than that it might be later compared with the architecture of other areas of the Gulf. It is also important to document what is there – and what can be remembered – as there is now very little left in Qatar that is truly original. Whatever the architectural characteristics are in the region, the key to an understanding of Gulf architecture is to begin with the basic unit: the house. From the standpoint of urban design, the house is private and should not display itself to the street outside. Only one or some of its external walls will face the street and that is maintained in as unassuming a manner as possible. If there are openings other than a door, then they must be screened and it should

be impossible to see into the area occupied or used by the household. This is also true for door or gate openings, which usually have screen walls behind them guarding the privacy of the household. Privacy is paramount in Islamic households. The key point to understand the manner in which Qatari houses and their plots are used, is that there is a significant separation of the male and female spaces. Certainly a difference in scale of the house can make the layout less or more complicated, but all houses should fulfil the requirements of privacy.

Privacy is an issue of the utmost importace in the Islamic world. In old Qatari architecture, it was preserved by providing a men's area in the house where all the visiting guests would reside, called the *majlis*.

Regarding the entrance to the house, in the majority of cases in Qatar the main entrance was the only entrance; however, in a number of places in the Islamic world there would be a family entrance used exclusively by the women of the family.

The majority of cities and towns in the Islamic world have been designed as compact clusters where façades are blind, houses share the same walls and the streets form very narrow alleys. This type of design, which is also widespread in Qatari architecture, was supposed not only to preserve the extended family tradition, whereby all the houses owned by one family were built near each other, but it also succeeded in maintaining a certain degree of privacy within and outside the house. Furthermore, narrow streets generated shaded areas, highly needed in such hot climate.

Exploring Qatari Architecture
A Brief History of Qatar

This chapter explores the history of Qatar since the dawn of the human presence till nowadays. The sources of this chapter are the historical studies found in the official websites linked to Diwan Amiri and Carnegie Mellon University in Qatar.

First Qataris: The Dawn of the Human Presence and Earliest Flint Tools

Pre-9th millennium BC

Most authorities now agree that at present no conclusive evidence exists of Paleolithic man having inhabited the peninsula of Qatar. When the Arabian Gulf was dry, some 70,000 to 44,000 years ago, early man may have wandered across what was then a marshy plain, but no signs of human occupation from this period survive. This late date for the occupation of the whole of eastern Arabia, including Qatar, has only recently been accepted.

The pioneering Danish archaeologists who were the first to work in Qatar in the 1950s and 1960s saw no reason to dispute the assumption by their predecessors in the Middle East that the Arabian peninsula had been inhabited for some 55,000 years. The Danish prehistorian Holger Kapel classified a large collection of stone tools into four groups, and in 1967 he published the *Atlas of the Stone-Age Cultures of Qatar*. Group A, which he considered the earliest, included massive, primitive-looking hand-axes found on ancient shorelines far removed from today's coast. The three other principal Stone Age industries which followed culminated in Group D, which included superbly-crafted tanged arrowheads.

It was not until the excavations in Qatar by the French mission from 1976 onwards that an entirely new set of dates was assigned to Qatar's pre-history. Excavations at Al Khor on the east coast proved that Group A was not a Paleolithic industry. The site under investigation contained hearths, tools, shells and fish teeth and yielded carbon 14 dates of 5340–5080 and 5610–5285 BC. Nearby was an area covered in flint tools and flakes, representing three clearly-defined levels of occupation. Group A and Group C tools in the same layer, together with a fragment of Ubaid pottery from Mesopotamia, showed that the Group A tool-making industry could not have been either Paleolithic or earlier than the other groups.

The Beginning of Agriculture

9th to 5th millennium BC

The increase in rainfall that occurred between 8000 and 4000 BC made eastern Arabia a more hospitable place than it had been. It is this period which saw the gradual emergence of Neolithic cultures throughout the Middle East. Domestication of animals and cultivation of plants evolved in Egypt, Turkey, Iraq and Iran.

In Qatar, the wandering population of hunters and gatherers learned to harvest wild cereals. Two limestone querns found at Al-Da'asa on the coast south of Duhkan may have been used for the preparation of wild grains.

The making of pottery is thought to have begun around 6000 BC. Pottery from Al Ubaid, a small site near the ancient city of Ur in Iraq, began to turn up in Qatar less than a thousand years later. Early Ubaid pottery is thin, greenish in colour, and characterised by lively painted designs in red or dark brown. Since the discovery of Ubaid pottery in the Eastern Province of Saudi Arabia in 1968, it has been found on over forty sites in Saudi Arabia, five in Qatar and recently at Umm al-Quwain and Ras al-Khaimah in the northern Emirates. Clearly, people were able to travel long distances at that time, making short, coastal hops between settlements. The earliest craft were probably constructed of bundles of reeds lashed together, or of palm-frond ribs. Small inshore fishing craft made of palm-frond ribs, known as *shashahs*, were in use in the Gulf until a few years ago.

The First Seasonal Settlements

5th to 4th mill. BC

Between about 5000 and 3500 BC the coastal areas of Qatar and neighbouring lands were inhabited by a population that survived by hunting, gathering and fishing, and living in temporary campsites to which they returned annually. Middens of shell and fish-bone accumulated at such seasonal sites. No trace of their shelters remain, but possibly they constructed palm-frond huts similar to the *barasti* that were widespread in the Gulf until the oil era. Southern Mesopotamian fishermen working the rich fishing banks off the Arabian coast may have visited these sites from time to time to salt and dry their catch, bringing pottery with them and giving it to the local inhabitants or perhaps exchanging it for fresh meat.

The first Ubaid potsherds in Qatar were found by the Danish expedition at Al Da'asa in 1961 but were not identified until later. Post-holes from shelters survived at the site, and a poignant find was a neat stack of domestic implements: querns, a grinder, a pounder, a slab of coral. Whoever piled them so carefully clearly intended to return, but never did so.

Ubaid pottery of a slightly later date than at Al Da'asa was found at Ras Abaruk by the British Expedition of 1973–74.

An area 200 metres square yielded not only potsherds but quantities of flint debris and tools amounting to an estimated 11,000 kilos. The amount, plus the bones of mammals, birds and fish, suggests that the site was of a hunting-gathering-fishing camp visited seasonally over many years.

French excavations on low hills at Al Khor in 1977–78 revealed more pottery from this period, as well as fragments of stone vessels. Between 1977 and 1981, eight cairn burials out of a group of eighteen were excavated, dating from the Ubaid period. Each consisted of an oval pit over which a low cairn of limestone slabs had been erected. Four skeletons in flexed position remained intact. The graves contained shells, and bone and stone beads, including seven of obsidian.

Closer Relations with Mesopotamia

4th to 2nd mill. BC

Contact between the people of southern Mesopotamia and those of the eastern Arabian coast, including Qatar, continued over centuries. During the middle of the fourth millennium BC the world's first walled towns were built in the fertile plain surrounding the Tigris and Euphrates rivers. By the end of the third millennium Sumerian scribes began to make written records by pressing the triangular ends of reeds into clay tablets to make cuneiform letters. This was approximately the time of the reign of Menes, the Egyptian ruler who united Upper and Lower Egypt and so opened the way for the great civilisation that was to flourish for millennia along the banks of the Nile. The link between Sumer and Egypt was almost certainly via the Gulf.

In the early third millennium BC Sumerians settled on Tarut Island off the Saudi coast, some 100 kilometres north-west of Qatar. The earliest inscriptions mentioning 'the land of Dilmun' are understood to refer to the eastern coast, including Tarut. Later, from 2450–1700 BC, Dilmun, a peaceful trading civilisation, was centred in Bahrain. Sumerian city states traded silver, textiles, oil and precious resins for building timber, stone and copper. The trade was channelled through the Gulf, and Bronze Age cultures sprang up and flourished along both coasts. Third millennium cuneiform tablets refer to Magan, centred in what is now Oman, and Meluhha in the Indo-Pakistan region.

That Qatar played its part in this complex trading network is evident from the presence of Barbar pottery, a product of the Dilmun civilisation, at two sites: a depression on Ras Abaruk peninsula, and a small island in the bay of Khor Shaqiq, near Al Dakhirah, where excavations by the Qatar Archaeology Project took place in 2000.

The Influence of the Babylonian King Kassite

2nd and 1st mill. BC

By about 1750 BC the local societies of the Gulf had entered a period of apparent decline. Southern Mesopotamia, which had previously acquired most of its foreign materials from the east and south-east, was now reoriented towards the north and west. Kassites from the Zagros mountains had assumed power in the middle of the second millennium, and Dilmun became absorbed into Kassite Babylonia. The only archaeological site in Qatar dating from this period lies on the southern shores of the small island in the bay of Khor Shaqiq. Here, crimson and scarlet dyes were being produced from a species of murex, a marine snail. Elsewhere, the dye is known as 'Tyrian purple' owing to its large-scale production at the great city of Tyre in the Levant, and Khor Island is the first such site to have been discovered in the Gulf. The middens of crushed shells contain the remains of 3,000,000 snails. Quantities of coarse Kassite pottery was found, which are the remains of large vats used in the dye production. Scarlet and purple-dyed cloth was much in use in Kassite and post-Kassite Babylonia, its use was controlled directly by the ruler and was confined to immediate members of the royal family and to powerful religious figures. Khor Island provides the first evidence that this dye did not come exclusively from the west.

No evidence of Iron Age settlement has yet been found in Qatar, although elsewhere in eastern Arabia Iron Age villages have been uncovered, whose inhabitants cultivated dates and cereals. Camels had been domesticated, first as milk animals and some time later as beasts of burden, as early as the third millennium, and it may be that some of the inhabitants of Qatar had by this time become nomadic pastoralists, herding not only camels but also sheep and goats.

The climate was now much drier than in the Neolithic period.

Alexander the Great and the Seleucid Period
1st mill. to 3rd century BC

Much later the use of the camel as a riding animal developed, and in the 9th century BC camel-riding Arab warriors make their first appearance. They were the descendants of the Amorites, a people known to the Sumerians and the Hebrews.

By the sixth century BC nomads and settlers were becoming interdependent, not only for the exchange of commodities but for the operation of overland trade using camels, a a development that augmented the traditional trade routes.

Alexander the Great conquered Persia in 326 BC and went on to enter the Indian sub-continent, having a substantial fleet constructed near present-day Karachi. He then ordered his Cretan admiral Nearchos to explore the coast of Arabia in preparation for a proposed conquest of the region. The exploration took place, probing the entrance of the Gulf at Ras Musandam. But Alexander's sudden death, three days before the campaign was due to begin, ended the plan of conquest.

His vast empire was divided among his generals. The eastern portion was taken by Seleucis Nictator, who set up his capital at Seleucia on the west bank of the Tigris. At this time the city of Gerrha, on the eastern coast of Arabia not far from Qatar, became a major centre for both land and sea trade between Arabia and India. Pottery fragments from this period, known as Seleucid, occur in some quantity at Ras Uwainat Ali

on the west coast of Qatar and a nearby cairnfield on Ras Abaruk, consisting of over 100 burial mounds – the largest such concentration in the country – has been provisionally dated to the Seleucid era.

Classical Period: The Graeco-Roman, Parthian and Sassanian Influences
3rd c. BC to 7th c. AD

There is further evidence of human activity in Qatar during the Graeco-Roman period in the form of a fish-processing complex, again at Ras Abaruk. A stone building consisting of two rooms and a third open to the sea is located on an old shoreline on the north-west of the small peninsula. Nearby is a mound of fish-bones and several hearths. Some large smooth pebbles, possibly used as hammers, originate outside Qatar, suggesting that the site probably represents a temporary station where fishermen from elsewhere landed to dry and preserve their catch.

Around 140 BC, the rise to power of the Parthians, a Persian people, had begun to interrupt Graeco-Roman trade between Europe and India via the Arabian Gulf, and the Red Sea again became the main link between Rome and the East. But in 225 AD the Parthians were overthrown and the second great Persian empire, that of the Sassanid dynasty, was established. They established their capital in Mesopotamia at Ctesiphon and reversed the practices of their predecessors, controlling the trade of both the Gulf and the Indian Ocean and forcing the decline of the Red Sea as a rival commercial route. By 570 AD they succeeded in extending their control as far as the Yemen. Both sea and land trade routes were arteries, not only of trade, but of cultural influence.

The Sassanids traded a vast range of commodities and it is possible that Qatar contributed two luxury items: purple dye and pearls, to Sassanid trade.

A number of areas in Qatar provide archaeological evidence of the involvement of local people with the outside world during this period. At Mezruah, north-west of Doha, an oval burial cairn contained two skeletons, one with an arrowhead embedded in a bone of the forearm. A fine iron sword and some iron arrowheads lay in the grave, which also contained an almost intact Sassanian glass.

An intriguing feature was the hamstringing of camels around the grave: early literature refers to the sacrifice of camels around the grave of a hero, and also of horses. Near Umm-el-Ma' on the north-west coast a small settlement contained fragments of glassware and pottery including 'Sassanian-Islamic' glazed ware, and a fragment of red, polished ware dating to the second or third century AD. Such finds are evidence of a standard of living well beyond subsistence level.

The Rise of Islam
7th c. to 15th c. AD

By the end of the seventh century Islam had spread throughout the whole of the Arabian peninsula, ending the paganism practised by much of its population. Politically, the third to seventh centuries had seen a reversal in the fortunes of the Arabs of eastern Arabia. The trading opportunities they had once enjoyed had reverted to the control of the Sassanids, Byzantines and others. The call to embrace Islam came in 627–29 AD and the Christian governor of the Hasa Oasis in the Eastern Province of Saudi Arabia quickly adopted the new faith and sent a delegation to the Prophet in Medinah. Others followed suit. Within a short time Islam had helped to do away with the old tribal rivalries by teaching the equality and brotherhood of all Muslims. This new ideology was to provide an inspiration to Arab Muslims and introduce a new era of expansion and exploration, as Islam was taken to the furthest corners of the civilised world.

In the year 750 the Umayyid dynasty, based in Damascus, was overthrown by the Abbasids, who were descended from the uncle of the Prophet. The capital was relocated to Baghdad and this had far-reaching political and economic implications for the Gulf as, inevitably, trade benefited from the wealth and sophistication of the Abbasid empire. This was the golden age of trade in the Gulf, which was to last until the tenth century. Merchants traded with India, China and East Africa and the port of Suhar in Oman rose in importance. This period of adventures by merchant seamen gave rise to the stories of Sindbad the Sailor. The demand in Abbasid Baghdad for pearls undoubtedly enriched the pearl fishers and merchants of Qatar; however, few accounts of Qatar's fortunes exist from this period. The geographer Yaqut al Hamawi, who died in 1229, referred to rough red woollen cloaks being exported from Qatar, and also commented that the markets for horses and camels in Qatar were renowned.

The inland settlement of Murwab near Zubara dates from this period. It consists of some 250 houses, a fort and two mosques. The fort is the oldest in the country and was built on the site of a still earlier fort that had been destroyed by fire. The style of both is similar to forts in Iraq dating to the eighth and ninth centuries. Sherds of fine quality ceramics and glassware give a hint of the relative affluence of the town-dwellers. Two other smaller settlements in the area are contemporary. Murwab is the only sizeable ancient settlement in Qatar not situated on the coast.

In the thirteenth century the island of Hormuz, at the mouth of the Gulf, established itself as a new maritime power and by the mid-fourteenth century had gained control of Gulf trade.

The Gulf entered into a new period of prosperous commerce and Hormuz became famous among European trading nations.

The Portuguese Influence
15th c. to 17th c. AD

In 1498 the Portuguese confirmed a direct sea route to India by rounding the Cape of Good Hope, and they set out to create a new maritime empire. Their aim was to divert the rich trade from India and the Far East to Europe via the Cape, away from the Red Sea and the Gulf. Amid scenes of extraordinary brutality on the part of the conquerors, one by one the Arab ports fell to the Portuguese. In 1515 Hormuz was captured by Admiral Albuquerque and, shortly afterwards, Bahrain. In 1520 Qatif in eastern Saudi Arabia was sacked. Throughout the 16th century, Hormuz remained the base from which the Portuguese controlled the Gulf as far as Bahrain.

Meanwhile, in the northern Gulf, the Ottomans from Turkey had established themselves, taking over Basra in Iraq between 1534 and 1546 and making several unsuccessful attempts to dislodge the Portuguese from their strongholds. But eventually the task of maintaining control over the Indian Ocean routes, so far from home, proved beyond the resources of the Portuguese. In 1622 the Safavi ruler Shah Abbas I of Persia, who was allied with Britain, ousted the Portuguese from Hormuz.

Fort after fort fell to the allies, and the Portuguese were finally expelled from Muscat in 1650. They continued to trade in the Gulf, as did the Venetians, but their days of power were over.

The British Influence
17th c. to 1939 AD

Between 1630 and 1700 the Dutch East India Company, which had been set up in 1602, dominated Gulf trade along with the English East India Company formed two years previously. Portuguese trade had been monopolised directly by the crown, but this was a new era of 'merchant adventurers' from Holland, England and, later, France.

Ottoman power was gradually weakened.

In 1620 the Persians took control of Basra; even so Ottoman authority persisted in a reduced form until 1680, when it yielded to the ascendancy of the indigenous Arabs under the leadership of the Bani Khalid, who dominated eastern Arabia.

As for Qatar itself at this time, life continued to centre around the immemorial activities of pearling and fishing, with Bedouin pastoralists grazing the interior. The main east coast settlements were Al Wakrah, Al Bidda' (later to become Doha), Al Huwailah and Al Ghuwairiyah. Al Huwailah emerged as the principal pearling port of the early eighteenth century.

On the north-west coast Murair fort was built in 1768 to protect Zubara from land attack, and the following year a ship canal two kilometres in length – a remarkable engineering achievement for the period – was dug from the sea to the fort to facilitate the unloading of supplies. Zubara remained vulnerable from the sea for the next hundred years.

Meanwhile, in 1745 Sheikh Mohammed bin Abd al Wahhab began preaching adherence to orthodox Islam, and this led to a powerful reformist movement that swept the region. It was taken up by the Al Saud of Najd, who reached Al Hasa in 1793, replacing the Bani Khalid. Zubara gave shelter to some of the refugees from Al Hasa, and as a consequence of this Zubara was besieged in 1795 by the Saudi commander, along with Al Huwailah.

By 1820 the British had grown concerned that turbulence in the Gulf could interfere with their trade with India, where they had become the imperial power. Their intervention among the ruling sheikhs resulted in a General Peace Treaty.

The following year Qatar was deemed to have broken the new treaty and the East India Company's cruiser Vestal bombarded Doha with their cannon and set the town on fire – although few of the inhabitants of Doha knew of the treaty's existence. The first Maritime Truce took effect from 1832 and, brokered by the British, helped to outlaw warfare during the pearling season from May to November, and the truce was generally popular. But in 1841 a further bombardment of Doha was launched by the British. A more serious breach, however, was to take place in 1867 when Doha and Wakrah were sacked by a combined force of ships and men from Bahrain and Abu Dhabi. The following June the Qataris, though outnumbered, courageously counter-attacked Bahrain.

The Emergence of the Al-Thani and the Beginning of Modernity
19th c. to 1939 AD

The upshot of this conflict was the receipt of compensation by Qatar and the emergence of Sheikh Mohammed bin Thani Al-Thani as the most influential man in the country. Sheikh Mohammed had recently moved from Fuwairat to Doha. The family stemmed from the Arab tribe Tamim, whose descent is traced back to Mudar Bin Nizar in the eastern parts of the Arabian peninsula.

The treaty ratified on 12 September 1868 effectively marked the end of interference on mainland Qatar by the country's neighbours, and the consolidation of Mohammed bin Thani's status as the internationally recognised ruler of the country.

The eclipse of Saudi power in the later nineteenth century led to renewed interest by the Ottomans in the Arabian peninsula. They sent a deputation to Doha to persuade Qasim, the son of Mohammed bin Thani, to accept the Turkish flag. The British did not intervene but made it clear they recognised no Turkish rights to Qatar.

The following year, 1872, saw the arrival of Turkish troops in Doha and the occupation of a fort. For the next forty years Qasim bin Mohammed Al-Thani charted a course between the Ottomans and the British. Qasim was a man of courage, tenacity and skill, and managed to maintain his position as the chief personage and recognised ruler of Qatar while balancing the two super-powers. But he resented Turkish interference in Qatar's internal affairs and their increasingly oppressive demands for tribute.

Matters came to a head when the Ottoman Wali of Basra, Nafiz Pasha, paid a visit to Qatar in 1893, accompanied by 300 cavalry and a regiment of infantry. Qasim retired to his fort at Wajbah, some 15 kilometres west, and declined the Wali's invitation to visit Doha. On 26 March 1893 Nafiz Pasha made a surprise attack at night on Qasim's headquarters, but the Qatari warriors bravely routed the attackers, who withdrew to Doha Fort.

The Ottoman defeat was a landmark. Qasim's reputation and popularity were firmly established. Although he went into semi-retirement soon afterwards, allowing his brother Ahmad, and later his son Abdullah, to deputise for him on many matters, he continued to exercise control over broad policy. He constructed roads to connect the main towns of the country, and set up religious schools and one secular school. On his death at an advanced age in 1913, he as succeeded by Abdullah.

In 1915 the last of the Turks left. By this time Britain and Turkey were fighting on opposite sides in World War I. The Anglo-Qatari Treaty of 1916 guaranteed British protection of an independent Qatar from both land and sea attack on the premise of Qatar's neutrality in the World War, and secured the establishment of postal and telegraphic services in Qatar. The World War left prevailing authority in the region with the British. Meanwhile, nationalistic movements were arising in countries bordering the Gulf.

The 1930s saw a time of severe economic hardship when the Western world was in the grip of a recession and the demand for pearls fell. In 1933 the Japanese developed the cultured pearl, which dealt a crippling blow to the Gulf pearl industry from which it never recovered. The population of Qatar at this time dropped steeply.

At this low ebb in the fortunes of Qatar, a new hope appeared. Although the possibility of the existence of oil in the region had been realised as early as 1908, when oil was discovered in southern Iraq, followed by a treaty in 1913 with the ruler of Kuwait that secured British companies the rights to oil exploration, little happened in the southern Gulf for many years. It was not until the American oil company Socal struck oil in Bahrain in 1932 and then negotiated a concession with Ibn Saud, that the British began to take an active interest in the oil potential of the Arabian peninsula. They focused their attention on Qatar.

News of the attractive terms offered by Socal to Ibn Saud reached Qatar, and the British had to convince Abdullah that he should favour the more modest offer made by the British-controlled Iraq Petroleum Company (IPC).

No one was yet to know the true potential of the oil that lay beneath the territory and any geological evidence was largely the preserve of the oil company, which took care not to exaggerate to Abdullah his country's potential. However, he proved a shrewd negotiator and was able to extract various concessions from the British, including further guarantees from external attack. On 17 May 1935 a document was signed granting the Anglo-Persian Oil Company, a participator in IPC, exclusive rights for production, refining and marketing of petroleum, as well as for natural gases and other by-products. After a series of down payments, Abdullah was to receive royalties of 3 rupees per ton.

The Contemporary Development of the State
19th c. to 1939 AD

Oil was finally discovered at Dukhan in October 1939, but World War II put a stop to production. In 1942 the three appraisal wells were sealed and the company's staff packed their bags: prosperity was to be delayed. Meanwhile, there was more hardship, with the sharp fall in revenue from pearling, and food shortages. Many Qataris temporarily emigrated. It was not until December 1949 that the first ship left the shores of Qatar bearing a consignment of crude oil.

By 1944 Sheikh Abdullah had handed over much of the management of the country's affairs to his son Hamad, a popular leader, respected for his faith, ability and breadth of vision.

Yet Hamad himself suffered ill health, and died in 1948, while his young son Khalifa was still being prepared to succeed in his role. Ali, Hamad's eldest brother, was appointed ruler in 1949 when Abdullah abdicated because of old age, with Khalifa bin Hamad as the Heir Apparent. In 1960 Ali abdicated in favour of his son Ahmad, with Khalifa as Deputy Ruler. Then in February 1972 Khalifa assumed power from his cousin, endorsed by the ruling family and the people of Qatar. The country had become formally independent of Britain's protectorate role in September of the previous year. In June 1995, Sheikh Hamad bin Khalifa Al Thani acceded to power.

Traditional Islamic Architecture
Principles and Dimensions of the Built Environment

The tradition of Islamic architecture embodies principles of physical environment and social organisation. These principles have been established in the islamic architecture to create a place. This chapter aims to explore some of the principles which Islamic architecture has set up for other societies and their living environment.

Physical Environment Dimension

In the past the traditional physical environment was not based on the aesthetics of buildings and streets. The city of the past was built within a scope of very simple principles that are required to understand the gradual transformation of the urban pattern form of the old Islamic cities. The tradition of Islam in relation to the physical environment grew to protect the environment and to maintain the privacy of people and their accessibility to public spaces. The Islam as tradition aimed to preserve certain values that have been set to be a guidance for everyday life.

Eisenberg (in Mortada 2003) argues that at every scale – the natural environment, the urban environment down to the house or the building – there are principles based on the larger objective supporting the social values of Islam. This author adds that a balance between the use of resources and their preservation is needed. At the urban level, the requirements are to fulfil the objective of social integration and the provision of people's needs. Eisenberg continues saying that at the house scale the preservation of privacy is required to be maintained, which has a strong impact on the design of the house. It can be argued that the old city formation was the result of the combination of all the three scales mentioned above.

The domination of the mosque in the early Muslim built environment is very common in the old traditional districts. The location of the mosque in the old urban environment was intended not only to maintain and support faith, but it was also a mark structure creating a public space which could be seen from different angles of the streets.

Social and Economic Values

Whatever the architectural characteristics are in the region, the key to an understanding of Gulf architecture is to begin with the basic unit: the household.

Privacy

From the point of view of urban design the house is a private unit and should not therefore display itself to the street outside. Usually only one of its external walls would face the street, and this is maintained in as unassuming manner as possible. If there are openings in the wall other than a door, they should be screened in order to make it impossible to see into the area occupied or used by the household.

This is also true for door or gate openings, which usually feature screen walls behind to guard the privacy of the household – privacy is paramount in Islamic societies. One key point to understand the manner in which Qatari houses are devided is that there is a significant separation of the male and female areas of the house and its spaces. Certainly a difference in scale of the house can make the layout less or more complicated, but all houses invariably should fulfil the requirements of privacy.

Relationships of the Owner and His Plot

It should be borne in mind that many residential developments have considerably more spaces, both internally and externally. In addition, in the men's area of the house there would be accommodation for guests. Sometimes a guest would sleep overnight on the floor of the *majlis*, but at least one room with associated bathroom facilities would be a preferred solution. You can see from the diagram how the site is organised to provide privacy. Essentially there are four kinds of space, whether internal or external:

- private
- semi-private
- semi-public
- public

Access to Housing

In different parts of the Islamic world the architecture and planning of the sequence of spaces was handled differently, perhaps as a reflection of the degree of importance the different societies attached to this hierarchy, but also as a consequence of the amount of land available and the degree of safety against attack, as well as the degree of comfort in terms of insulation from noise and nuisance. For example, a house in the *medina* of Fez, Morocco, features a sequence of four stages to access the public street: first, an angled exit from the courtyard leads to a private corridor which, in turn, gives onto a blind alley that leads you to the public street. However, the entrance to a house in Tunis and other cities would have a small room off the main thoroughfare or blind alley that served as a semi-public space, but which also provided *majlis* privacy to the rest of the house by means of further turns or screens.

In Qatar, houses might open onto either a blind alley or a public thoroughfare. In both cases there was usually a space incorporating either a dog-leg or right-angled turn in order to provide privacy.

Two further points are worth of attention here. First, that the positioning of the street doorway to a house was often a concern. Generally, it was felt that doors should not open directly opposite one another, even on large streets, as there was an argument that harm could result. It appears that the issue at stake was primarily privacy, but there were also issues relating to the uses that might develop around the opposite entrance. Sometimes a complicating issue was the rights of or duties incumbent upon the property owners, as these varied with their house's position in relation to the entrance of an alley. The second point to make is that, when writing about the entrance to a property, essentially what is referred to is the men's entrance. In the Islamic countries there is what is known as family entrance. It allows women and family to access the house and it maintains privacy. In contrary, in Qatar, there is only one entrance for the majority of houses. This entrance has two doors. The big door is for family and goods and the small one for guests' access.

The Essence of Qatari Vernacular Architecture

The objective of this chapter is to describe the roots of Qatari architecture and to provide with more detailed illustration of house design. The house was considered very important social space at that time.

Certain coastal examples of Qatari architecture suggest that their builders either came from Iran or were influenced by its architecture. Similarities are seen to exist between Iranian and Gulf architecture, the main difference being due to the amount of finance available for construction, although there are also slight architectural differences. In contrast, the builders of houses in the interior of the country were influenced more by the architecture of the Najd. This particularly applies to the fortified houses constructed at locations like Rayyan, Wajbah and Umm Salal Muhammad. Further evidence of the origins of the people who lived on the coast and inland can be seen in the family names: those on the coast having many Persian names, and those inland sharing the same names as peoples elsewhere in the Arabian peninsula.

With regard to the builders, the same elements of construction and building techniques both in south Iran and in Qatar were almost similar. Examples of these works are the Doha Museum at Feriq al Salata and the re-building of Sheikh Khalifa bin Hamad's house in the new Diwan al Amiri in Doha. The town of Zubara itself is a different example, having being constructed by the members of the Al Khalifah who settled on this tip of Qatar and ruled Bahrain from there. Despite the examples of the architecture of the interior, coastal architecture for the mass of housing in Qatar followed the inexpensive models of the other side of the Persian/Arabian Gulf but, of course, in a more concentrated pattern as family housing groups were joined together near the shoreline. The littoral village of al Jumail, between al Ruwais and al Zubarah in the north of the country, is typical of the abandoned villages around the country and illustrates how little remains of buildings constructed of *hasa* and *juss* if they are not maintained for a few decades. In the early 1970s al Wakra had many old buildings that have now, for the most part, disappeared. This row of buildings had their first floors facing the sea to benefit from the on-shore breezes.

Al Jumail was a relatively small fishing village and you can see that, compared with it, al Wakra was better off as its economy depended more on pearling. The more affluent merchants were able to build houses that matched more closely the similar models already established elsewhere in the Gulf. Sheikh Abdullah bin Vassim Al Thani – the great-grandfather of the present ruler of Qatar, for instance, employed an *ustad* or *benna* – a master builder from Bahrain to construct the palace complex he developed in Feriq al Salata, to the east of Doha. Similar but better organised buildings could still be seen in Wakrah, in the early 1970s. There it was possible to see the remains of a considerable number of relatively good quality buildings, including a number of wind towers, which were more numerous there more than anywhere else in Qatar. At first sight this might seem correct but it is in fact a long way from the truth. Not only do the various cultures differ in many ways, but so do the environmental conditions that have influenced the characteristics of the constructions. In addition, the length of time that the States have had to create their structures and the amount of funding available for materials have also played their role. Dubai, for instance, is very humid compared with Doha, with Manama in Bahrain perhaps falling between them.

Architecture in Qatar

This section in this chapter aims at exploring the main patterns in house design. These patterns have been analysed in a study carried out by Yarwood and El Masri in Al Muharraq area, Bahrain (Yarwood and Masri, 2006).

House Form and Layout

The house is the smallest urban unit in the socially generated urban pattern. Generally speaking, the form of the house comprises four elements. The first is the courtyard, which forms the heart of family life. It is open to the sky and provides a source of ventilation and sunlight. The courtyard was also considered a private space where women can carry out domestic activities such as washing, cooking, and storing. It was also a place of social interaction where family members could meet and talk. The number of courtyards would vary from one to four depending on the size of the family and its wealth. The second element is the various spaces that line the courtyards. Apart from the kitchen, stores and animal stall, all rooms are multi-functional, but their utilisation depends on climatic conditions. A room may be used for sleeping, eating, socialising and so forth. Ground floor rooms may be used in cold weather and upper rooms in hot weather, during which period people would sleep on the terraces. Also the upper room would gain heat on a still summer's day, but having a low thermal capacity this heat would quickly be lost at night, thus it might be slept in at night as it would be cooler than the ground floor. Ground floor rooms would lose heat through the night and could be used on a still day. However, a wind would cool the upper room more effectively than the lower room.

Building Design in Qatar

The most important design considerations are privacy and territoriality. Spaces are segregated on the basis that male visitors are separated from the family, young men from young women, servants from others, and passers-by from residents. The social function and hospitality is so important that the *majlis* access route is always to some extent separate from the family territory. As the family grows, older son may take a room in the house for a time. In this case separated plot, territory, and new access will be established. The general qualities of housing groupments represent unified units. It is resulted from the common structural module and the open space known as courtyard. The street doorway – and sometimes the door between courtyards calls for visual reinforcement, celebration, strengthening of the place, and transition between spaces – courtyards and lower and upper rooms.

The climate and geographical nature of Qatar both played a role in the nature of the country's architecture. The Gulf is an arid desert region, but the fact that it borders the sea modifies the climate in certain important aspects. Rainfall is light but in certain areas humidity can be very high. Thus roofs are flat and always aim provide shade in spaces leading to rooms and courtyards to provide comfort. Due to the quantity of sunlight and the strong heat, window openings – in the rectangular "Al Darish" form – are very small when compared with the very large walls, making almost blind facades. In ordinary rooms, the windows look out into the courtyards. With regard to the *majlis* and upper rooms, the windows open onto the courtyards and streets. In addition, there are openings for ventilation and sunlight known as *badjeer* that are mostly found in *majlis* and the upper rooms, but not on the ground floor.

The Use of Space and Spatial Qualities

Shade was given to the front of the house by covering the circulation, which commonly projected from centre of the house. Both the terrace and the veranda were designed to provide shade so that the members of the household had shaded spaces for sleeping, washing, storing, and sitting.

Rooms in a house had no particular designation other than the washroom and the *majlis*. All the rooms could be used for any purpose by anybody in the family, the only restriction being the privacy required for the male and female members of the family, and the privacy of the area allocated to the family's normal activities. Cooking was usually carried out in the courtyard or in a shaded space on the *liwan*.

Food was served on dishes or bowls placed on a *sufra* (a circular woven mat in a room of the house), or on the veranda, depending on the weather and time of day. Rooms had no specific function apart from the *majlis*, while washrooms were used by day and night throughout the year for a variety of purposes. Traditional Qatari houses consisted mostly of one or two rooms, with an internal bathroom attached to each room.

The water closet was usually built inside one of the corners of the courtyard. The *majlis* sitting room was totally separate from the house rooms, and usually located near the main entrance of the house. In spite of the simplicity of this type of traditional houses, it has a courtyard, which considered a breather of the residents of the house. It receives big amounts of light and sun heat during the day, a thing which we miss in most of the buildings of today. The middle of the courtyard was utilized for constructing a shelter of palm stems and its branches where people used to sleep on its rooftop during the nights of summer. Also a part of the courtyard was utilized for breeding goats, one of the wide spread customs in Qatar and Arabian countries at that time.

(Al Kholaifi, 1990: 124) adds that every house there is a courtyard and it represents the source from where the sunlight and ventilation and also from Badjeer in the walls. The houses vary from the space they occupied. The rich people usually have larger space than other groups. In this larger space, they have room for guests, room for women and section for servants and an enclosure for animals. He adds that the majority of old houses had a water well inside them, where water supplies acquired for washing clothes, cleaning kitchen wares, showering the courtyard and irrigating the trees, if any.

The House Decoration

The houses of rich people in Qatar and the Gulf states were characterized with the carved gypsum decorations, mostly of geometrical style, and sometimes plant pictures. The same applies to the wooden doors, particularly its peaks, and windows. Windows might be decorated with glass of brilliant colours. The owners of the houses had diversified its decoration from both inside and outside. From outside, the walls were decorated with rectangular wall recesses with pointed and semi-circular ends and arches. Inside the rooms, there were the inscribed gypsum decorations used for plastering walls. They were either geometrical or plant figures decorations being carved in specific places and organized in the form of rectangular, lobed or semi-circular panels. This is in addition to various types of friezes under the level of the wooden roof. It often looks like the saw teeth or the graded pyramid. No room was without 'Rawashin' which are rectangular recesses, 70 × 50 cm approx., depth 25 cm approx., used for putting lamps, toilette equipments, rose water jugs and so on.

SHORELINE

SHORELINE

N

Urban Development of Qatari Cities and Towns

The previous chapter, on *traditional Islamic architecture: principles and dimensions of the built environment*, described how Islam has generated different lifestyles that have in turn had a great influence on architecture in the Arab world. In the past, the factors that affected town development, the form of individual buildings, the manner of house construction, and the styles of Qatari architecture were the climate, the availability of resources and building materials, a strong desire for privacy, and close family and neighbourly relationships. Generally speaking, Islamic urban centres evolved over long periods of time in which the individual skills of generations of *craftsmen* added variety and a diversity of styles to the environment. This chapter considers Qatar's four largest urban centres: Doha, Wakrah, Al Khor and Umm Salal Muhammad.

The majority of Qatari urban centres witnessed similar growth to other Islamic cities. As Figure 1 (Doha 1937) demonstrates, the towns of Qatar originally developed on the coast for two reasons: fishing and trading. However, the urban development of Doha, Wakrah, Al Khor, and Umm Salal Muhammad was also affected by the most typical characteristic of the traditional Islamic city: the unity of architecture represented by the sequence of spaces in the *mosque, suq, palace* and *private home*. It is this trait, plus the introduction of new architecture and style, that has maintained the identity of Qatari culture. The growth of the collective form of housing arises from the extension and the subdivision of inherited properties, which creates an intensification of land-use.

Mortada (2003) analyses how traditional Islamic principles affect people's physical environment. He argues that the Islamic town is based on three scalar elements – the natural environment, the urban environment and the house – and that these were the major forces in the shaping of urban centres and compact residential quarters. In the section that follows, the four largest Qatari cities are considered in relation to Islamic, urban and social principles.

As already stated, fishing and pearling constituted the primary economic activities of the past. In consequence, Doha, Al Khor and Wakrah grew up on the coast. Two other important factors that contributed to the growth of these three centres were the natural environment and the availability of materials and resources. The traditional Qatari house developed out of the use of local materials and the need for sustainable living: for instance, roofing materials were provided by the leaves and trunks of palm trees that grew in groves around the towns. Stones and mud were also used by families in the construction of their houses, who were assisted by the local *ustad*.

Mortada writes that the distribution of urban functions in the traditional Muslim environment was mixed, and was mainly driven by social integration. He says that in the traditional environment, every individual had equal access to public spaces and religious and commercial facilities. The pattern followed in most Qatari cities was of a centrally located mosque and *suq* surrounded by residential neighbourhoods. The integration of the mosque and the *suq* in residential quarters gave inhabitants easy access to these places without the need for traffic systems. The importance attached to family privacy was not encroached upon by the location of religious and commercial facilities in public spaces.

The compact form of residential areas in traditional Islamic urban centres was a precise reflection of the values placed on social interaction, extended family, neighbourly relationships and the preservation of privacy. Thus it can be argued that Qatari cities have been formed not only by urban and architectural planning, but also by the social dimension. Mortada claims that the Muslim urban environment contributes to the

Fig. 1 Doha, 1937

Fig. 2 Doha, 1947

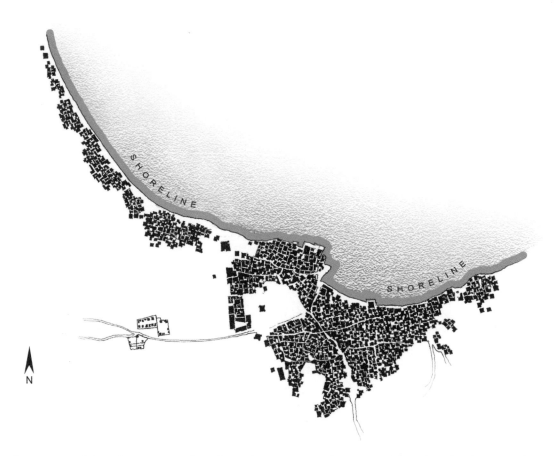

achievement of the Islamic principles of social interaction, strong family ties and good relations with one's neighbours, and that the urban environment, the house and social integration are interrelated. Figures 1-3 demonstrate that the physical attachment of dwellings to one another as a result of social integration limited the size of neighbourhoods and reduced the walking distance to religious and commercial facilities.

Strong family ties, neighbourly relationships and privacy have also contributed to the morphological development of Qatar's cities. Figures 1-3 show that the streets in the old city of Doha were narrow but they served the community of the past. Mortada points out that in the planning of Islamic cities, the hierarchical system of road width regarded streets as no more than the gaps between houses wide enough to meet the demands of movement and communication. He adds that determining the width of a road by its functionality sustained urban compactness, helped to offset the impact of the climate, and supported the principal of social interaction.

Exploring Qatari Cities

The city of Doha used to be known as Al-Beda'a, an important town on the east side of the Qatar peninsula. Al Rostamani (1993) tells us that Doha consists of nine neighbourhoods (*fareeq* or *furqan*), and some sources claim that Doha was built after Wakrah. The Al Thani family built their palaces and mosques in specific locations in the centre of Doha for reasons of symbolism, protection against the climate, and military purposes. The layout accords with the Islamic urban tradition in which the ruler's palace lay at the centre of administrative, political and upper-class social life. This formed the physical and functional core of Doha, from which the city grew in different directions. There are several interesting maps that were drawn from aerial photos taken during the twentieth century. Maps of Doha (created in 1937, 1947, 1952 and 1959; figures 1-4) reveal the city's slight expansion northwards and southwards and enable its approximate boundaries at different times to be established.

The fluidity of the city along the coastline is interesting. It was this growth that provided the basis for the gradual process of land reclamation which allowed the town to grow. Examining the tendency of certain street lines to reflect the growth process, we see that the main trading routes along the shoreline and fortifications by-pass the dense, narrow alleyways of the old town. The seafront in Figure 1 shows residential quarters close to the shore where goods were landed. The

Fig. 3 Doha, 1952

SHORELINE

SHORELINE

SHORELINE

N

Fig. 4 Doha, 1959

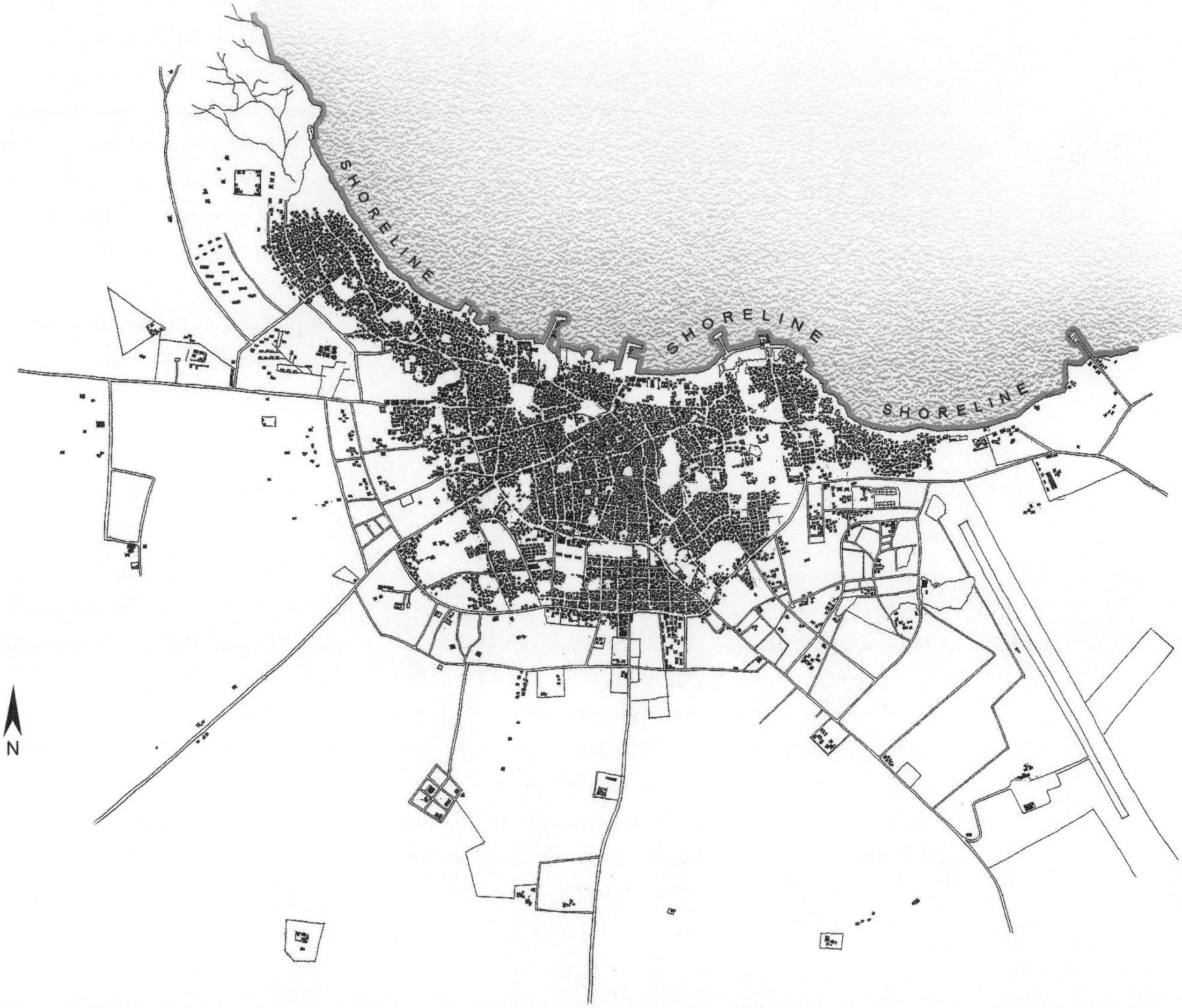

SHORELINE

SHORELINE

SHORELINE

N

houses there may well have been built and inhabited by merchants for this very reason.

The old city of Doha can be thought of as a family or housing zone. The spatial arrangement parallels the social pattern in the sense that socially related families clustered together, perhaps for reasons of extended family, security and power. As the town grew, families expanded across new roads, which mostly ran along the coastline. Each extended family would create plots for its constituent families and secondary roads would be built to give access to them. With the development of the family tree over the generations, however, each plot would be subdivided many times over. The consequence was traditional Qatari housing in which the different sections are close to each other and functionally shared, thus enhancing social interaction within the family and between neighbours. Islam encourages an extended form of family to maintain strong social ties. Mortada explains that this social structure helps to prevent families from splitting up. The preference for the extended family to live in a single building or in a series of houses close to one another meant that the Muslim-Arab house was never complete. As family grew, so did the house. The road pattern modelled the social structure of the community. The pattern was the result of neither engineering nor physical features but purely social relations. And because the distances between houses and the religious, educational, commercial, and other facilities in a town were short, walking was the preferred means of transport.

Figures 1-3 show the integration between the private and public realms in the built-up area. Public realms were mainly the mosques and *suqs* in the centre of the city, and private spaces primarily the residential quarters. The compactness of the built-up area resulted from the configuration of residential clusters, narrow streets and open spaces. Furthermore, the residential blocks were small and the dwelling units similar in shape and size, and maybe even in height. The majority of old Qatari houses had courtyards, which helped to create a natural air flow and maintain a low temperature inside the buildings.

A typical narrow street in the old part of Doha encouraged face-to-face contact between pedestrians, and the tiny squares surrounded by and providing access to dwellings enhanced interaction between residents and thus social cohesion. The city's larger roads started in the centre, where the mosque and palace were located, and gradually diminished in size, form and function as they radiated into the residential area. The organic fabric and street hierarchy were dictated by the location of the main buildings, the mosque, *suq* and palace. This traditional hierarchy of outdoor spaces and street width established a hierarchy of privacy and social integration.

Figure 4 (Doha 1959) illustrates the rapid growth of the capital at that time. The 1950s saw the beginnings of development along the shore, construction of the road infrastructure, and the first major new building. Government buildings were constructed.

It is thought by some that Wakrah was the first urban centre to be established in Qatar, built even before Doha. Its first inhabitants made a small living from fishing but the little evidence that remains indicates that Wakrah was relatively wealthy, partly due to pearling. The buildings in Wakrah, both in their arrangement and decoration, were some of the best in the country, though it is interesting to see that there is an *arrish* in the foreground, a pitched-roofed building which would have been roofed with palm fronds. There were many old two-storeyed houses in Wakrah, most of which faced the sea so that their backs were to the west with its hot, afternoon sun and the *shamal*. They were also protected by *badgheer*, which allowed cooling winds to flow through the building but which could be closed in the event of rain or dust storms.

Umm Salal Muhammad is a town in the centre of the country and is different from most of the other urban developments in Qatar for that reason. Its climate is dry, and it has a small gardened area of date palms with ground crops beneath them supported by a reservoir of water contained by a small dam. Around this resource residential quarters began to grow and extend. However, compared with Doha and Wakrah to the south, Umm Salal Muhammad was relatively less developed. Constructed in a flat landscape, the town had a tall lookout tower from which warning could be given in the event of attack.

Al Khor was a much larger coastal town based on pearling and fishing. It was built on the slopes of a protected bay on the Arabian Gulf leaving room only for the fishing boats on its shore.

[1] In Qatar, the term craftsman is referred to by the word *ustad*.

Qatari Architecture

Al Kholaifi (1990) argues that Qatar and other Gulf countries have benefited from what has remained from the old architecture, which dates from the period between the seventeenth century and the beginning of the twentieth century. He has categorised Qatari architecture as follows: religious (mosques), civil (castles, houses, and souqs) and military (forts, towers, and walls). Each category has its particular function.

This chapter of the book aims at providing with an introduction to different buildings established in the past. This includes military buildings, domestic houses and mosques. The next chapters in this book, are arranged into many parts, provides a detailed analysis of military buildings, public buildings, mosques, palaces and domestic houses.

Military Buildings

Fortified buildings in Qatar fall into two general groups: buildings constructed specifically as fortified structures, usually within the colonial period, and those that developed a fortified character for protection.

The first type is typified by the forts at Al Zubara, Doha and Wakrah. This last fortification has a form of machicolation with a limited function. There are two levels of *'ayyin* from which to look out of or shoot, but they are designed to permit shooting straight ahead and do not allow for enfilade fire along the face of the building. The machicolation, however, does allow the defenders to deal with anybody who gets below them. The second type of structure – fortified housing – can be found at Umm Salal Muhammad and Doha. Umm Salal Muhammad is a special case as it features fortified housing as well as two watch towers. In consequence this site does not have the large footprint seen at Al Zubara and Doha forts, which are essentially protected courtyard developments.

The courtyard type of development was constructed more securely with particular attention paid to the weaker points of the structure. This typically resulted in tall circular towers at the corners of the structure to give greater security. Its two adjoining towers provide enfilading fire should attackers attempt to breach the wall. The reason for the rounded corners is that the desert stones with which walls were constructed are relatively small and irregular, making them difficult to bond together, particularly at the corners. There was no attempt to trim the stones to regular sizes and square them up, and this led to the corners of small buildings being reinforced internally with mangrove poles across the angle, and, where the walls were defensive, the corner was thickened and rounded, giving no easy point to attack. The fort at Zubara in the north-west of the country illustrates this point well. Although there is a square-sided structure forms part of the fortification, the main towers are rounded and battered and of considerable thickness to provide strength. An additional feature is the reinforcement of the towers at their junction with the ground, which helps resist a mechanical attack as well as weakening by water ingress. It is also worth noting the extent to which the towers project from the main walls. Internally this allows a small entrance to the towers from the first floor parapet, while giving a greater periphery from which to observe and defend the building.

Mosques

The mosques in Qatar have always been simple, comprising a simple room with its *mihrab*, which indicates the direction of Mecca, an entrance *sahan* and *burj* from which traditionally the faithful are called to prayer. Some mosques at Madinat al-Shamal in the north of the country, show not only the manner in which many old buildings have been allowed to deteriorate, but something of the character of the small mosques that were built all over the country. The *burj* in this case is typical of many small mosques, though a different shape. Generally mosques are rebuilt larger – and with a tall *burj* – to reflect the increased populations of the area they serve. Perhaps this is one of the reasons why there are few small mosques in existing communities, though this example used to serve a population that has moved on and abandoned its buildings. These structures represent a very definite architectural stage in the development of the country.

An old mosque in Wakrah demonstrate the characteristic shape of the early mosques in Qatar. These small buildings, with their tapering towers and simple *mihrab*, could be seen all over the country. Many of them have now been replaced by more modern constructions, which are thought to serve the community better. The building was relatively easy to construct, with the towers' battered walls and domed finish built manually by a relatively unsophisticated labour force. The result is a beautifully simple combination of forms that are sculptural in essence and suited to purpose.

In a recent reconstruction of a mosque near Umm Salal Muhammad, the minaret represents a later architectural type than the one in Wakrah and was developed for the call to prayers to be made more easily.

Domestic Houses

The first dwellings were simple and served the purpose of providing not only shelter and security, but also of making a visible claim to the land about. For the most part the first houses in the interior were small and made from mud bricks with, perhaps, an admixture of straw (known as *libbin*) and a pitched roof covered with palm branches. The width of the single room was determined by the span of the palms, which was approximately two metres. Little remains of such constructions today though, until the beginning of the 1980s, some were still visible at a number of settlements, particularly at Na'ijah, a little way south of Doha. More permanent houses were soon constructed from desert stones and

mud *or juss* mortar with palm branches for the pitched roofs. This type of construction is referred to as *arrish*. The patterns left by some of these developments can still be seen in the desert and work has been carried out to determine the extent and character of the constructions. The overriding reason for the choice of location for a settlement of this kind was the provision of water for the family and animals. The *bi'r* was dug by hand and would have a channel leading from it into which water could be poured and from which the animals could drink. These houses initially contained a single internal space and had just one opening: this was the doorway at the centre of one of the long walls of the building, which provided the source of ventilation and light. The photograph shows the ruins of a number of small buildings in a desert settlement. One of them was designed for a pitched roof covered with palm fronds – *arrish*. These structures have now all gone. The majority of the family's activities would have taken place outside the house, as was the custom in tented encampments, though it is probable that buildings of this kind were used by an individual rather than a family, as the right to use the land was established. The houses were loosely grouped some distance from each other. Their two most common characteristics, which they shared with tents, was to turn their backs to the prevailing north-westerly wind – the *shamal* – and to have a *bi'r* in the immediate vicinity.

Use of Space and Spatial Qualities

Shade was given to the front of the house by the simple expedient of covering the mangrove poles that commonly projected from the front of the building. The covering would have been initially a woven mat but, with progress, *juss* was later laid on top of the mat in an attempt to form a waterproof finish. Both the roof and the veranda covering were laid to convey water off the building rapidly and thus minimise the possibility of ingress. Roofs of this nature need constant mainte-nance but the materials were readily available and it was a simple job to effect. In the less well finished build-ings – which represented most desert buildings – the mangrove poles projected different lengths, there be-ing a reluctance to trim such a valuable resource. Rooms in a house had no particular designation other than the *hamam* (washroom) and the *majlis*. The *hamam* was di-vided from its adjoining space by a *qatiya* – a wall up to head height designed to give some degree of priva-cy. Sometimes, as in this example, there is *naqsh* deco-ration at the top of the wall. The important point to note is that the *qatiya* has to be clear of the ceiling as it is imperative that air circulate in this kind of space. For the same reason there was also a need for air to circu-late between rooms in larger houses. All the rooms could be used for any purpose by anybody in the fam-ily, the only restriction being the maintenance of pri-vacy between the male and female members, and pri-vacy reserved for the areas where daily activities were performed. Cooking was usually carried out in the courtyard or in the shade on the *liwan*. Food was served on dishes or bowls placed on a *sufra* (a circular woven mat) in a room of the house, or on the veranda, de-pending on the weather and time of day. Rooms had no specific function apart from the *majlis* and *hamam*, and were used all year round for a variety of purposes. In some houses particular members of a family might man-age to take over a specific room for themselves, which was, I suspect, a natural consequence of there being more consumer items around which needed space for storage and use.

MILITARY BUILDINGS

Merwab Fort (Abessi Era)

Introduction

Merwab is built on a fertile slope 4 kilometres from the coast and 15 kilometres north of Dukhan, between Al-Numan and Umm-Al-Maa. The fort was built on the ruins of an older fortification. There are about 250 houses around the site, constructed in groups. The largest group, built in a crescent configuration to the north of the fort, consists of 170 houses. Two other small groups exist, one to the west, and the other 1 kilometre away on the southern side. Excavation has revealed the ruins of two mosques on the boundary of the northern group. Furthermore, a group of tombs of different sizes has been discovered to the west of the south group of houses, and other, scattered tombs to the south of the fort.

The Second Fort

The fort is one of the largest remaining in Merwab Islamic Village. The general shape is a rectangle, with four round towers at the corners and five semi-circular towers. The semi-circular towers are located as follows: one each in the middle of the eastern and western walls. The north wall has an entrance 140 cm wide at the centre. The entrance opens onto the courtyard through a rectangular corridor.
The courtyard is surrounded to the north and west by 12 rectangular rooms of different lengths, the largest on the south-west corner. These are accessed from the main courtyard through doors 60 cm to 80 cm wide. The opening in the north wall is not the only entrance: there is also a side entrance 90 cm wide on the west side of the south wall, which was discovered in 1984.

The Walls

The walls are built of unfinished rocks and mud and are 140 cm wide in the south-east wall. The eastern wall acts as a retaining wall for the rooms. Its thickness varies between 40 cm and 60 cm. The height of these walls does not exceed 1 metre. In the south-east corner of the internal court is a well 150 cm across that decreases in diameter as it descends. The well was the main source of drinking water for the residents of the fort.

The First Fort

The second fort, which is rectangular in shape and is bigger in size, may have been built on the foundations of the earlier construction. Nothing is visible of the earlier construction's walls except the south and east walls, and a few bits of the north wall at its east end. Only three of the corner towers of the original fort still survive, one on the north-east corner, another on the south-west and the third on the south-west corner. Also, there are two towers in the middle of the east wall and one at the middle of the south wall. The west wall probably had one semi-circular tower. The French Commission that undertook excavation work on a part of the south wall and on some houses in the village between 1979 and 1981 dated this site to the Abbasid era.

• Aerial perspective of Merwab fort. The fort is characterised by a big courtyard and a number of towers

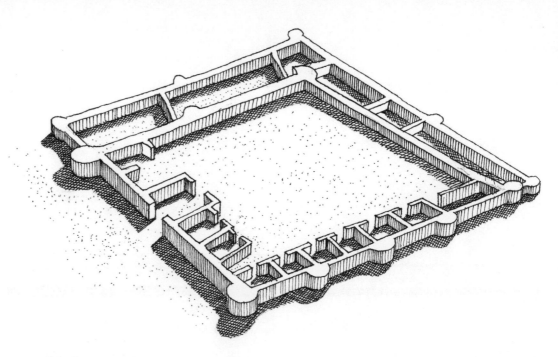

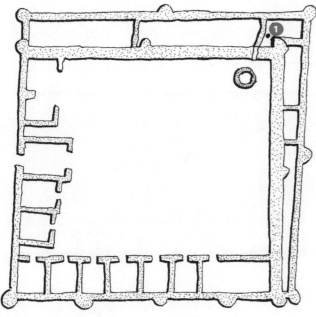

• This view is indicating the well which was a source of drinking at that time

• This view is indicating one of the towers

• Floor plan of Merwab fort. The rooms in this fort are of different forms and sizes. The structure of the rooms has defined the courtyard

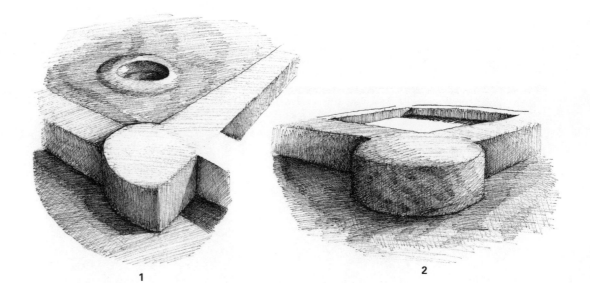

1

2

• Simplicity is the feature of all elevations of this specific fort

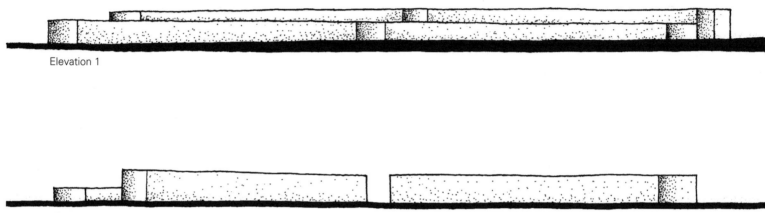

Elevation 1

Elevation 2

Elevation 3

Elevation 4

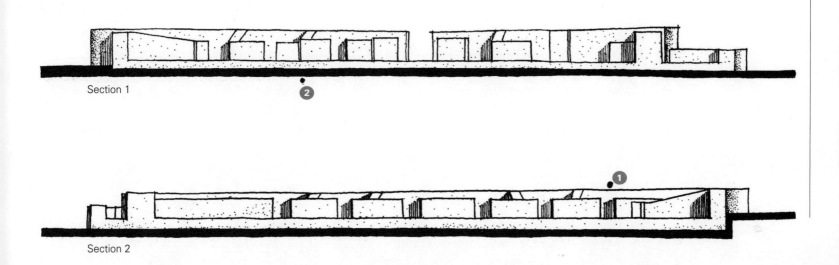

Section 1

Section 2

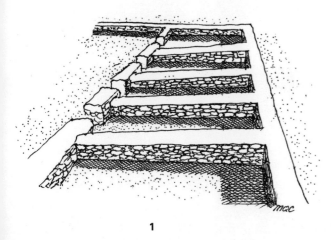

1

• This view is showing the rooms and material used

• The rooms and openings are almost similar

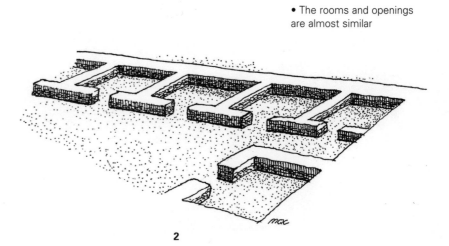

2

Al Zubarah Fort
(1937)

Introduction

Zubarah Fort is located to the north-west of Qatar peninsula, 105 kilometres from Doha. It was constructed by local builders in 1938 during the rule of Sheikh Abdullah Bin Jassim Al Thani. Its purpose was to defend the west coast of Qatar.

Description

The fort has a square plan with a wall 4 metres high and 1 metre thick, with round towers at each corner. Three of the corner towers are decorated with pointed parapets. The upper level walls and towers are fitted with small openings that offer protected observation and firing positions.

The fort was built of stone quarried in nearby hills, with mud as a bonding agent. The ground level has eight rooms on the west and south sides, while the east and north walls have longitudinal *iwans* that look onto the court through square arcades. On the north-east corner of the eastern *iwan* there is a washing area adjacent to a well 15 metres deep. A room exists under both the north-east and south-east towers, while the other towers are built on solid ground. Two staircases lead up to the four upper rooms on the first level of the fort.

• Aerial perspective of Al Zubarah fort. The fort is characterised by four towers. To mark the entrance one of the towers is designed to be different in shape and form

• The floor plan is simple with a courtyard and four towers

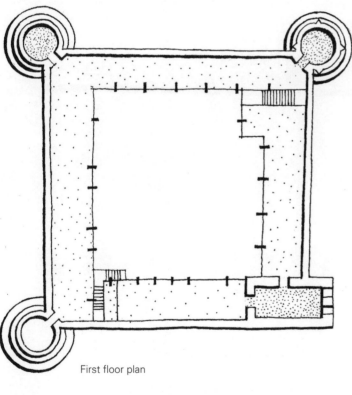

First floor plan

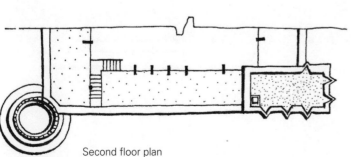

Second floor plan

• The perspective is showing the entrance and how it is marked by one of the real towers

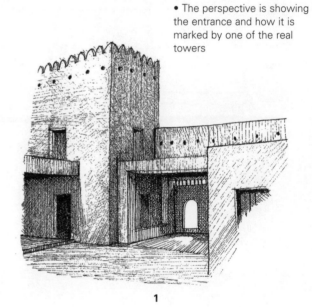

1

• All the rooms into the courtyard. The roof is accessible through the towers

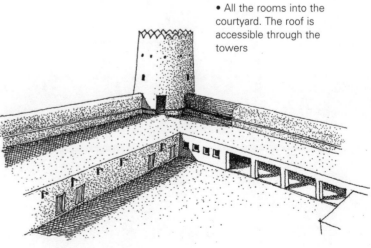

2

• This figure is showing the main entrance and some of the openings. The upper part of the towers has specific treatment

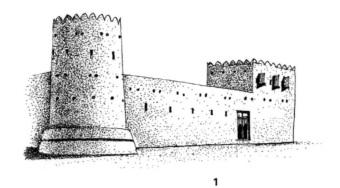
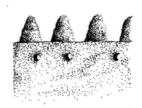

1

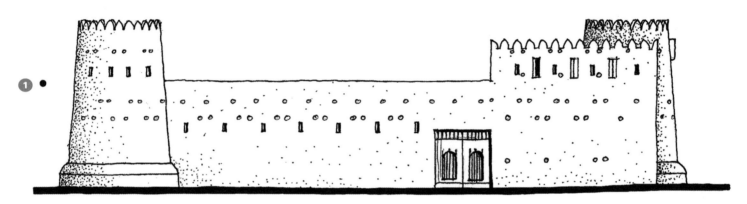

South elevation

• The elevations are of simple design with very few openings

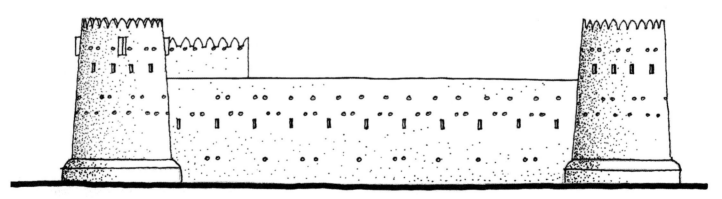

North elevation

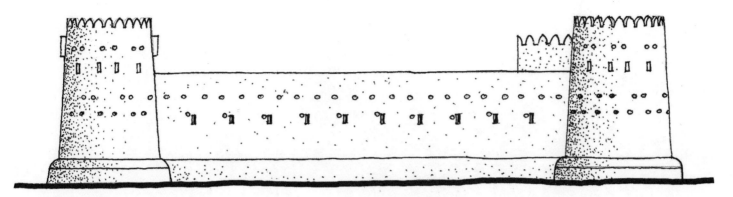

West elevation

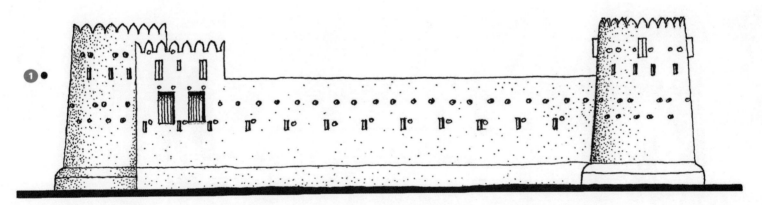

East elevation

• This view shows different
windows at one of the
towers

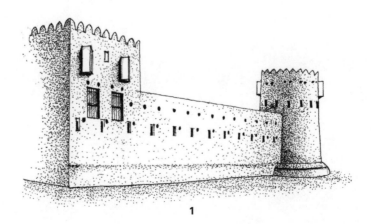

1

• Doors are all of the same
design. In this perspective
the stairs lead to the roof

1

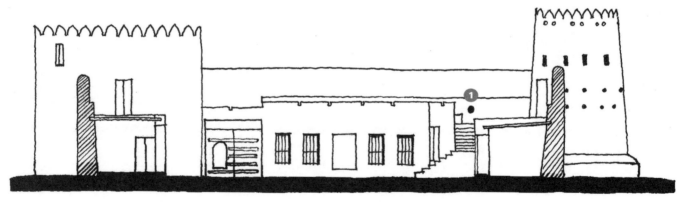

Section A

• This view shows entrance
to the shaded gallery

• A typical shaded gallery.
It is designed for walking
to the towers

1

2

Section B

Aarkyat Fort (South of Al Areesh) (18th century)

Introduction

Aarkyat Fort is one of several old military forts on the road between Zubarah and Madinat-Al-Shamal, close to the north-west coast of Qatar. The exact date of its original construction is not known, but coins and other artefacts found by archaeologists at the site date it to more than two hundred years ago, to at least some time during the eighteenth century. Ruins of buildings at nearby Zubarah City indicate that it was a thriving town by 1765, and evidence suggests that Aarkyat Fort dates from the same period. The present fort was partially renovated in 1988 but is once more falling into disrepair.

The name "Aarkyat" means "wells" in Arabic, so it was likely that Aarkyat Fort, like other forts in the same area, was built to protect the sources of water, the region's scarcest and most precious commodity. There was, in fact, a freshwater well 5 metres deep at the fort. There are ruins of a village close to the fort, so no doubt the fort was intended to protect the local inhabitants' water supply.

Within 5 kilometres of the fort are the ruins of four more villages: Al-Khuwair, Fareehah, Al Areesh, and Ain Mohammed. Zubarah City itself is only about 12 kilometres away to the south-west. Historically this area was the most settled part of Qatar due to its proximity to the sea and to Bahrain, a regional trading centre along the sailing route between India and Mesopotamia. Later, during the twentieth century, as Doha became Qatar's most important city, the north-west coast declined in importance as the Qatari population moved to and consolidated in Doha.

Architectural Description of the Fort

Aarkyat Fort is approximately rectangular, measuring roughly 22 × 38 metres, with corner turrets extending a further 2 or 3 metres. It is laid out in a typical military fort style with narrow rooms arranged in linear fashion around three sides of a large central sand and earthen courtyard. The only entrance is a 2.8 metre opening in the metre-thick front wall. The exterior walls surrounding Aarkyat Fort are relatively low, as far as military forts go, standing only about 3 metres high or less. Another striking feature of Aarkyat Fort is the total absence of architectural ornamentation: it is an unadorned, utilitarian structure and in that sense is a classic piece of military architecture. Even the walls are very smooth without any architectural articulation.

The only distinctive feature of the fort is the crenellated circular turret at the south-west corner, which is slightly more than 7.5 metres in diameter, rising about a metre higher than the adjacent west exterior wall and 2 metres higher than the south wall. There are rectangular turrets at the three other corners of the fort. Each of the turrets has one or more very small square openings (less than 20 centimetres wide) high up on the walls, providing some light and air, but primarily intended as gun holes for firing at attackers. The tops of each turret, except the one at the south-west corner of the courtyard, can be accessed by an outside stairway at each of the other corners of the courtyard, though for some reason one only goes halfway up the wall.

About a dozen rooms line three sides of the courtyard, most of which have doors that open onto the courtyard. None of these rooms has any windows. The rooms inside the three rectangular corner turrets are accessed through adjoining rooms that open onto the courtyard. The larger rooms were used as barracks, and the smaller ones for storing ammunition or other articles. There is also a small mosque just outside the exterior entrance, adjacent to the large circular turret at the south-west corner of the fort.

The existing configuration appears to be the result of an expansion of the original fort, which doubled the size of the courtyard to its present dimensions. The remains of the rock walls of the earlier configuration stretch across the middle of the courtyard and clearly outline several rooms that ran along what was the original east wall.

The fort was constructed using traditional materials, primarily horizontal layers of rock, covered on exterior surfaces with thick layers of mud plaster. Some walls, however, particularly along the front and rear facades, are constructed of adobe[1] brick not commonly used in Qatar, despite its greater strength and durability. The roofs over the rooms surrounding the courtyard were all constructed in the traditional manner, consisting of *danshal* wood beams, overlain with *basgill* and *mangharour*, and topped with a layer of rocks crowned with *tanqa al-tiin* mud plaster over the exterior roof surface. There are *marsams* along the outer parapets.

[1] Adobe brick is large rectangular sun-baked brick made from mud mixed with straw. It is very heavy, has good insulating qualities and is very durable. There are intact adobe buildings in the south-west United States that are more than one thousand years old. It has enjoyed widespread use as a traditional building material in many arid or semi-arid regions around the world, though it was not commonly used in Qatar.

• Aerial view indicating the courtyard and the foundations four turrets. One of the turrets is circular

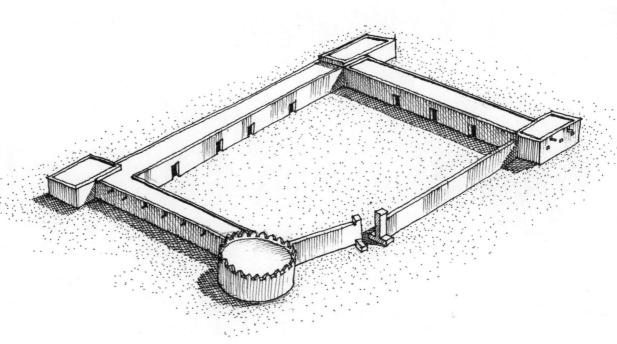

• The courtyard in this fort is of irregular form. The rooms are also of different shapes and sizes

• This image is showing rooms that could have been built as extension to the fort

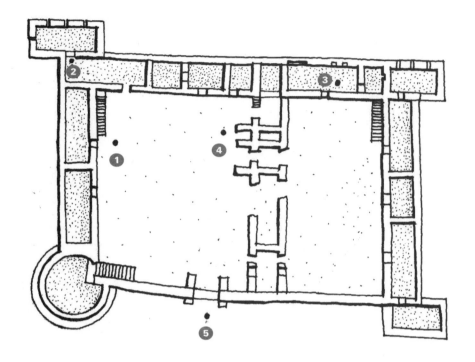

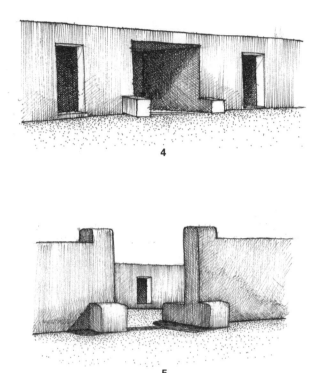

4

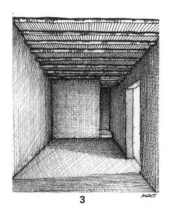

5

• The entrance to the fort

• This is an example of stairs in the fort
• Interior of one of the rooms
• Another example of the inside of the room

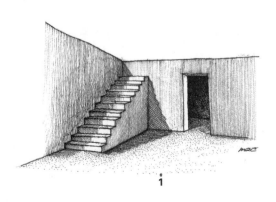

1

2

3

• This perspective is showing
one of the towers

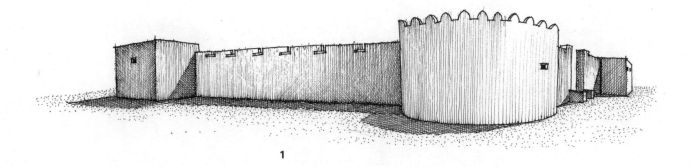

1

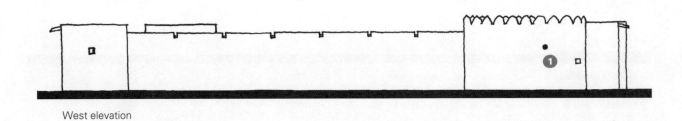

West elevation

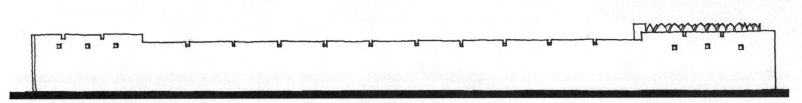

North elevation

• This is the common form
of the towers which are
different from the former one

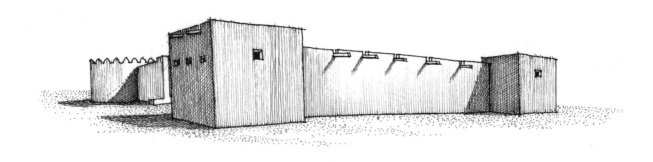

1

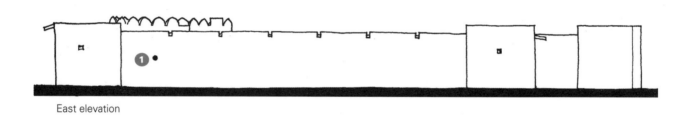

East elevation

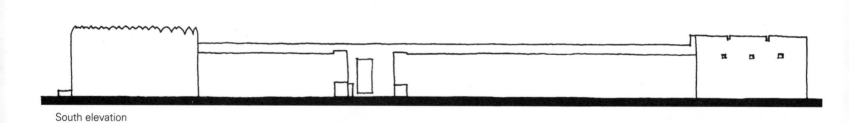

South elevation

• The floor plan is a simple
rectangular form

• This is a simple perspective
of one room

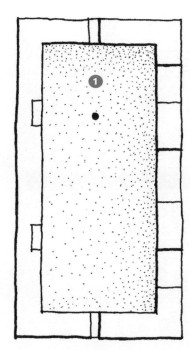

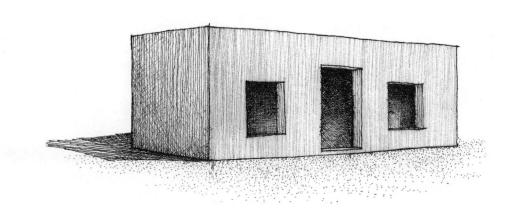

2

• The perspective inside
the room is showing the
recesses and materials used
for the ceiling

1

Elevation

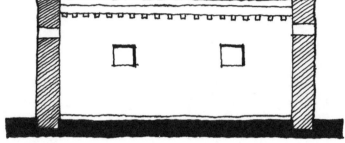

Section

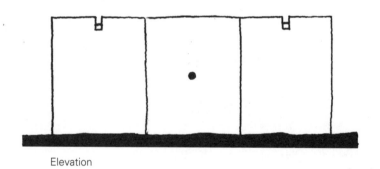

Elevation

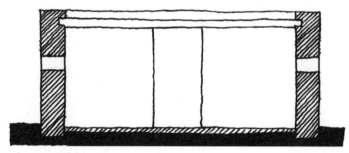

Section

• The floor plan in this case is different because of the recesses inside the room

• Perspective of the room

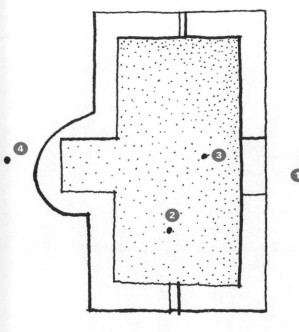

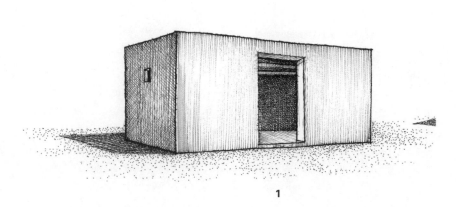

1

3

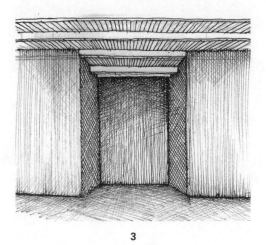

2

• The entrance to the room

• The interior of the room

4

• Perspective of typical circular recession

Umm Slal Mohammad Fort (Umm Slal)
(Late 19th century)

Introduction

Umm Slal Mohammad stands on the old North Road 20 kilometres from Doha. The area is named after its founder. The fortress was distinguished by its high tower that looked down on the North Road, but nowadays it stands approximately 700 metres from the new highway. The old village was surrounded by a wide wall of stone and mud that took many years to finish. Around 1910, the founder of the village, Sheikh Mohamed Bin Jassim Bin Thani Al Thani, built a fortified residence that is still standing. Umm Slal Mohamed is considered one of the loveliest places in Qatar; it has many farms and a big lake that stores water for several months after the rainy season. Currently, the village has many wells and a complete urban settlement with houses and palaces.

The current layout of the village was initiated with the construction of the residence belonging to Sheikh Mohamed Bin Jassim Bin Thani, which is generally referred to as a fort due to its general shape and design. The Sheikh, who was born in 1881, used to live in this house during the winter season with his brother Sheikh Abdullah, while in the summer they moved to Barazan Tower.

Architectural Description of the Fort

The plan is a long, narrow rectangle measuring approximately 36 metres by 9 metres. It can be divided into two distinct but attached parts, the women's *majlis* and the men's *majlis*. The women's *majlis* is the main part of the house since it contains all the facilities. It can be accessed through two staircases, one leading into the *Liwan* and the other to the first floor. The *Liwan* is an arcaded space that measures 8 metres by 3 metres. One of its square arches is closed and the space behind it is used for storage. The columns supporting the arches each measure 100 × 60 cm, and stand approximately 350 centimetres high. The top of the sides of each column are adorned with a small corner decoration.

The women's *majlis* is a very shallow space, less than 3 metres deep and more than 14 metres long. Wall recesses decorate its interior in an irregular manner. The recesses have no consistent size or width. The *majlis* also acts as a connecting room to other spaces inside the house. On the far left of the *majlis* there are two doors, one leading to a room where the dishes are kept and cleaned – an entirely closed space measuring no more than 8 square metres.

A door in the wall opposite the main door of the *majlis* leads into the Masbah or bathroom space (20 square metres) partitioned into two spaces. This bathroom has three windows on the north-west wall, one is now blocked and another window on the north-east wall has been used to create an opening for an air conditioning unit. The Masbah gives access to an external swimming pool.

Two staircases are located on the north-east side of the women's *majlis*. One leads down to the dates room and the other up to the first floor. Date rooms are usually rectangular spaces with a sloped floor, with the lowest section at the point of access to the room. The purpose of the room is to extract the juice from dates, with the juice running down the sloped floor into a collection channel. This room measures approximately 10 square metres.

The men's *majlis* consists of a section of a *Liwan*, three rooms and a toilet. It is built on the south-west side of the main building, with the two parts separated by a thick wall 2 metres high. At the southernmost corner of the house, a room with rounded corners and three interior wall recesses can be accessed from the courtyard level. The rest of this area can be accessed through a staircase leading to the

Liwan level. The front wall of the *Liwan* is an arcade with very narrow arches supported by two large columns each measuring 100 × 80 cm. These three arches are undecorated and have simple geometry.

From the *Liwan*, a large room can be accessed through the entrance door. The decoration of this space consists of some wall recesses with no regularity or rhythm in their layout. On the north-eastern wall of this *majlis*, a staircase leads to the roof and upper rooms, while at the east corner a door leads to the small bathroom. From the south-west wall of the *majlis*, a door provides access to another adjacent room with rather simple decorations consisting of three wall recesses.

The first floor can be reached by means of two staircases, one at the north-east end of the building, which concludes on the first level in a staircase room. The other is located in the men's section and leads to the roof and a second level approximately 16 metres above the level of the courtyard.

• This perspective is showing Umm Slal Mohammad fort. This fort is different from the others because of its form and shape

• Ground floor plan. In this fort the plan is a long, narrow rectangle. There are two parts divided by two courtyards. The women's part is the main one since it contains all the facilities

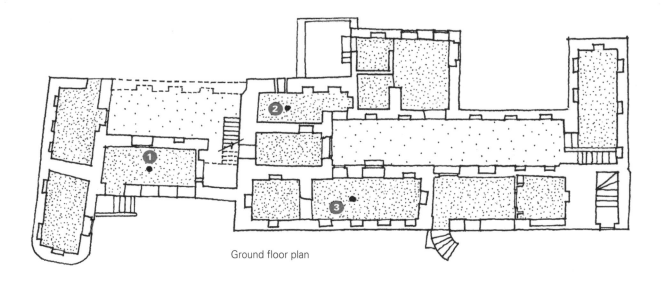

Ground floor plan

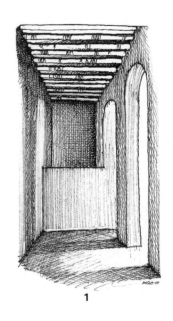

1

2

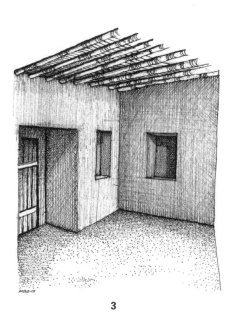

3

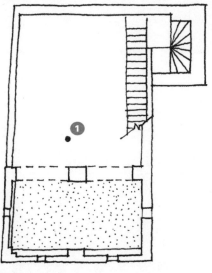

Third floor plan

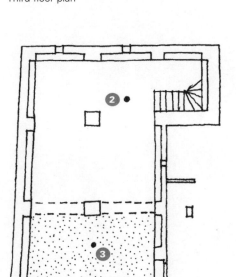

Second floor plan

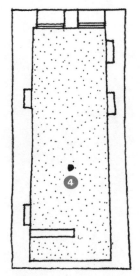

Mezzanine floor

• The entrance to the room

1

• This figure shows stairs leading to the upper floor
• The view to the veranda

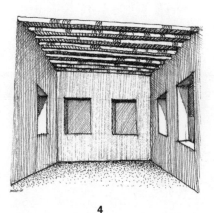

2

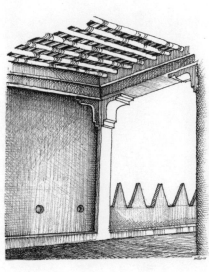

3

4

• The entrance to the fort and
the tower are indicated in this
perspective. The tower could
have been used as watch
tower so as to control the
views through the small
openings on it

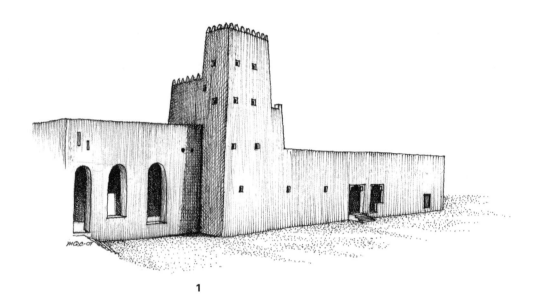

1

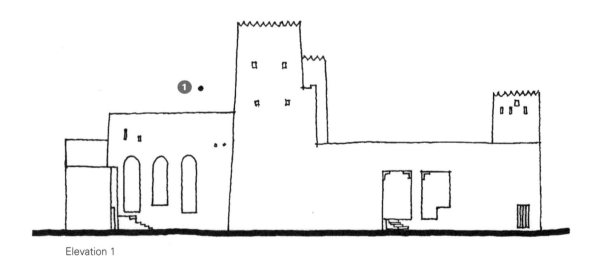

Elevation 1

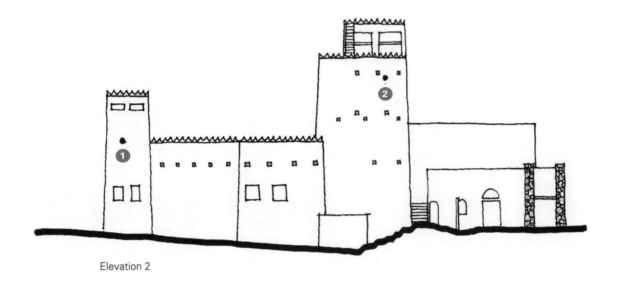

Elevation 2

1   2

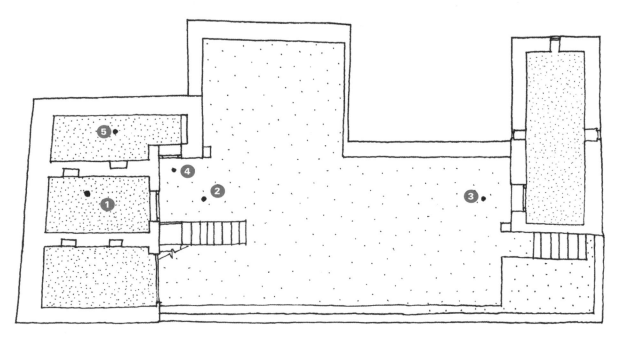

First floor plan

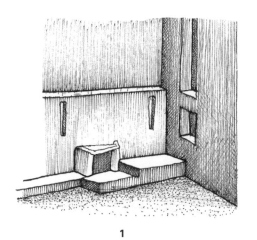

1

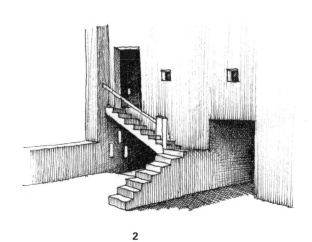

2

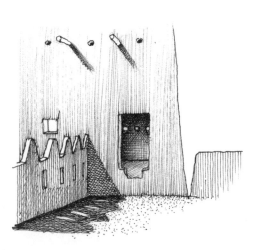

3

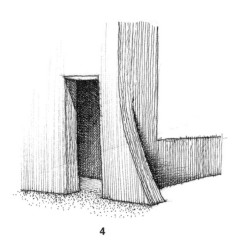

4

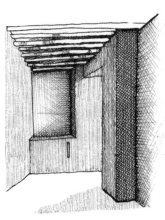

5

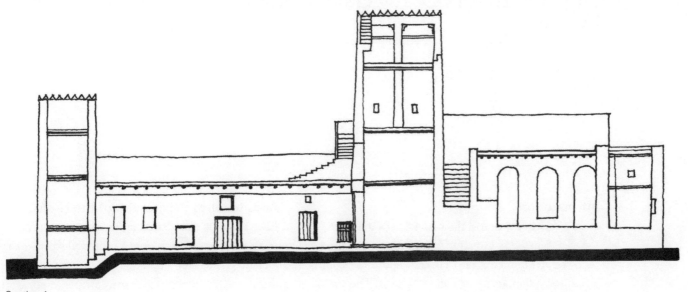

Section 1

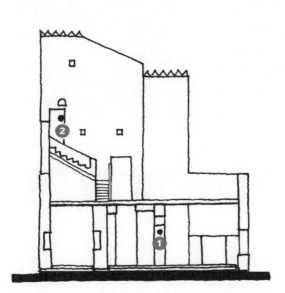

Elevation 2

1

2

Al Khor Towers (3 Towers) (Al Khor) (1930)

Introduction

Al Khor is one of the major towns in Qatar outside of Greater Doha. It lies approximately 50 kilometres north of the capital. Al Khor is a port town famous for its fish and pearls. The towers in Al Khor were built around 1900 to serve two main purposes: to allow the people of the town to maintain a watch over the town and to act as a defensive building. The height of the towers allowed guards to watch both the sea and the land, while the 60-centimetre thick walls provided safety from which to protect the town.

Architectural Description of the House

Each tower is cylindrical with a diameter of four metres. They are built out of mud and stone quarried locally. The towers stand eight metres high and are decorated at the top with arrow shaped units around the parapet. Openings called *mazaghel* allowed the throwing of stones and various other materials in times of attack. The building has a ceiling of *danshal* wood beams overlaid with *basgill* and *mangharour*. The guard was able to reach the roof but was obliged to climb ropes to do so.

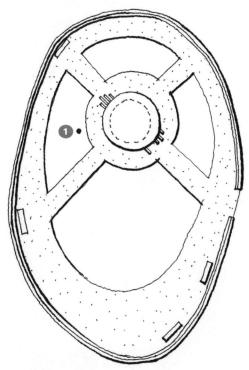

Floor plan

 Circulation

 Open private space

• Floor plan. The tower was built to allow the people of the town to maintain a watch over the town and to act as a defensive building
• Each tower is cylindrical with a diameter of four meters and eight meters high
• The towers are decorated at the top with arrow shaped units around the parapets. Openings called mazaghel allowed the throwing of stones and various other materials at the time

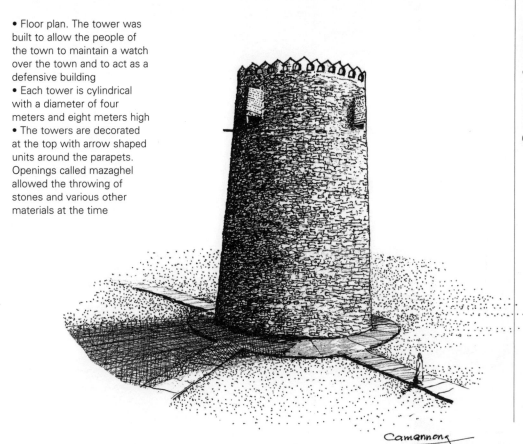

1

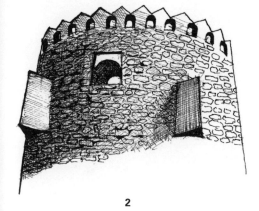

2

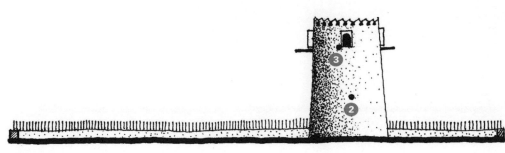

Elevation

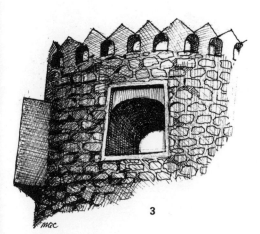

3

Section

Tower B

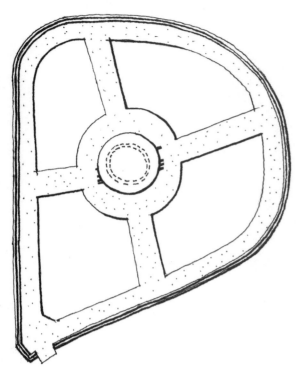

Ground floor plan

 Circulation

 Open private space

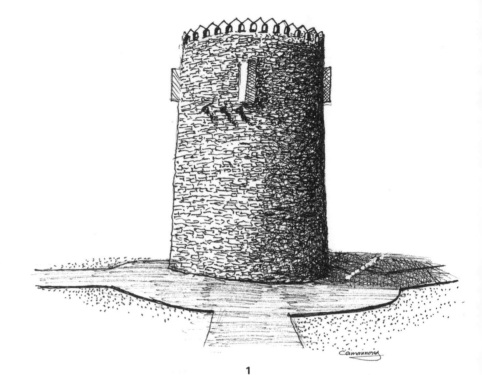

1

Elevation

Section

2

Tower C

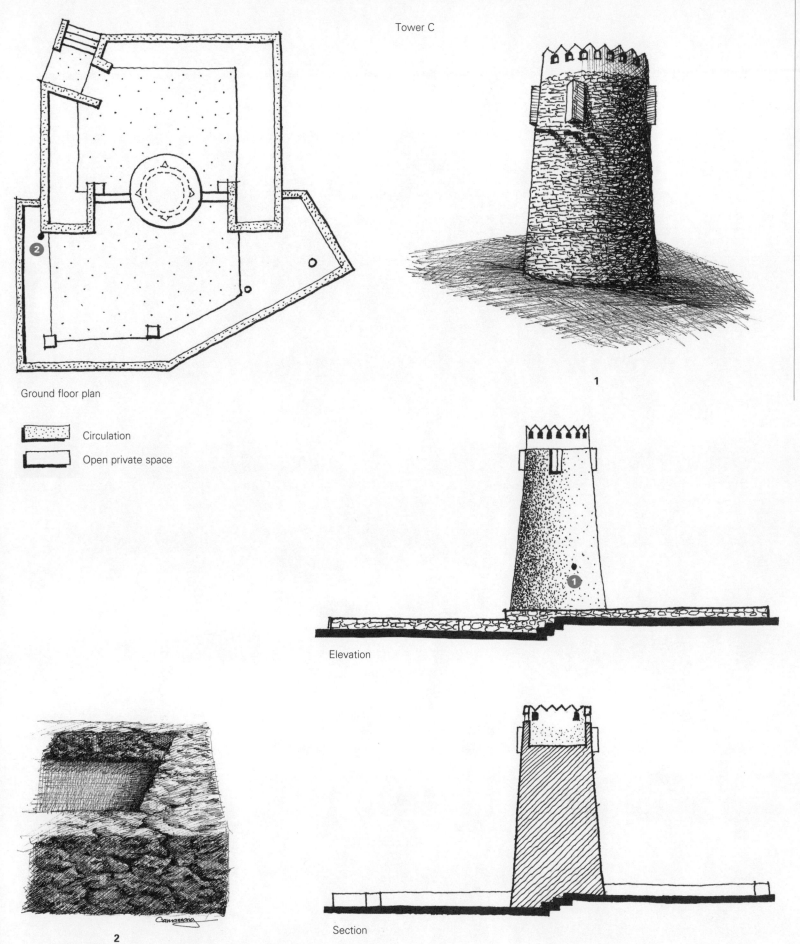

Ground floor plan

Circulation

Open private space

1

Elevation

2

Section

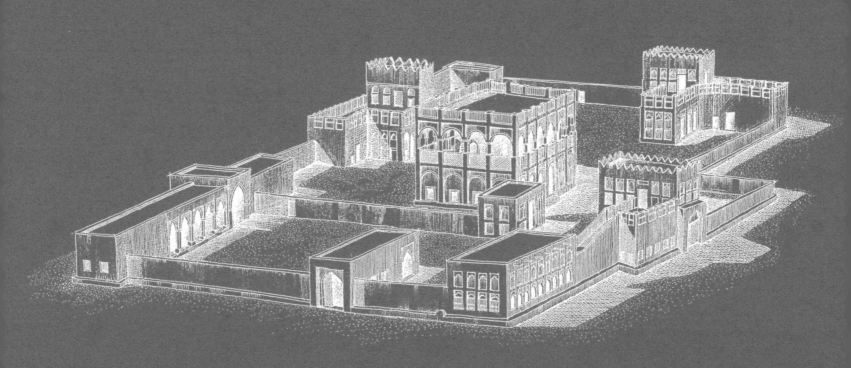

PALACES

The Old Amiri Palace
Doha, Qatar

This section provides with a detailed description and analysis of the old Amiri palace carried out by the Supreme Council of Culture.

Historical Background

The gulf that lies between the land masses of Persia and Arabia has provided the easiest means of contact between the inhabitants of the two regions, whilst direct communication between the Eastern and the Western worlds took place via the two great rivers that flow into its head waters. In short, it is a region where Arabs and Persians have always intermingled and the traffic between Mesopotamia and India used to pass. These have been the historical constants of the region over the last two thousand years, and they were contributory factors in the construction of a building erected there about a century ago.

This interesting building was the seigneurial residence of Sheikh Abdullah bin Qasim Al Thani, Sheikh of Qatar. It was built in response to specific historical developments. When after a generation the circumstances changed, it was superseded in its functions and (such is the incidence of change) it has now become a historical monument preserved with due respect and concern.

The circumstances governing its building were as follows. During the nineteenth century a controlling interest had been exercised over the affairs of the Gulf from the sea by the government of India. However, towards the end of the century, the imperial government at Istanbul extended its energies beyond its Arab province of Iraq and penetrated into the Gulf region. North-eastern Arabia (*Al Hasa*) was incorporated into the Ottoman Empire and Qatar became the imperial frontier, with a Turkish garrison established in Doha. Istanbul met Bombay in East Arabia – Turkey in Europe confronted England in India.

These developments by no means reduced the significance of the Al Thani family. Day-to-day affairs were still very largely under their control and patronage and in fact they negotiated some balance between English and Turkish interests. To discharge these functions a new "family seat" was built up. Whereas for security reasons the Turkish authority with its garrison occupied the higher land in the central part of Doha (Qal'a el Askar), an area on the eastern outskirts of Doha was chosen for the Al Thani's headquarters. This was situated at a discrete remove from the centre of the town but gave immediately onto harbourage and could be thus approached directly from the sea. The area was called Feriq al Salatah (the Salatah district, named after the Sulaiti tribe). Here Abdullah, the son of Qasim (Jasim) the paramount Sheikh, set up to act as Governor of Doha, and thus the overseer of its sea-borne life and a liaison officer with the Turkish representatives. At the end of the century Sheikh Abdullah began to build his family residence. Here he lived with his wife, and in due course he added the Baits of his sons Sheikh Hamed and Sheikh Ali. From here he managed the day-to-day affairs of Doha and its provinces. Eventually the events of World War I caused the departure of the Turks and in November 1916 Sheikh Abdullah received Sir Percy Cox, the British Resident in the Gulf. An agreement was signed whereby Qatari affairs of state were arranged on an understanding with British representatives, while Britain guaranteed Qatar protection against external aggression. Shortly afterwards, in 1923, Sheikh Abdullah and his family quitted the Old Amiri Palace to reside at the seat of government in the central part of Doha town. Thirty years later, through the enlightened understanding of the Amir of Qatar and in accordance with the interest that the people of Qatar show in their past, the building has been restored and reconditioned to form in itself a fitting monument of Qatar's past and at the same time to serve as the centre of the magnificently planned museum.

Description of the Building

The complex was not the result of an overall plan conceived and worked out at one time.
The assemblage grew by addition and adaptation. Thus it is that identification and explanation of all detail cannot be given in a word. Uses changed. Secondly, the dilapidated structures have been reconditioned to form part of a museum. They have now a new function quite different from that of a Sheikh's family residence. In this way some of the characteristic installations and arrangements of past times are not found since they would conflict with the present day purpose.

As preserved, the most important apartments of the complex are the following.
Family dwelling of Sheikh Abdullah
Family dwelling of Sheikh Hamed
Family dwelling of Sheikh Ali
Watchman's quarters
Quarters of the mosque janitor
Public apartments of East Gate-house
Public apartments of North Gate-house
Public apartments of coffee reception hall (the little *majlis*)
Public apartments of Assembly Room (the inner *majlis*)

It should be noted that an original main gateway in the west wall has been superseded, while the present main entrance set in the south wall next to *10* is an entirely modern structure – its presence dictated by present functional necessities.

Additionally there were various apartments for functionaries at the east of the enclosure between *9* and *10*. An extensive kitchen area existed in the north-west part at present fronted by the new museum. There were storage facilities (for fodder, dates etc.) near and to the west of the present main entrance.

If the position and nature of these various apartments are considered, it is apparent that when fully developed the complex of the Old Amiri Palace consisted of a private domestic area to the west and a public or reception quarter to the east. This was indeed so and the division was marked by a partitioning wall. To the west lay the family dwellings, kitchen and stores – i.e. the *Haramlik* of the establishment, to the east the arrangements such as gate-houses, guest halls, assembly halls, schoolroom, offices, etc. – the *Selamlik* or *Diwaniyah* of the establishment.

As has been stated, this disposition was not an original design but was achieved by piecemeal extension. Initially Sheikh Abdullah bin Qasim Al Thani built his dwelling place (his *bait*) – structure 4.

The essential parts of this structure are exactly those which may be seen in any of the old surviving houses, e.g., at Wakrah. The plan consists basically of one or two rooms at ground level, fronted by a veranda or porch. These rooms are entered from the long side and are thus technically "broad rooms". One such room is partitioned off across an end by a screen wall that does not rise to the full height of the room, giving a private alcove itself in the form of a broad room. An external staircase leads up to the terrace roof of these rooms, and in one corner a tower-like upper storey room rises. The roofs are sheltered by tall parapets and that of the tower crowned with crow-stepping. The walls are largely fitted with windows and other openings and devices for the controlled admission of light and air. The basic plan is subject to minor variations and may be added to, as in the present instance of Sheikh Abdullah's house. Such additions generally develop (as here) an L-shaped plan, and this in turn predicates an enclosure or *housh*. In essentials, however, the dwelling is open looking and not dependent on an enclosed court for its functioning. The houses of Sheikh Abdullah's sons – Sheikh Hamed bin Abdullah (5) and Sheikh Ali bin Abdullah (6) – were constructed on the same standard plan and when these were erected, the monumental complex began to take shape. Each of these residencies doubtless had some sort of *housh* before it, but additionally the space to the south and west of the residences of Abdullah and Hamed was enclosed by a strong wall to form a large courtyard entered by a main gate (now suppressed) in the west side. At the south-west angle of this enclosure an apartment (7) was built for a watchman. Thus was developed a protected and guarded compound into which the family and visitors could enter mounted and leave their camels or other chattels under guard before passing into the domestic apartments. Following this came the full-scale development of the property into an official residence. Enclosure walls were extended eastward to the strand or foreshore (virtually high water mark) so that the sea almost washed the east and north walls – since to the north of the complex in place of today's reclaimed ground there was a harbour inlet, dense with moored shipping.

The main Sea or Harbour Gate was in the north wall (1). This takes the form of a small porch set before an entrance passage which is built up with a second storey into the semblance of the battlemented tower. To the east of the gate passage is set a public waiting room. From the terrace roof of this chamber, access is given to the "room over the gate". This gate provides an axial approach to the Coffee Hall – Reception Hall (2) set inside, and it would appear that the two buildings were planned in common by the slightly skew setting of the latter. Certainly they make an effective and pleasing ensemble.

The small porch or portal which is now set out from the wall in front of the Gate is decorated with stucco work and opened on each side with arches set above embrasure seats for guards etc. The entrance-passage room is flanked with benches (*mastabas,* or *datchas* as they are called locally). This is where those on business or attending audience can congregate. This is an ancient institution of the East – "He went down and sat in the gate", etc. The room which flanks the gate to the east is designed for public affairs and accordingly all the walls are open at ground level with ranges of low shuttered windows (*derishas*) to permit the most effective lighting and ventilation for the weather conditions obtaining. The terrace roof of this room and the tower room above the passage form an extensive and well appointed apartment. These quarters attached to the Gate together constituted the official bureau of the Sheikh's scribe (*katib*) or private secretary, and his dwelling place. There is also a memory that for a time they were used as a religious school (*madrasah*) for the children of the city's more important citizens. The guest reception room or Coffee Hall (*Mahal el gahwah*) has a charming simplicity and forms a pleasing contrast to the more substantial buildings set around it – its off-square lines in plan and its asymmetrical arrangement give it a sort of rustic quality. It is a pavilion with an open arched façade which shows to good advantage when entry is made through the north gate. There are low windows in the side wall and externally the walls are ornamented with blind arcading.

The other surviving gateway, the East Gate (9) is different in character. This provided for comings and goings in the vicinity – e.g., to visit the mosque that once stood outside the palace just south of 10. Sheikh Abdullah would go out by this door and seat himself at a bench (datche) in front of 8 or 10 to greet and be greeted by passers-by. Accordingly the structure is less pretentious than the north gate, consisting of a simple passage room set flush with the outer wall and devoid of any superstructure. Its design incorporates the age-old defensive device known as the "bent approach" – i.e., the entry requiring a right-angle turn to avoid the possibility of hostile forces rushing straight through into the interior. Although at the Old Amiri Palace the military significance is very attenuated, the arrangement has distinct advantages in the circumstances. It renders the gate-chambers less exposed to public view and in this way a very convenient and pleasant of attendance. Likewise it provides for a more refined approach to the complex of buildings in that they are not thrown open to view immediately with the opening of the Gate but are revealed by degrees with a delayed and cumulative effect. Inside the passage chamber the walls are lined with benches, aired and lighted on the north with low windows. It is all a very good piece of design. On stepping through the inner portal of the Gate chamber the visitor is immediately confronted by the main façade of the *Majlis* (8) which is set in the north-east corner of the compound (6).

This, the most formal public compartment, comprises a single large chamber entered by a door in the middle of the long side – i.e., it is a broad room. On all sides it is opened up by ranges of low windows set at ground level. On the north and east these windows looked out onto the shores of the Gulf immediately adjacent, while on the south and west they surveyed the internal court and its activities. In this fashion they make the best of whatever cooling ventilation might be available. The large airy hall was spread with carpets and those here assembled rested on cushions propped against the wall. The refined and elaborate interior decoration further lent an air of repose and dignity to the chamber. Above the ranges of windows the walls were decorated with two registers of stucco panels, the upper register arch headed; and as an additional mark of distinction there was a moulded and painted timber ceiling.

In the south-east quarter of the complex there were apartments of lesser note. In the angle of the enclosure it is said that originally there dwelt one of Sheikh Abdullah elder brothers. However this building (10) came to shelter the keepers of the mosque (now demolished) which then stood hard by just outside the walls. Additionally, built along the eastern wall between 10 and 9 were quarters provided for two retainers of some significance – the household steward and the coffee maker.

The foregoing gives an indication of how the complex of the Old Amiri Palace took shape in the years at the beginning of the present century. However, in 1918, after the withdrawal of the Turkish authorities, Sheikh Abdullah caused new and very impressive buildings to be erected in the compound for his private dwelling – as befitted his new dignity. This is 3. It was constructed by a famous Bahraini builder, Abdullah bin Ali el Mail, in a form and style which then obtained for important buildings in Bahrain. Certainly its added height supplied the element of dominance over the surround appropriate to Sheikh Abdullah's new circumstances.

In plan as in other respects this building differs from the earlier structures. The plan is rational and centralised – consisting essentially of a central chamber surrounded by galleries, balconies and minor rooms. There are two storeys and an important terrace roof.

The central hall on the ground floor is approached from North and South by way of porches, while to the east and west of it lie chambers, closets, stairs, etc., and the walls of the central hall are articulated by a continuous range of low windows. These windows in the east and west walls communicate with the peripheral chambers, so they here provide borrowed lighting and ventilation. To emphasise the significance of this hall used for public reception, it was given a painted timber ceiling. Set into the floor at the west end are two cists covered with stone slabs. These are for the storage of valuables etc. and are called *Khazinat* (treasuries). There is also a larger one in the adjacent room to the west.

The upper storey repeats the central chamber of the lower floor but this is open on all sides to a surrounding veranda. This veranda is arcaded and the round arches of the arcades, rising above the remaining buildings of the complex, make a distinguished architectural feature which is a tribute to the abilities and taste of the architect Abdullah el Mail. The arcades are screened by lattice-work panels to give the private living a viewing space – very agreeable in the cool of the evening. The central chamber is ornamented with elaborate arched windows surmounted by stucco panels, and a cornice gives onto a painted timber ceiling.

The stairway in the south-west corner continues up to a terrace roof surrounded by a balustrade. The elevated terrace compensated for the low lying site in affording outlook and control over the town and harbour.

In connection with this worthy building it is worthwhile recording one or two interesting memories which subsist regarding its architect, Abdullah el Mail. He apparently gained the reputation of extreme virtuosity in his craft bordering on the uncanny (a sort of *Div-band* or demon builders). For example, he was never seen to make plans of calculated dimensions, etc. but arranged everything in his head. Equally, he is said to have informed Sheikh Abdullah that this building would stand in good order for 40 years but then would require attention. And this apparently proved to be so.

Having indicated the disposition in plan of the complex, it now remains to say something of the style and construction of these buildings. This is a uniform entity of considerable interest. As in all good building the style and construction are wedded so closely that it is difficult to assert which is the controlling factor.

The significant materials of construction are rubble, gypsum, plaster and wood. The rubble (*hasa-*) supply was supplemented from a source close to hand – the sea, where coral rocks yielded serviceable building stone. This was gathered in the form of lumps, etc. (*hasa bahri-*) and was also quarried as thin slabs (*faraush-*) specifically intended for partition walls. Gypsum plaster in this area is called *juss-*. The raw material (hydrous calcium sulphate) was burned, pulverised and sieved. The fine powder was sometimes mixed with lime. It gave a very quick setting plaster for rendering and ornamentation. Wood was freely employed in the form of poles, stalks, trunks, etc. (of mangrove, tamarisk and palm). Squared sections of timber, carpentry and joinery were for fittings and in the nature of luxury work. Elegant windows, shutters, doors, etc., were a feature of better houses. The hard wood employed came from East Africa or India. Teak and mahogany were favoured and all this is made apparent in the term employed for the work, *Siyami*; for example, an ornamental hardwood window is termed a *Shibbak siyami* (a Siamese window). Other auxiliary materials were used in roofing, where palm ribs (*jareed-*) for a lattice and palm leaves of cane matting (*mangoor-*) provided a base for the pebble and plaster terrace.

The craft of bold and formal wood-working, probably owed much to shipbuilding activity in the Gulf. Massive doors spoke for themselves and the metal studding which gave them strength equally strengthened and ornamented their appearance. Equally impressive are the striking wooden water spouts (*marzam-*) that punctuated the upper register of walls. Painted colour was kept to a minimum and applied in the main only to bring out construction – e.g., on the pole and lattice ceilings (*saqf danche-*) and, where used, colours were strong primary ones. A few remarks must now be made about the use of these Old Amiri Palace buildings. Their social background was a mixed one of Bedouin and commercial life, which have always accorded one with the other in Arabia. For considerable periods the members of the Al Thani family would take advantage of favourable weather conditions to move about the open country of the interior, sleeping in tents, and in some senses this assemblage of individual dwellings (*buyut-*) was an immobilised Bedouin encampment (*manzil-*).

Thus, in addition to the family dwellings, there are appointments that reflect the public aspects of tribal life – for instance, a place for deliberation and a place for hospitable refreshment.

However, this is but part of the background. The hard dealing associated with sea-borne commerce (and particularly with pearling), plus the political commitments, suggest a comparison for the Al Thani sheikhs with the merchant princes of an Italian city-state. Indeed the early *palazzi* in Florence have a functional *raison d'être* not unlike that of the Old Amiri Palace.

The private family life of the several dwellers within the complex was an unrestricted and agreeable one. Apart from the separation of the public quarters to the east of the compound, there was little in the nature of segregation. This again accords with Bedouin practice and indeed travellers' remarks that, compared with the towns of the Nejd under Wahabi control, the womenfolk entered freely into the life of the community. Accordingly family dwellings were not arranged to provide for a distinct *haramlik* of limited access. An end of a ground floor room is screened off to provide private place, and this was used for any of the variety of purposes that demand privacy, such as washing (there was no convenient source of water near the Palace and it had to be brought from a spring some distance away).

Finally, in considering the usage of these dwellings, a salient fact must be borne in mind that is not in any way peculiar to the locality but operates generally in the East. European domestic organisation based on heavy furniture sets aside specific rooms for specific activities – dining rooms, sitting rooms, bedrooms etc. Eastern furniture is minimal and portable. Thus rooms are differentiated according to climatic functions rather that social activities. In this fashion any room may be used and turned about for dining or sleeping etc; but one room or balcony is used in the noontime and another in the cool of the evening, one room is used in winter and another in summer for this or that purpose.

The Work of Restoration

When his Highness Sheikh Khalifa bin Hamad Al Thani conceived the project of transforming the remains of the Old Amiri Palace into an integral part of the Qatari people's heritage, more than the restoration of a monument was involved. The old buildings and their ambiance were to form the nucleus and setting of a civic centre demonstrating Qatar's concern and respect for its past. In this way a new museum building has been incorporated in the irregular area previously occupied by kitchen shelters and their appurtenances. Additionally, something of the original marine siting (since cut off by land reclamation) has been suggested by a pool lake roughly simulating the old shoreline. This pool will display traditional sailing vessels for which the Gulf was famous, and a pavilion at the landing will house a maritime museum.

Such features exceed the dictates of restoration proper and mark the project as one of "Development and Restoration". Although this is obvious in itself, it is perhaps not equally obvious that it affects details of the restoration work on and about the old buildings themselves.

The restored and developed complex of the Old Amiri Palace has a new and different function from its original one as a seigneurial residence – and these new functions must be planned for. Manifestly, the requirements of circulation and access are entirely changed. These questions have involved some treatment of the Old Amiri Palace complex which varies from that of the standard practice in restoration of monuments. However the guiding principle in the work has been to conserve and recreate as far as possible the spirit of the original construction.

• Overall aerial view of the palace. The assemblage of this monumental building grew by addition and adaption

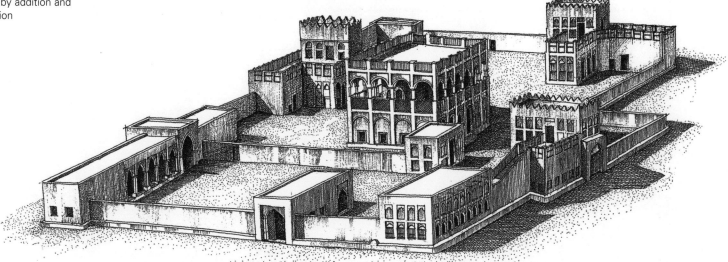

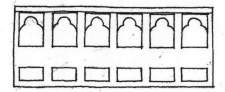

Elevation of wall A

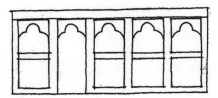

Elevation of wall B

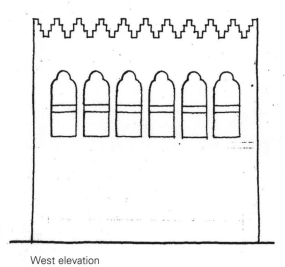

West elevation

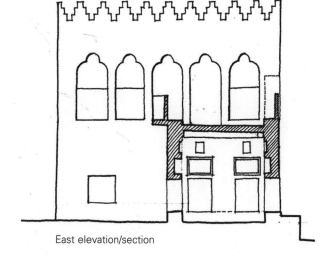

East elevation/section

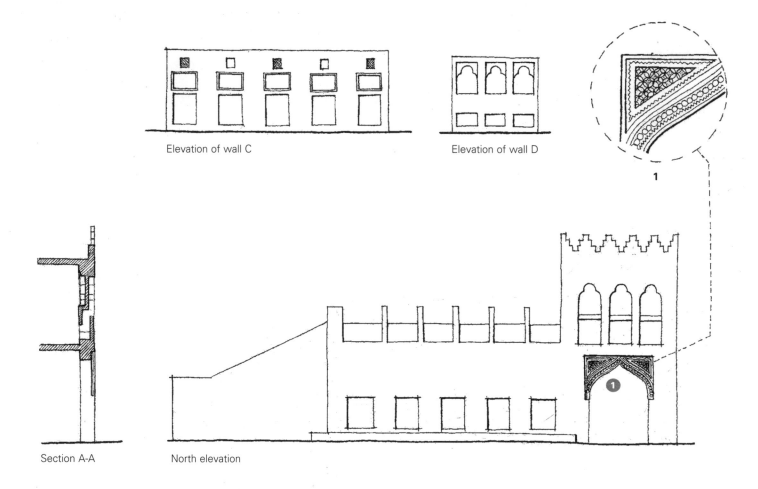

Elevation of wall C

Elevation of wall D

1

Section A-A

North elevation

1

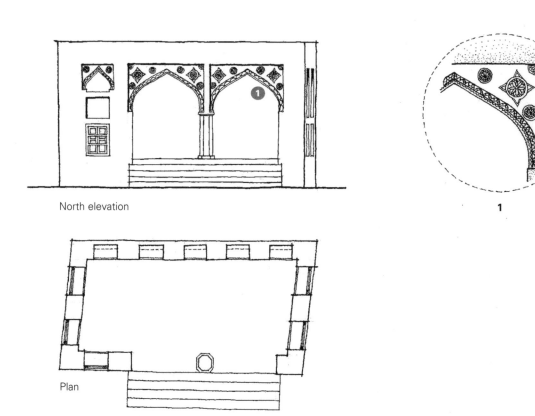

North elevation

1

Plan

• The plan consists basically
of few rooms at ground level,
fronted by a veranda

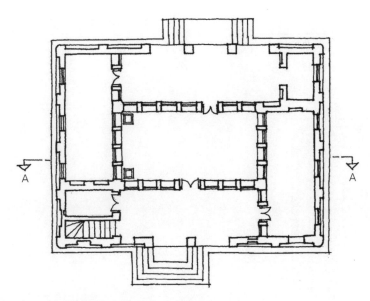

Ground floor plan

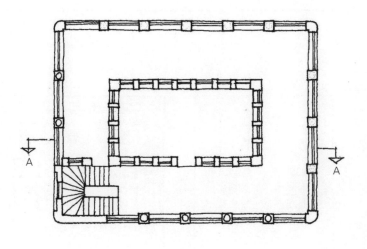

First floor plan

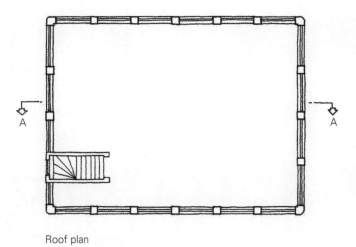

Roof plan

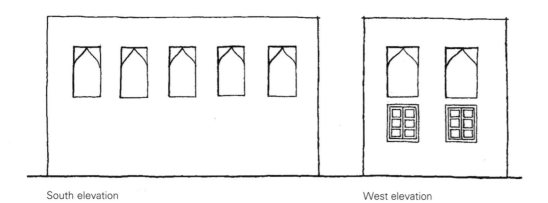

South elevation

West elevation

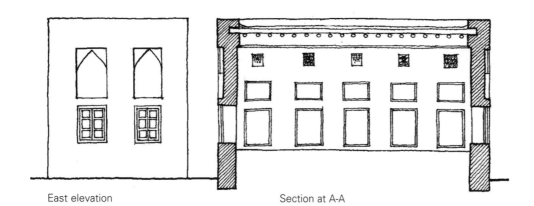

East elevation

Section at A-A

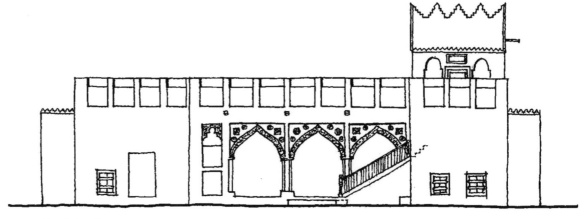

Front elevation

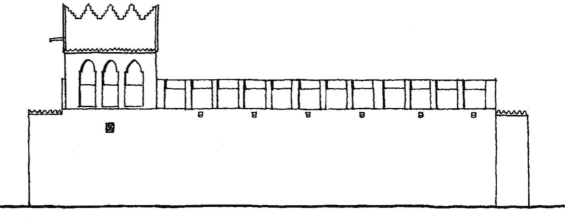

Rear elevation

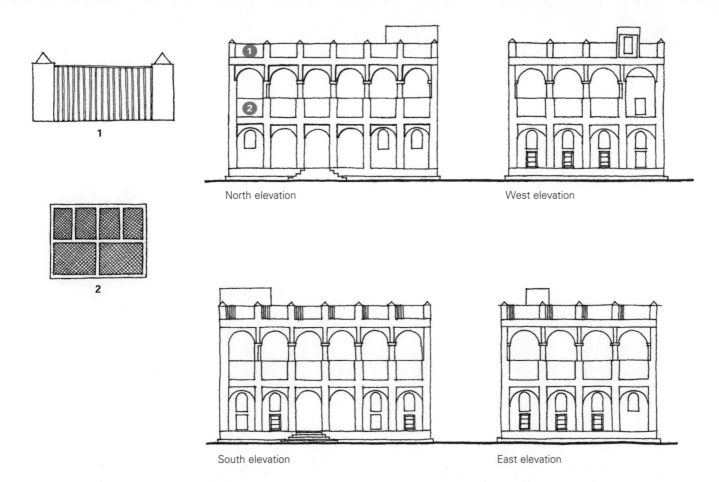

1

2

North elevation

West elevation

South elevation

East elevation

• The walls are largely filled with windows and other openings and devices for the controlled admission of light and air

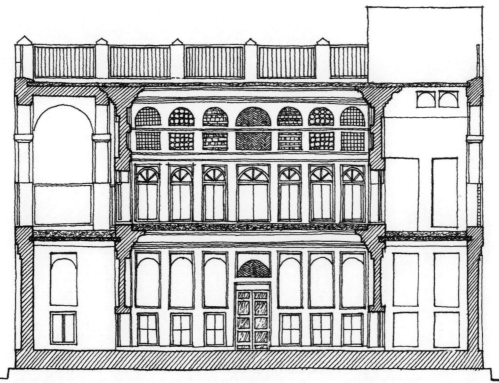

Section A-A

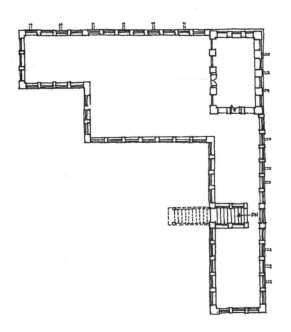

First floor plan

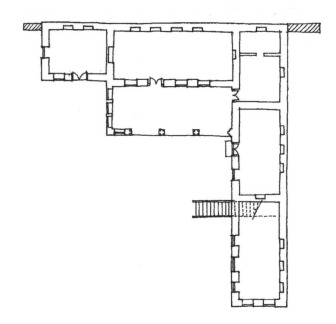

Ground floor plan

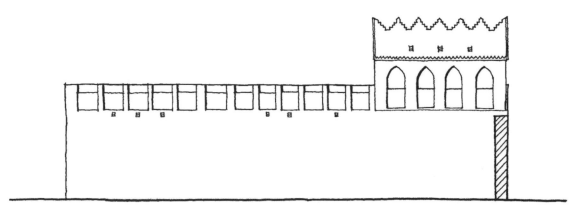

West elevation

East elevation

78

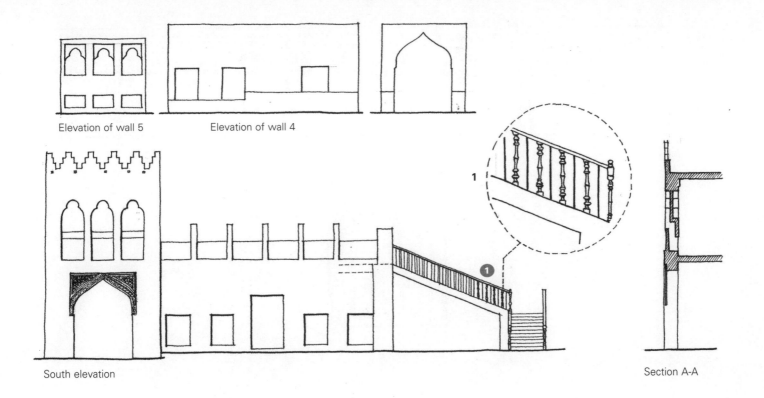

Elevation of wall 5

Elevation of wall 4

1

South elevation

Section A-A

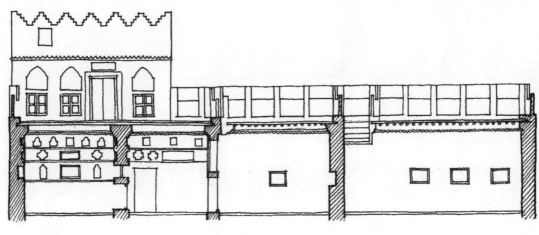

Section B-B

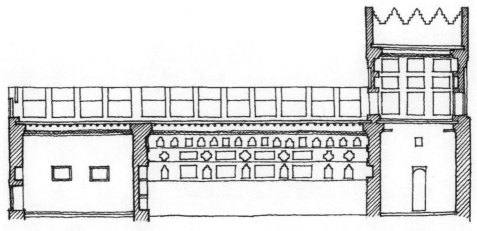

Section A-A

Section at A-A

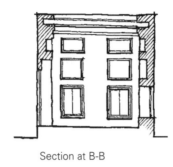

Section at B-B

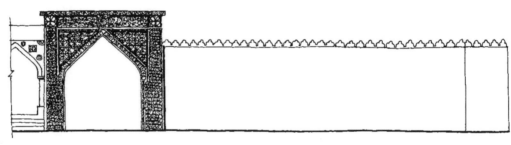

North elevation

South elevation

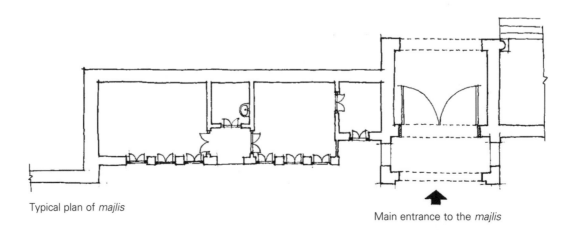

Typical plan of *majlis*

Main entrance to the *majlis*

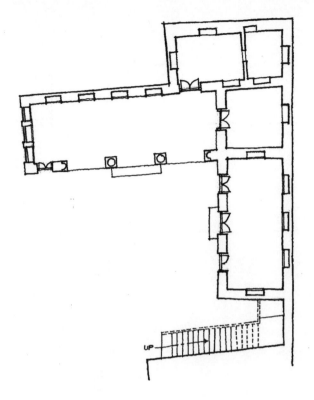

Ground floor plan

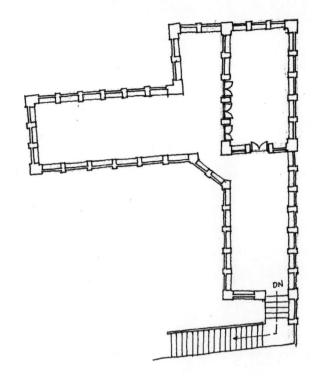

First floor plan

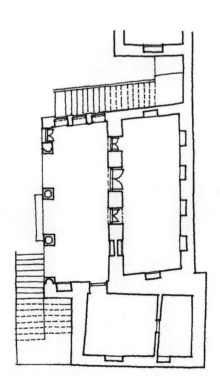

Ground floor plan

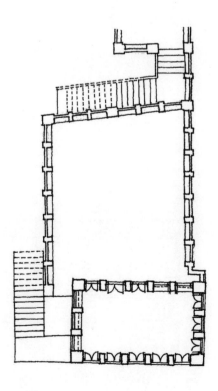

First floor plan

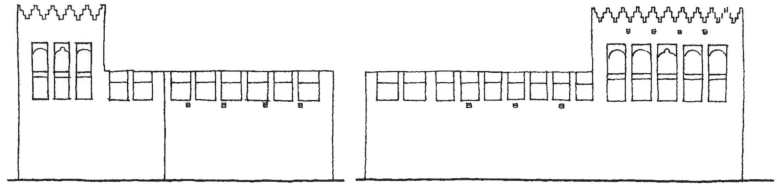

South elevation

West elevation

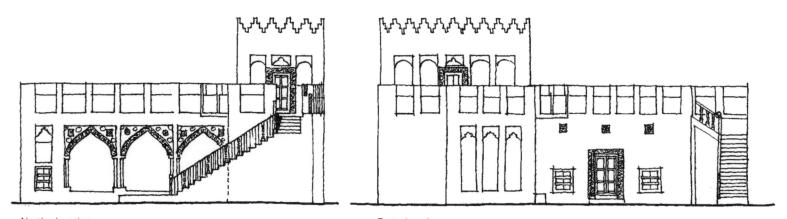

North elevation

East elevation

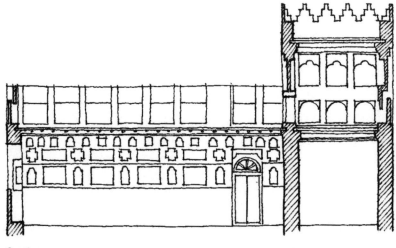

Section

Elevation A

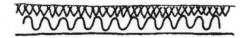

1

Elevation B

Elevation C

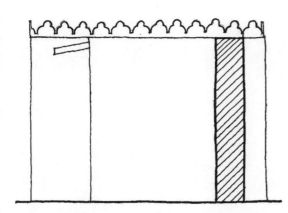

North elevation

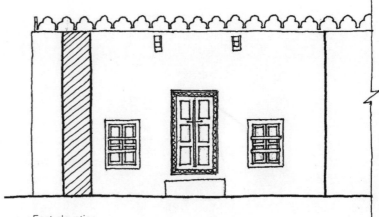

East elevation

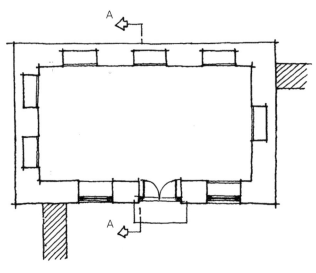

Plan

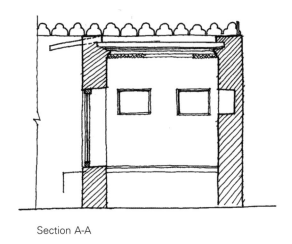

Section A-A

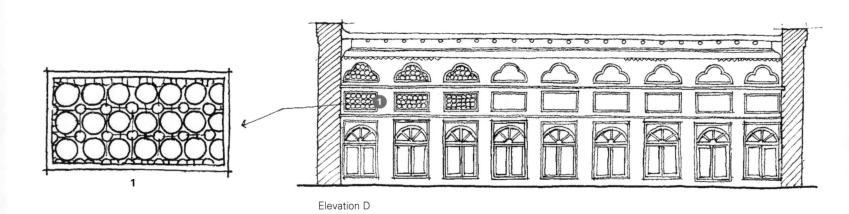

1

Elevation D

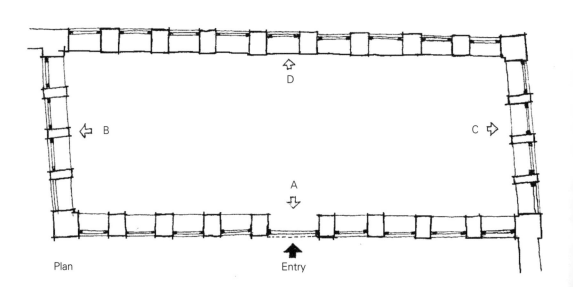

Plan

B

C

D

A

Entry

North elevation

East elevation

South elevation

West elevation

East elevation

North elevation

1

Section A-A

Plan

2

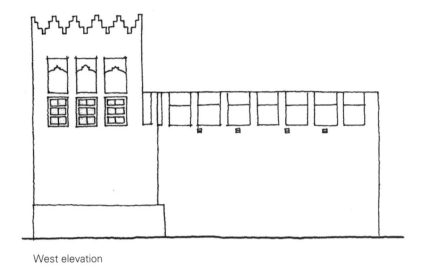

West elevation

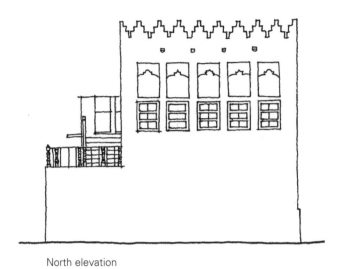

North elevation

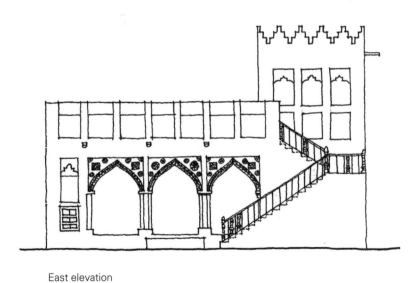

East elevation

Section A-A

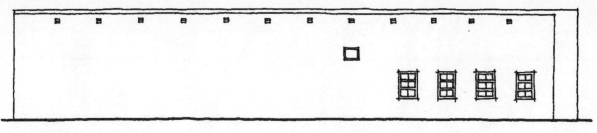

South elevation

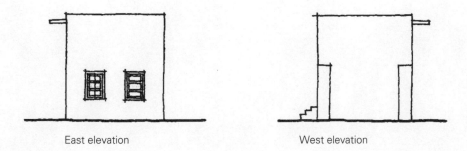

East elevation   West elevation

North elevation

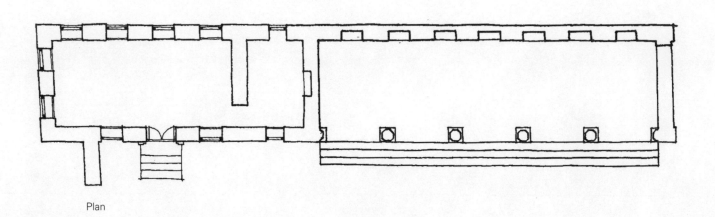

Plan

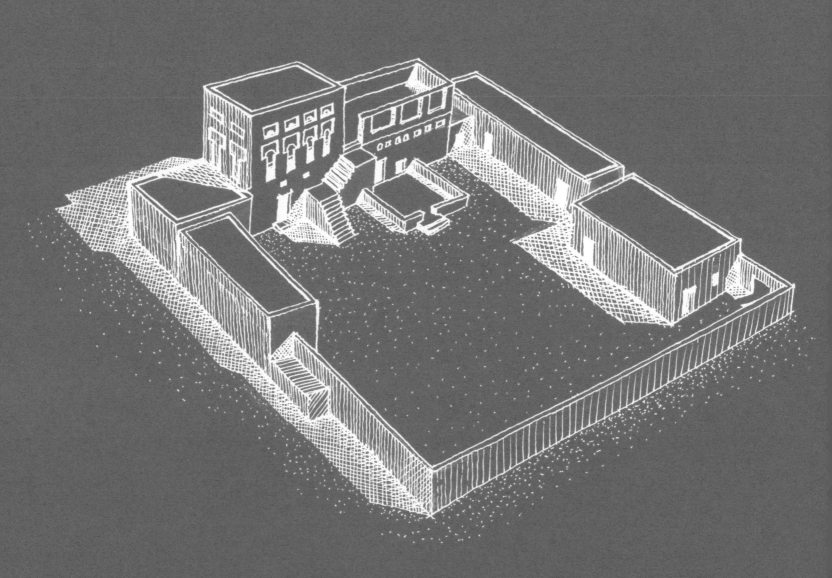

DOMESTIC HOUSES

House in Rodat Al Hamamah (Al Keesha) (1945)

Introduction

This house – a modest winter farmhouse built in 1945 but now abandoned – stands in a farming district about 3 kilometres north of the village of Al Kheesah. A scattering of occupied houses lies nearby.

The site itself is flat and barren with virtually no vegetation. Nevertheless, there are some trees and bushes in the area, particularly to the east and south just outside the walls that surround the old house. This fact indicates that working wells existed in the area to support farming sometime in the past.

The nearest paved road is the recently completed North Relief Road, which passes about 1 kilometre to the east. The area lies just after the north edge of Doha, and the adjacent Al Keesha area has been earmarked by the Municipality for future residential development.

Architectural Description of the House

The house extends along the north edge of a walled compound, roughly rectangular in shape, that measures approximately 22 by 29 metres.

The closed-in portion of the house is long and narrow, only about 3 metres wide. Rooms are arranged in a linear fashion along the rear of the compound, which also serves as the rear wall of the house. Another room abuts the west wall of the compound. An open porch, a little less than two metres wide, extends along the east half of the front façade.

Overall, this old farmhouse is austere, very much a utilitarian structure, and virtually devoid of architectural ornamentation. It is a typical example of the North Arabian style of architecture, characterised by blank external walls and a square building form. There are almost no decorative elements in the house, and only one remaining window, which faces the front porch. Once there were two smaller windows in the rear wall of the same room but these have been filled in, leaving only small square openings. Other architectural elements common to old Qatari houses such as *raushans* and interior alcoves are not found in this simple house. There are not even any *marsams* along any of the parapets, just niches cut out to allow water to drain from the door.

There are three main rooms, each with an exterior door that opens onto the courtyard. A fourth door, also facing the courtyard, is located in the middle room but has been blocked with concrete blocks and plastered over with mortar on the exterior. Inside, the ceilings throughout the house are constructed in the traditional manner, consisting of *danshal*, wood beams overlain with *basgill* and *mangharour*, and finally with a layer of rocks topped with *tanqa al-tiin* mud plaster on the exterior roof surface. These roofs are the only major traditional element of what is otherwise a concrete hollow-block building and are now breaking up and sagging badly. The roof over the east half of the house, including the front porch, is more substantial than the roof over the rest of the house, with the use of heavier, sawn wood beams covered with closely spaced bamboo.

On the roof, roughly over the centre of the house, is a curious square tower-like construction, the size of a small room, which, for obvious structural reasons, is centred over a small room of the same size and shape directly below on the ground floor. This room looks like a watch-tower and gives the house a fortress-like look. The only access to this rooftop room is by an exterior stair along the east wall of the house, which leads across the roof to a door on the east wall of the room. There were once large rectangular windows on the other three sides of this room, but these were subsequently plugged with concrete blocks. On the front and rear sides, some of this block has been removed to create irregular openings in what appears to have been a crude attempt to create window openings again. The roof of the lower room has small decorative corner parapets that represent the only hint of architectural decoration anywhere in the entire house.

The wall around the compound is also constructed from concrete blocks and is still intact, though much of the outer layer of cement plaster has disappeared to reveal the blocks beneath. There is a small, single-roomed building at the south-west corner of the courtyard, constructed from blocks topped by a traditional roof. It has two doorway entrances facing north and east into the courtyard, no windows and was likely used for storage. The north entrance facing the main house has been filled with concrete blocks, then later, the top portion of the blocks was pushed out to recreate an opening.

• This house represents a typical example of Arabian style of architecture, characterised by blank external walls and a square building form

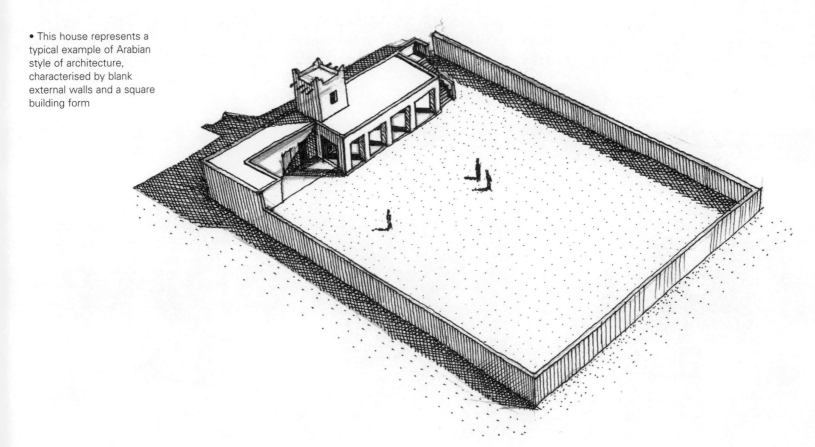

• Ground floor plan rooms are arranged in a linear fashion along the near of the compound, which also serves as the near wall of the compound

Private room

Circulation

Open private area

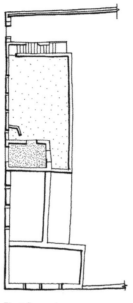

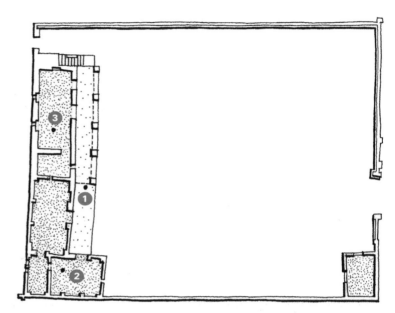

First floor plan

Ground floor plan

• Entrance to the room
• Inside, the ceiling throughout the house are constructed in the traditional manner

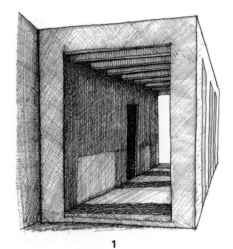

1

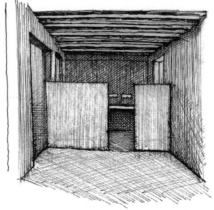

2

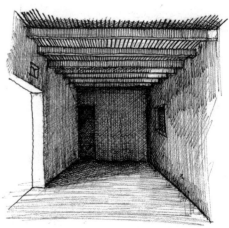

3

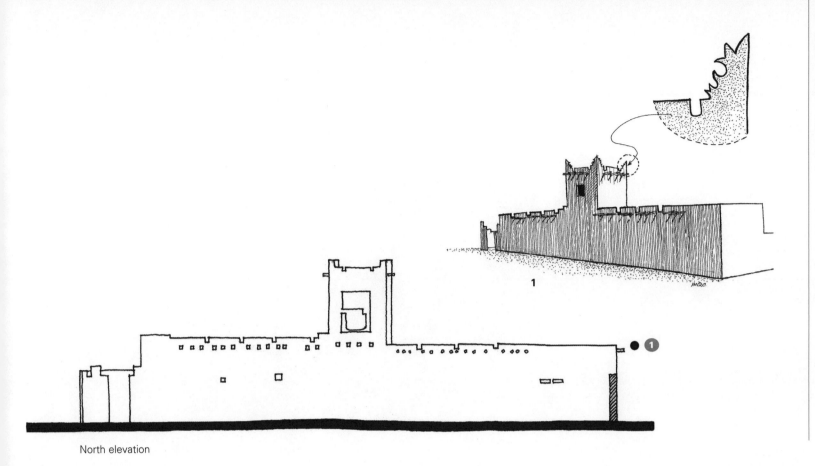

1

North elevation

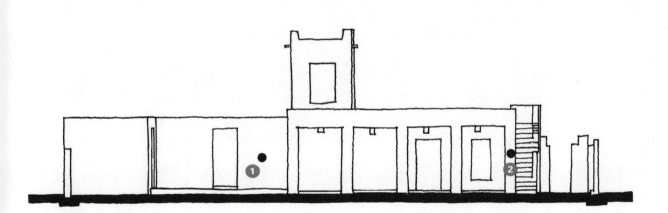

South elevation

• The only access to the
rooftop room is by an exterior
stair
• The room on the rooftop
looks like a watch tower
and gives the house
a fortress-like look

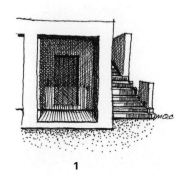

1

2

93

• Inside room

1

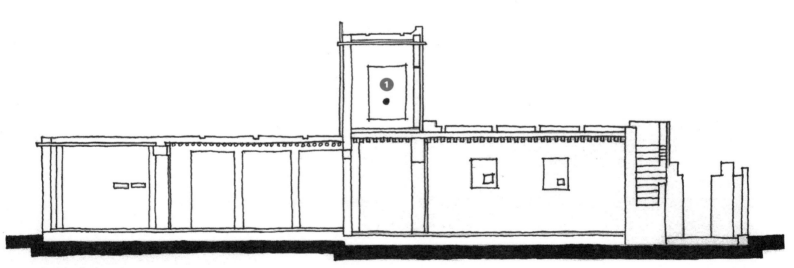

Longitudinal section

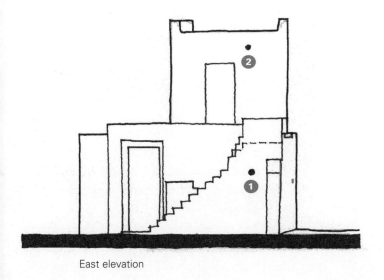

East elevation

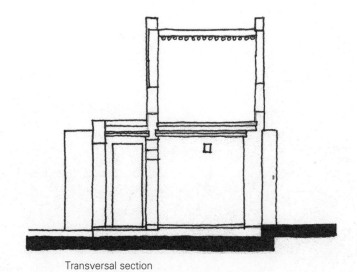

Transversal section

• Detail of the stair
• Entrance to the room
in the top roof

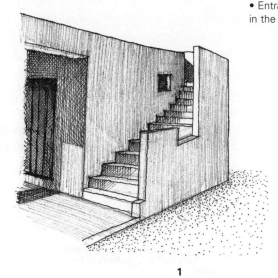

1

2

Abdullah Bin Saad House (Al Wakrah) (1940)

Introduction

Abdullah Bin Saad House is an important building in the sea-side town of Wakrah, 23 kilometres south of Doha. It sits at the south end of what was Old Wakrah Village. The Wakrah Municipality took ownership of the house in 1984 with plans to demolish it as part of re-designing Old Wakrah. In 1986, work started on restoring it as a museum and it was finally opened to the public as a working museum. The house has had many owners in the past, the last owner being Abdullah Bin Saad Al Mutallaq.

Architectural Description of the House

Abdullah Bin Saad House is an isolated building close to the shore. The nearest buildings are a set of ruins to the south-east, and some newer buildings to the west. The architecture is typical of the houses built in Wakrah in the early part of the twentieth century, and its plan follows the typical Arabic houses of the time. It comprises five rooms plus a *majlis* and an upper room, all of which open onto a central courtyard. The central courtyard also had a well, which was used for dishwashing and bathing. According to one source, the *majlis* was built after the house in AH 1359 (1922), which makes the original house date pre AH 1357 (1920). The date of the *majlis* is carved into the gypsum decoration on the centre column.

The house and the *majlis* are constructed primarily of stone and mud overlaid with gypsum, which is the traditional method. The roofs of all areas are made from *danshall* beams overlaid with *basgill* and *mangharour*. The final finish on the roof is mud and then covered concrete. Many of the original doors and windows have been restored. The Upper room, *majlis* and lower room have extensive gypsum details. The Upper room, in particular, is very beautifully detailed with many *badgheer* recesses and decorated wall vents. These are in good condition possibly having been carefully restored in the past. The lower room also displays gypsum carvings on the walls. There is a decorative cornice and several recesses present in the walls. The *majlis* also shows much decoration on the walls, arches and outer surfaces, including the date that it was built. This is an open building with a double arch and open windows across the courtyard side. It is also much taller than the other rooms of the house. The property is bordered by a stone wall, which is original.

• Aerial perspective of the house. The architecture is typical of the houses built in Wakrah in the early part of the twentieth century

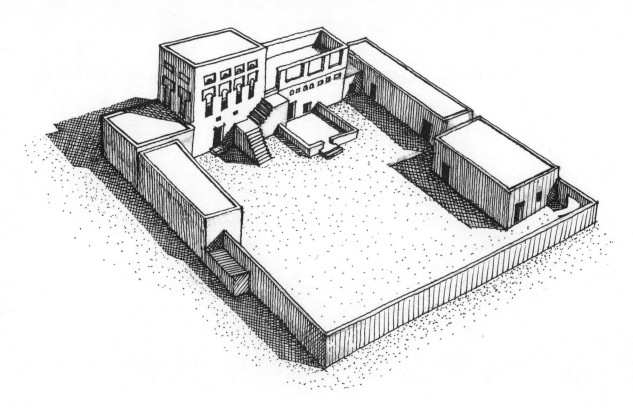

• Ground floor plan
The house comprises five rooms plus a *majlis* and upper room, all of which open onto a central courtyard

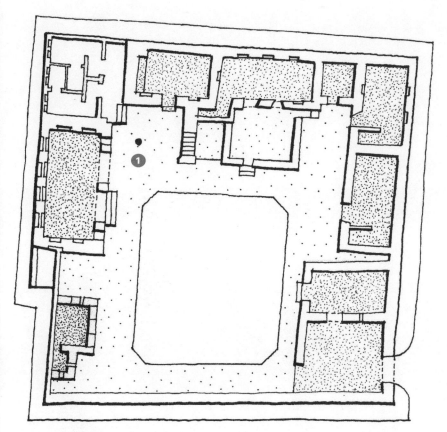

Ground floor plan

Private room

Circulation

Open private area

1

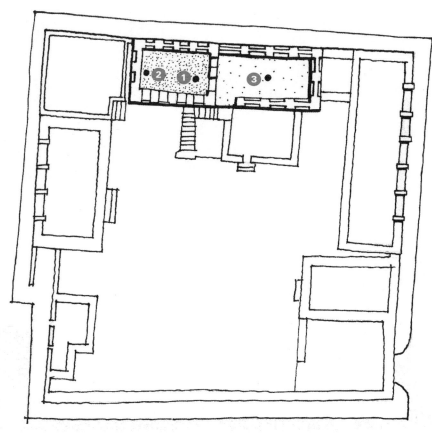

First floor plan

1

• The upper room is beautifully detailed with many *badgheer* recesses and decorated walls

2

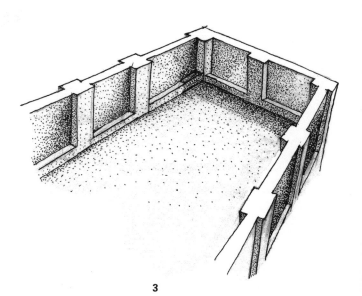

3

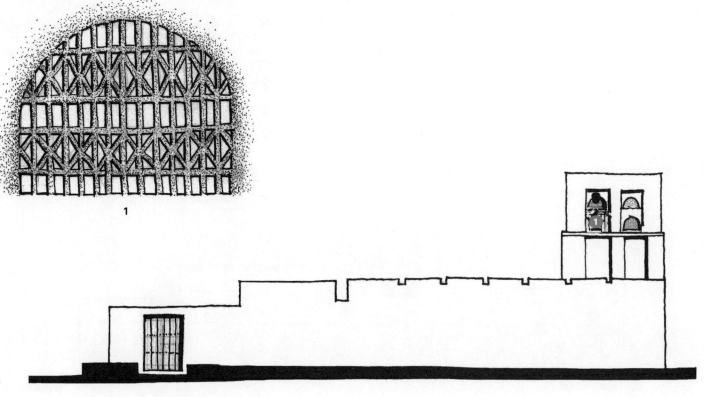

North elevation

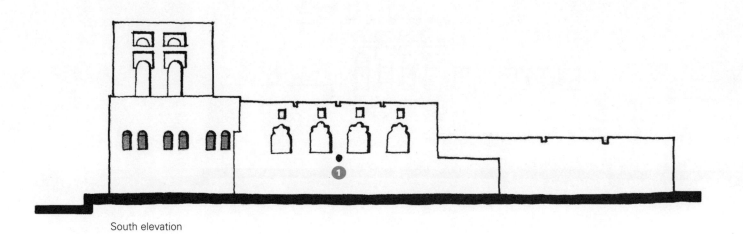

South elevation

• The *majlis* is an open building with a double arch and open windows across the courtyard side. It is also taller than the other rooms of the house

1

East elevation

West elevation

• The recesses on the external walls looking onto the street
• Decorative features on the recesses and badgheers

1

2

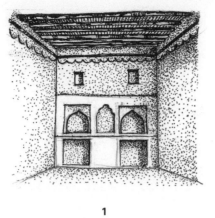

1

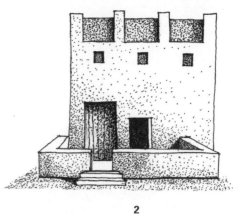

2

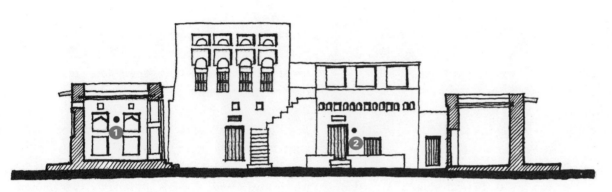

Section A

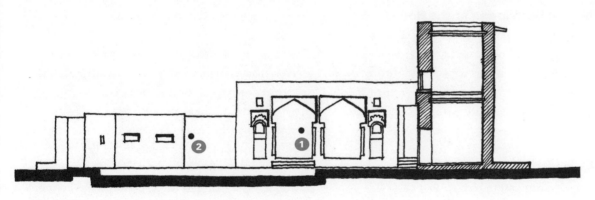

Section B

1

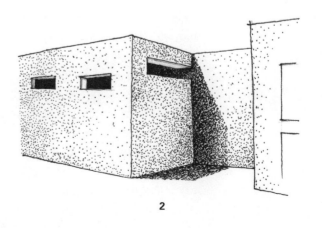

2

Mohammed Said Naserallah House (Doha) (1920)

Introduction

The house of Mohammed Said Naserallah is located in Old Doha in the Baharat Al-Juafairy area, now called Suqs. This area was a public market where most people's daily trade activities took place.

The house was built during the first quarter of the fourteenth century of Hijra, and has had several owners. The first owner was Ahmed Bin Mohammed Al-Imadi, who in turn sold it to Mr. Mohamed Bin Zein Al-Abadeen for 2000 Indian rupees. After that, it was purchased by Mohammed Said Naserallah.

Architectural Description of the House

The plan is a rectangle measuring 21 by 27 metres, with its west edge inclined creating a trapezoidal shape. Entrance to the house is provided through a gate on the south-east corner. In the entrance lobby, there is a staircase leading to the upper floor. The ground floor houses 11 different spaces surrounding a central court. The rooms are all rectangular in shape. Only one of these rooms overlooks the court through an *iwan*.

On the right hand side of the entrance, the first room encountered is a *majlis*. This allows the visitor access to it without having to pass by any of the rooms in the house, thus giving the occupants of the house their privacy. This *majlis* is beautifully decorated with external arched recesses above the window openings and wooden gutters between the recesses. The south-east corner of the building is treated by subtracting a square volume, this particular treatment, not seen in all old buildings, is intended to give more value to the entrance. Solid stone benches can be seen the whole length of the outside of the south wall and along parts of the east and west walls. The benches were of social importance since they were used by the local community and as places where passers-by can rest.

This house is one of very few Qatari houses that possessed wind towers or *malqaf*. The *malqaf* of this house is on the south-west corner, adjacent to the only room that has an *iwan*. The *malqaf* is the main decorative feature of this house. The section on the first floor has two square arches on each side fitted with decorations on the corners. The section on the first floor has three square arches on each side as well as two wooden beams between the two columns to hold them together as well as provide an element of decoration. The parapet of the tower is decorated on all sides with a very well moulded saw-tooth design.

The *iwan* on the ground floor is approximately 25 centimetres higher than the courtyard level, its square arches are supported by circular columns and fitted with decorations at their corners, a feature not seen elsewhere in Doha. The treatment of the arches is different from the treatment of the *iwan* on the first floor, which lies directly above this *iwan*. A wooden grill parapet fitted between the columns decorates the upper *iwan* and enhances its traditional feel. Another room on the first floor on the east side of the house overlooks the courtyard and can be accessed from the staircase at the entrance.

The first floor has a parapet surrounding all four sides. Like all traditional houses, this parapet is a *badgheer* since the occupants sometimes use the roof as a sleeping area during the summer.

• Aerial perspective of the house. The south-east corner of the building in treated by subtracting a square volume. This particular treatment is intended to give more value to the entrance. This house is one of very few Qatari house that possessed a wind tower or *malqaf*

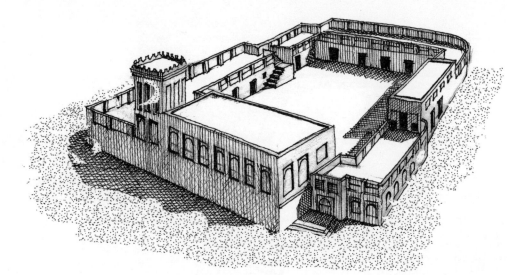

• Ground floor plan. The plan is a rectangle with its west edge creating a trapezoidal shape

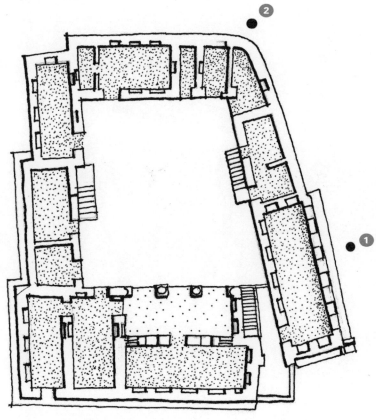

Ground floor plan

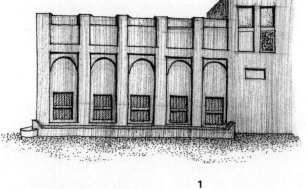

• The *majlis* is beautifully decorated with external arched recesses above the window openings and wooden gutters between the recesses

1

 Private room

 Circulation

☐ Open private area

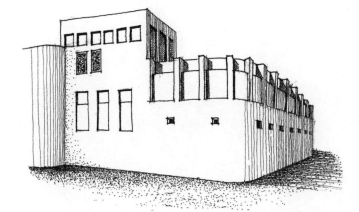

2

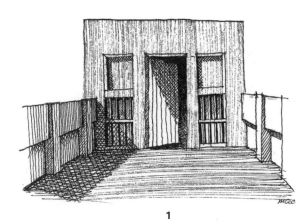

• View showing entrance
to the upper room

1

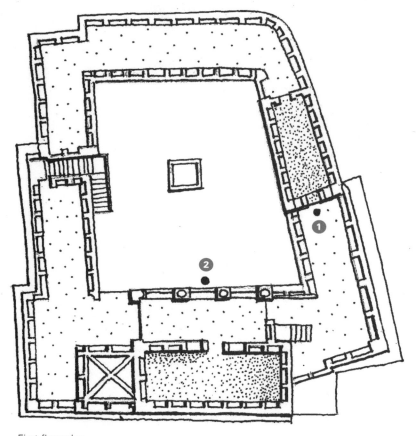

First floor plan

• This floor has a parapet
surrounding all four sides
houses, this parapet is a
badgheer since occupants
sometimes use the roof
as a sleeping area during
the summer

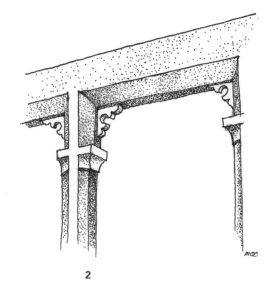

2

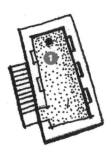

Mezzanine

• View inside the room
on the mezzanine floor

1

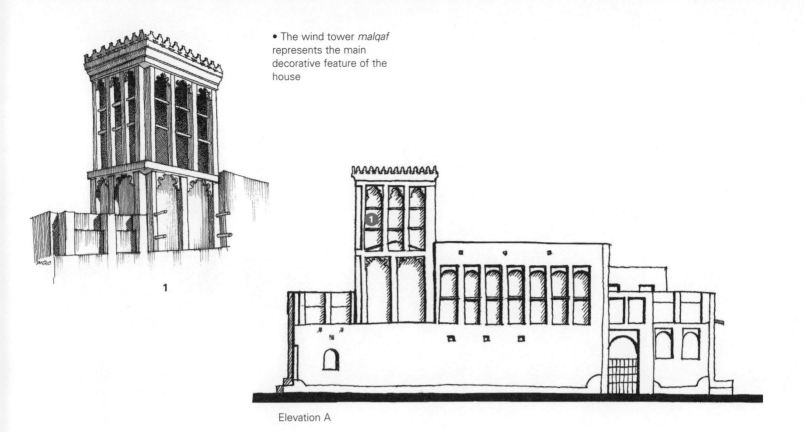

• The wind tower *malqaf* represents the main decorative feature of the house

Elevation A

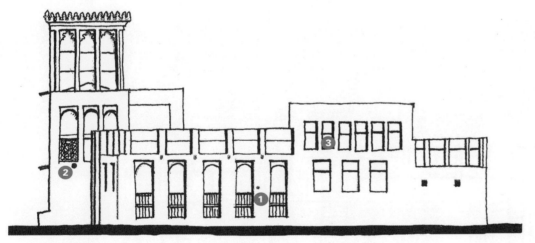

Elevation B

1

2

3

1

2

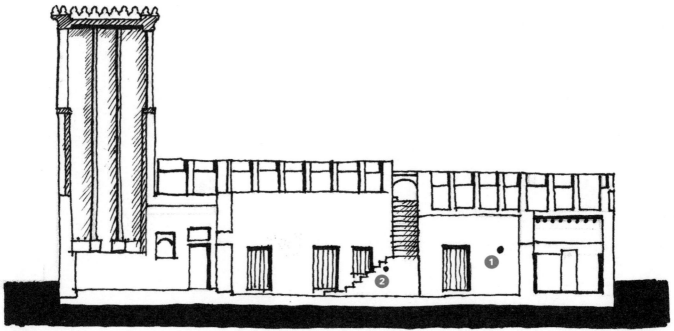

Section A-A

• View of decorative features
used in the wind tower

1

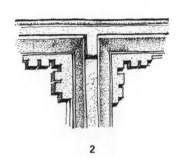

2

3

• The *iwan* on ground floor is
higher than the courtyard
level. Its square arches are
supported by circular
columns and fitted with
decorations at their corner a
feature not seen elsewhere
in Doha

Section B-B

Nasser Bin Ahmed Obeidan House
(Al Jasra, Doha)
(1940)

Introduction

This house belongs to the Obeidan family. Located just half a kilometre away from the Corniche, the plot is on Ukaz Street in the heart of Old Doha, at the Abdullah Bin Thani roundabout. Some sources mention that this house dates back to the start of the twentieth century; other sources record it as being built in 1940. In either case, the house has witnessed all the major changes that have occurred in Doha over the past 63 years.

Architectural Description of the House

Nasser Bin Ahmed Obeidan House is a large building, rectangular in shape, measuring approximately 42 by 31 metres. At the south-east end of the plot, a large section (14 × 20 m) has been sectioned off and a new building occupies the space, leaving a clear square court measuring approximately 19 metres on each side.

No doubt, at the time this area was sectioned off there would have been an original part of the building occupying the same area, 7 metres away from the boundary wall, providing more privacy for the main court as it would have been used by the family members. The missing part may have been a *majlis* open to the courtyard at the entrance gate.

The main building now consists of two major sections; one runs along the entire length of the north boundary of the plot and contains the main entrance. The second section is an L-shaped building that runs along part of the south and west walls. The L-shaped building consists of four rectangular rooms, similar in size. Each pair of rooms is separated by an open space measuring 2.5 by 4 metres. These spaces have recently been closed with either concrete blocks or plywood sheets so they can be used as rooms. Original ornaments are fitted on the walls inside the rooms; wall recesses, consisting of two parts, a lower rectangular part and an upper part closed with an arch. These recesses are approximately 20 centimetres deep. Where there are windows, they can be as deep as 40 centimetres. Under the *danshal* beams level, the ceiling is decorated with a cornice chamfered at the corners. Outside the rooms, 13 decorative octagonal columns border an *iwan* 2.5 metres deep. The surfaces of the corner columns are decorated with different shapes. The same details are used to decorate the side of the roof parapet that overlooks the courtyard, giving the house a more prestigious look. A staircase occupying the central corner of the L-shape provides access to the roof where a new room has recently been added on the north edge.

The other section of the house, running along the north wall, consists of a shallow rectangle 42 metres by 4 metres that houses 7 rooms, a staircase and the main entrance gate. The floor level of this section is no less than 45 centimetres above the courtyard level, which means both parts have the same height of floor slab, probably because they were joined on the west end, providing access from one building to the other. The rooms on the north wall have different decorations inside. Some rooms are fitted with vertical recesses that run along the height of the wall, while other recesses are divided in two. Other rooms don't show any type of decoration at all, suggesting that their function was different, probably service areas, kitchens or storage areas. This part has an L-shaped staircase leading to the roof area 4.3 metres above the courtyard level.

The ceiling of this house is totally changed. The original ceiling consisting of *danshal* wood beams overlain with *basgill* and *mangharour* doesn't exist anymore. Instead a new roof slab made of concrete has been built. An attempt to keep the old style has been made; the square wood and the thick hardwood used as the mould for the ceiling during construction has been kept and dealt with as an element that has the same look and feel as the original ceiling.

Although a part of the east wall is now constructed of concrete blocks, the boundary wall of the compound consists mostly of the original stone used. The external north part of the wall is the only part that shows what the building previously looked like, that is to say decorated with recesses along the length of the wall. On the north-east corner of the plot, the main gate was the only gate in Qatar decorated with *muqarnas* feature, a three dimensional honeycomb pattern that is specific to Islamic architecture. Unfortunately, due to heavy rain in February 1988, the top part of the gate was destroyed and never restored.

• Aerial perspective of the house. This house is a large building rectangular in shape

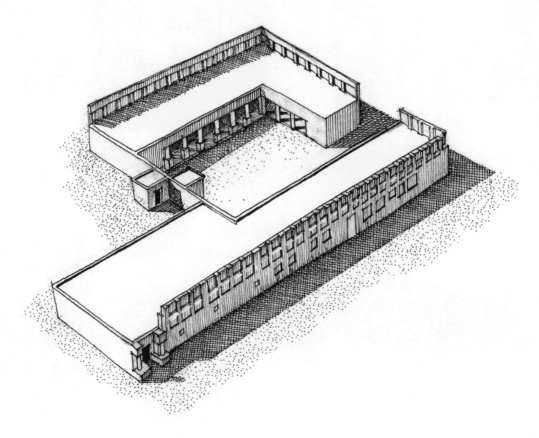

• Ground floor plan.
The building consists of two
major sections. The L-shape
section contains four
rectangular rooms similar
in size

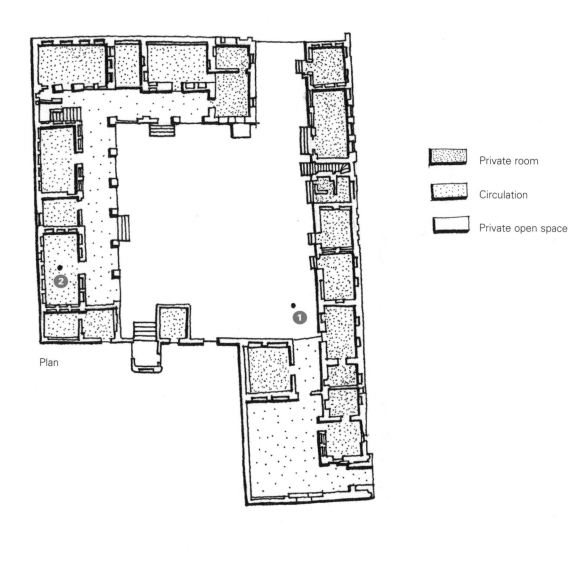

Plan

Private room

Circulation

Private open space

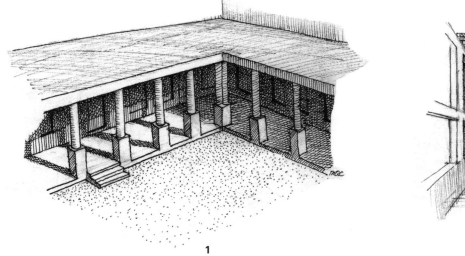

1

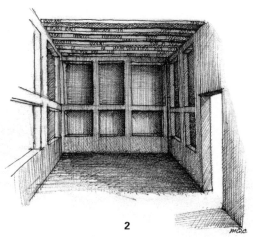

2

• View indicating the main
entrance to the house
and decorated external walls
with recesses

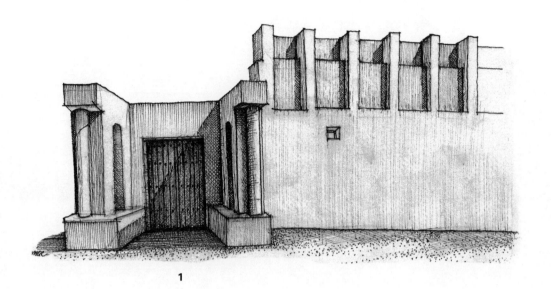

1

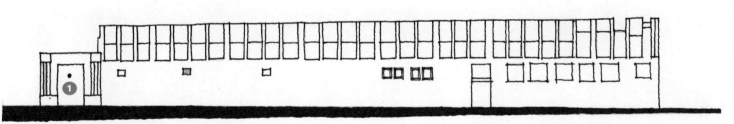

South elevation

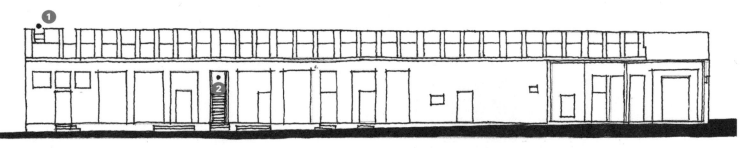

Section A

• View of the parapet

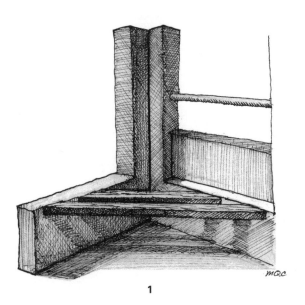

1

• View of the stair

2

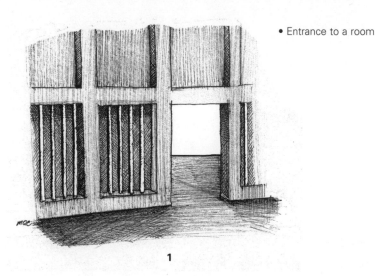

• Entrance to a room

1

Section B

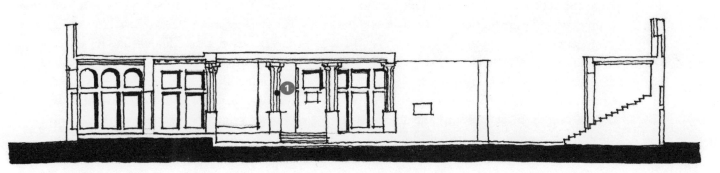

Section C

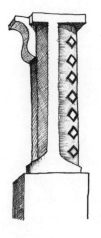

• Detail of column

1

Habib Ali Hassan House
(Behind Kahraba Street, Doha)
(1935)

Introduction

Located just behind Kahraba Street, Habib Ali Hassan House stands on a street corner in the busy centre of Doha. Bordered by two streets, this house is thought to have been built in 1940, however, photographs suggest that it was only in existence after 1956. In either case, the house holds an important position in the history of Doha and Qatar.

Architectural Description of the House

Habib Ali Hassan House is of average size for the period. It is almost square in plan, measuring approximately 23 by 24 metres, and is bounded on two sides by relatively new buildings. It consists of three distinct areas, which are all built around courtyards and were probably all built around the same period.

The main part of the house is U-shaped. It consists of seven rooms and a staircase leading to the roof. Curiously, this area contained two wells. One of these was in the main courtyard; the other was in what is now a room. Both are now dry and well hidden, having been covered with concrete.

The entrance to the main area of the house is through an ornate gateway and door containing a *khoka*. The gate faces what would have been a secondary street at the time. The entrance corridor is covered at the same level as the house. Originally, two doors led off from the entrance corridor, one into the first room (probably the *majlis*), and one onto the porch. The porch continues around three sides of the house, and has stone columns decorated with cement details in the upper corners. The corridor also opens out into the courtyard at its end. The roof appears to be original in most areas, consisting of *danshal* wood beams overlain with *basgill* and *mangharour*; however in many of the rooms, there is a modern plywood false ceiling.

The second section of the house consists of three rooms and is L-shaped. Its entrance is through a simple steel gate from the secondary street. There is one porch area, but this is not decorated with cement details in the corners as in the main part of the house. The main roof is again traditional, while many of the room ceilings are plywood.

The third section of the house is different in architectural style, suggesting that it may have been built later than the first two. There is no porch which the rooms open out onto. Furthermore, the porch that does exist has round concrete columns, rather than stone ones. This area consists of five rooms, though only three seem to be actively used. The smallest room is clearly used for storage as it only possesses a sand floor. All of this area has a traditional roof and all of the rooms, with the exception of one, have modern plywood false ceilings. The entrance is from the minor street, again through a simple steel gate.

• Aerial perspective of Habib Ali Hassan. The house is almost square in plan. It consists of three distinct areas, which are all built around courtyards

• Ground floor plan. The main part of the house is U-shaped. It consists of seven rooms and a staircase leading to the roof. The second section of the house consists of three rooms and is L-shaped. The third section is different in architectural style

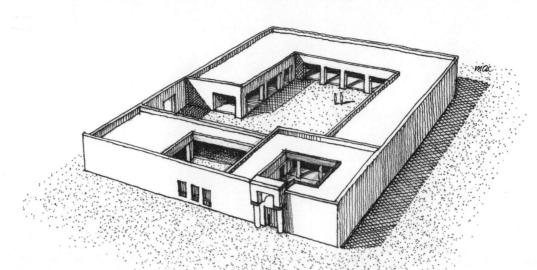

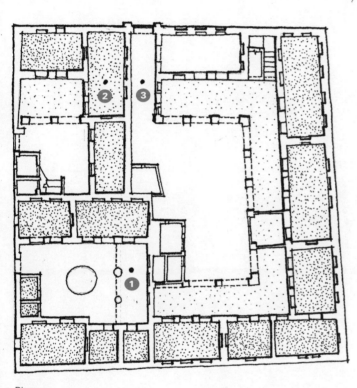

Plan

Private room

Circulation

Open private space

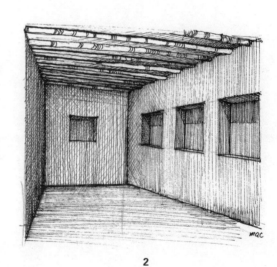

2

• The enhance to the house is from the minor street

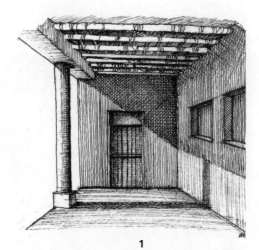

1

3

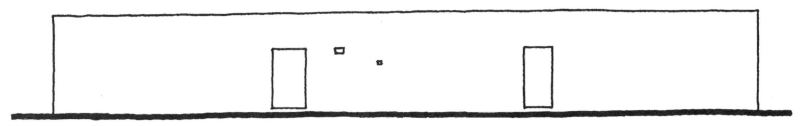

East elevation

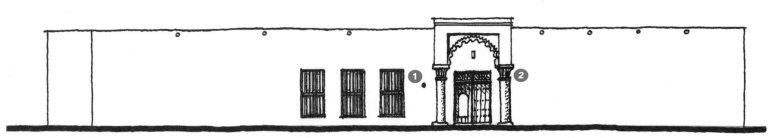

South elevation

• View of the main entrance
to the house
• Detail of the column used
in the entrance

1

2

• The roof appears to be traditional consisting of danshal wood beams overlain with basgill the mangharour
• Decorative element at the corner of the arches

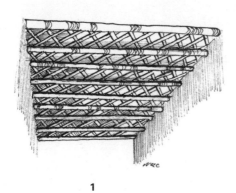

1

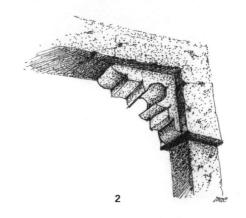

2

Section A

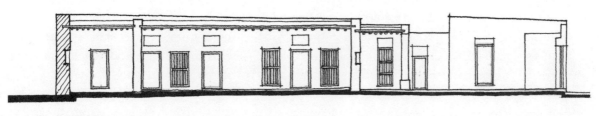

Section B

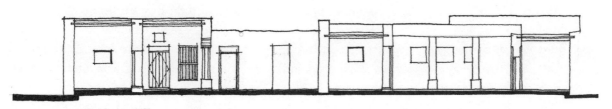

Section C

• View showing decorated arches in the liwan

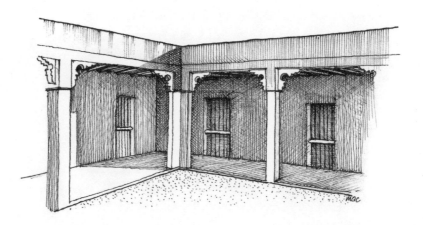

Faraj Hashim Al Ansari House (Musheirib, Doha) (1935)

Introduction

Located off Al-Maymoon Street in Asmakh, central Doha, Faraj Hashim Al Ansari House is a significant two-storey building. Its location in Doha's central business district dictates that its renovation should take priority and its potential re-use as consulting offices or other commercial premises is assured.

Architectural Description of the House

The house has two storeys that differ architecturally, suggesting that they were completed at different times. There were four entrances to the lower courtyard, three from the Sikka on the east side and the other from the south. The larger east entrance was probably the main entry point to the house. There have been many changes in this area, but it appears that there is no roof over the entrance, and that the house roof has recently been renovated. This may have been to provide for a new staircase to the upper level. The other two entrances from the east side led to staircases. The first of these has been blocked, as the staircase has been abandoned and used for storage. The second leads to two small rooms beneath the staircase. From the outside, the house is typical in that it has few windows or features. In the past it had *badgheers* around the north, west and south walls, but many of these have been removed or destroyed. A modern garage door has been installed in the north-west corner that services a garage.

The ground floor is built on a large courtyard and consists of 19 rooms. One of these, the garage, can only be accessed from outside the building, as all other old accesses have been blocked. There are two abandoned stairwells in the South-east corner and both are in very poor condition. One stairwell leads to the upper storey, the second leads to a blocked doorway to the Sikka on the east side. Under these stairs there is a small series of two rooms and a corridor, which opens off the stairwell from the Sikka. This entrance is no longer used and the rooms have a new door directly to the Sikka. In several rooms in the ground floor, new doors have been cut to access bathrooms. In the north wall, these bathrooms are located outside the boundary of the original house, with the doors being cut in the outer wall. A porch on all sides, made of concrete and overlaid with tiles, surrounds the courtyard. The rooms downstairs all show typical details in their walls and all have traditional roofs of "*danshall*" beams, overlaid with "*basgill*" and *mangharour*", however in many of the rooms, there is a modern plywood false ceiling. In some areas the traditional windows have been replaced by aluminium fixtures but many of the original doors remain.

The second floor of the house is different in architectural style suggesting that it may have been built later than the lower floor. The top floor is a collection of separate areas, rather than one continuous building. The rooms are built over the roof of the lower storey and have individual porched roofs. These have been constructed from square timber and concrete in most cases. The columns here are round concrete rather than the square stone of the ground floor.

• Aerial perspective of the house. This house has two storeys that differ architecturally

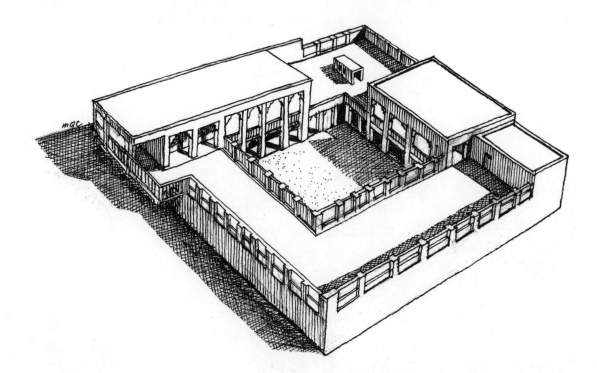

• Ground floor plan. This floor is built on a large courtyard and consists of 19 rooms

• Liwan and decorative arches are shown in this view

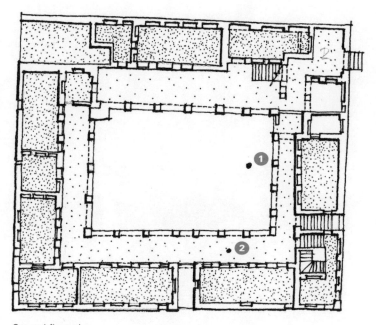

Ground floor plan

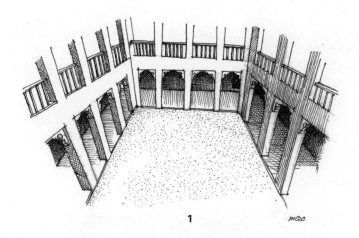

1

Private room

Circulation

Open private space

2

• The liwan has a traditional roof

119

• First floor plan. This floor of the house is different in architectural style suggesting that it may have been built later that the lower floor

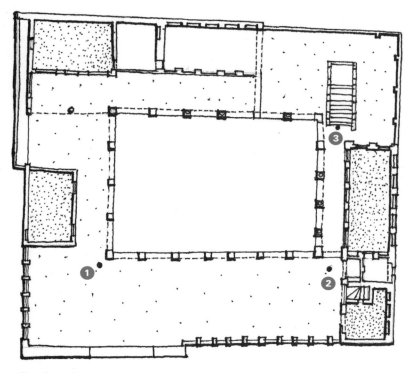

First floor plan

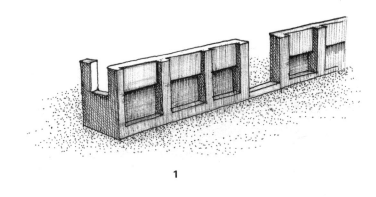

1

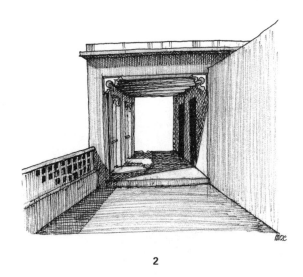

2

3

• View of the stair

• Main entrance to the house

1

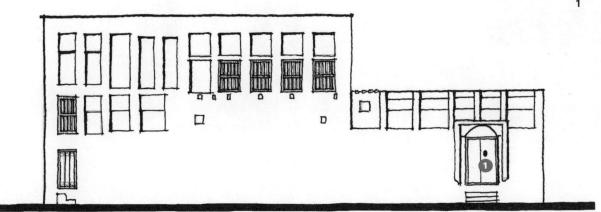

East elevation

• It can be argued that this balcony was added to the house since it does not reflect typical Qatari architecture

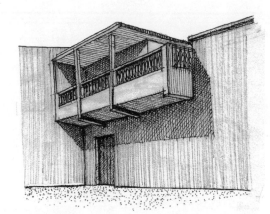

2

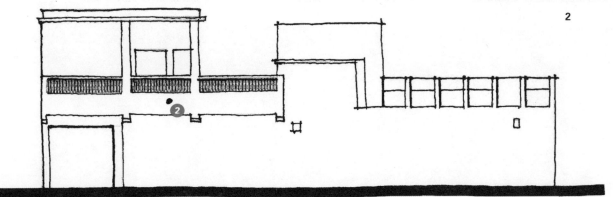

West elevation

• Liwan and decorated arches
are shown in this detail

• View detailing one typical
arch with decorative
elements in the corners

1

2

Section A

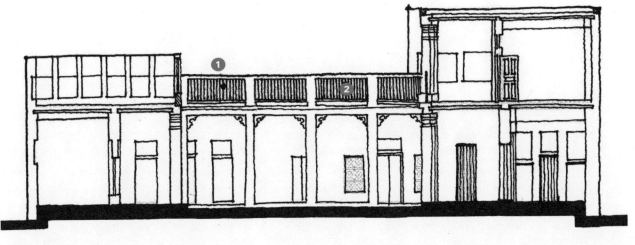

Section B

1

2

Sheikh Mohammed Bin Ahmed Al Thani House
(Al Asmakh, Doha)
(1940)

Introduction

Sheikh Mohammed Bin Ahmed Al Thani House is located off Maymoon Street in Asmakh, the central area of Doha. The Asmakh area of Doha is noted for its old and significant buildings, and this property is no exception. The Al-Thani family has a long and extremely important history in Qatar, having been the ruling family for many years and shaped the economic and social growth of the country. Sheikh Mohammed Bin Ahmed Al Thani House is important in many ways. The house shares a courtyard with a property owned by the same person (see pp. 128–131). Sharing a courtyard is unusual as this does not give either house privacy. From old maps of the area, it appears that the compound occupied a rectangle bordered by streets on all sides and contained within walls. It also seems that a significant part of this compound may have been built over earlier to build the commercial buildings now in the street frontages on the west and north sides. The house was used as offices for the military around 10 years after it was built, and before it was rented out as accommodation for labourers.

Architectural Description of the House

Sheikh Mohammed Bin Ahmed Al Thani House is part of a larger compound. This compound consists of two houses, a significant commercial section and many additional plywood and hollow block buildings. The house itself is an elongated L-shape of 12 rooms, not counting those constructed out of the porch. A large gate seems to give entrance to the compound, which is shared with the adjoining house (see pp. 128–131). It is not clear whether this was the only entrance. A porch extends the entire length of the building. Two staircases originally led to the roof but now rise to upper rooms constructed from hollow blocks and concrete on the roof.

The staircases are typical in that they turn through 90° on landings. The porch floor is made of concrete and the roof is made from the traditional *danshal* beams, overlaid with *basgill* and *mangharour*. The final finish on the roof varies as some areas have been covered. Many of the original doors and windows remain, and it appears that with the exception of the rooms on the roof the whole house was built at the same time.

The outer columns of the porch show concrete details in the top corners. These are of a similar style to many other buildings of the era. At the south end of the house, the column detail changes and a thicker base of concrete exists for a height of 1.5 metres. This detail is only seen in four columns at this end; all the other columns are of constant section. In the small section of the L, the column details at the top change to a simple arc, similar to that seen in house of Sheikh Mohammed Bin Ahmed Al Thani. The rooms in both sections of the house are simply decorated with no rectangular recesses or cornice details. There were interconnecting doors between each room, but these were closed when the house was used as military offices. Today the openings are filled.

• Aerial perspective. This house is part of a larger compound consisting of two houses

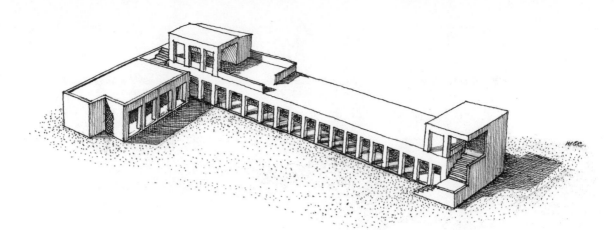

• Ground floor plan. This house itself is an elongated L-shape of 12 rooms

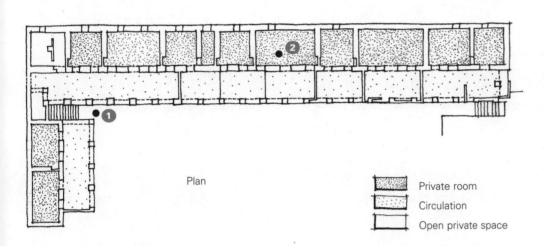

Plan

	Private room
	Circulation
	Open private space

1

• View of the stair

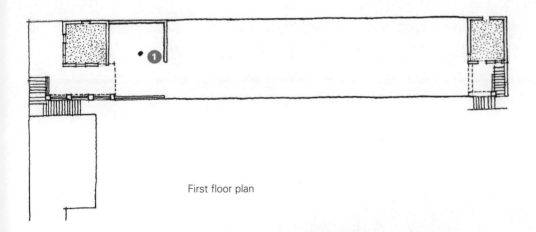

First floor plan

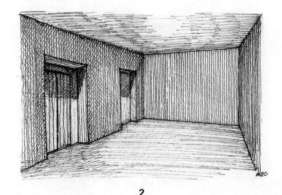

2

• Simple example of inside room with no decorative features

• This figure shows the extension room with shaded area. This room may have been built later than the lower floor

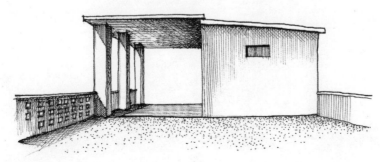

1

125

1

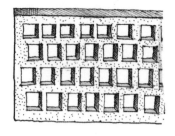

2

- The *liwan* and arches with their decorative elements in the corner
- Decorative elements used in the upper parapet

North elevation

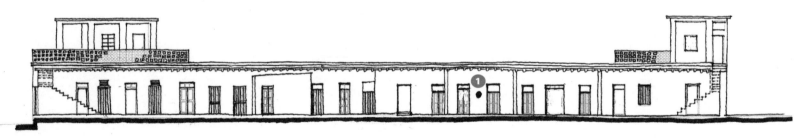

Section A

- View onto inside room. Traditional room is also shown in this detail

1

• Detailed view of the arches. Here the decorative elements used in the corners are different from the ones used in other arches

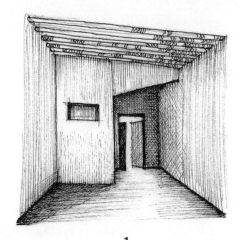

1

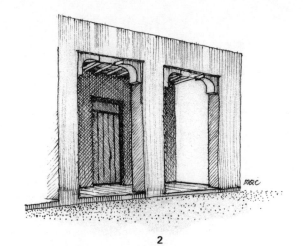

2

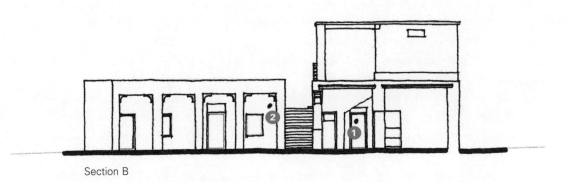

Section B

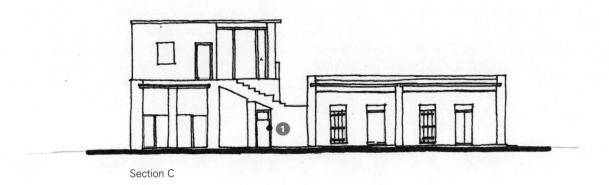

Section C

• Traditional roof used in the *liwan*

1

Sheikh Mohammed Bin Ahmed Al Thani House
(Al Asmakh, Doha)
(1940)

Introduction

This is the house that shares the compound of Sheikh Mohammed Bin Ahmed Al Thani House (see pp. 124–127), just off Maymoon Street in Asmakh, the central area of Doha.

The Asmakh area is noted for its old buildings, and this property is no exception.

The Al-Thani family has a long and extremely important history in Qatar, having been the ruling family for many years and shaped the economic and social growth of the country.

Sheikh Mohammed Bin Ahmed Al Thani House is important in many ways.

The house shares a courtyard with a property owned by the same person (see pp. 124–127). Sharing a courtyard is unusual as this does not give either house privacy. From old maps of the area, it appears that the compound occupied a rectangle bordered by streets on all sides and contained within walls. It also seems that a significant part of this compound may have been built over earlier to build the commercial buildings now in the street frontages on the west and north sides.

Architectural Description of the House

Sheikh Mohammed Bin Ahmed Al Thani House is part of a larger compound. At the time of the survey, this compound consists of two houses, a significant commercial section and many added plywood and hollow block buildings. The house itself is an elongated L-shape of 12 rooms, including those constructed out of the porch. The entrance appears to be through a large gate, which leads into the shared compound. A porch extends the entire length of the building. The porch floor is made of concrete and the roof is made from the traditional *danshal* beams overlaid with *basgill* and *mangharour*. The finish on the roof is mud covered with concrete. Many of the original doors and windows remain, and the house appears that it was built around the same time as house of Sheikh Mohammed Bin Ahmed Al Thani. The outer columns of the porch show concrete details in the top corners; however these are simpler than Sheikh Mohammed Bin Ahmed Al Thani House, the other house in the compound. The rooms are simply decorated with no rectangular recesses or cornice details.

• Aerial perspective of the house. The house is of simple rectangular form. It is sharing a courtyard with a property owned by the same person

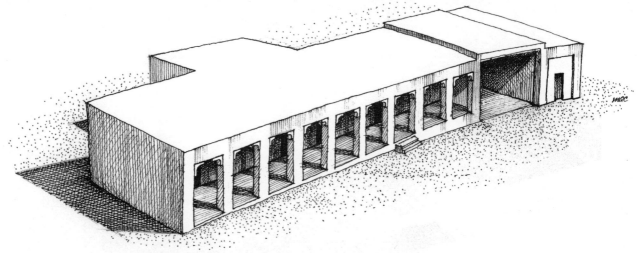

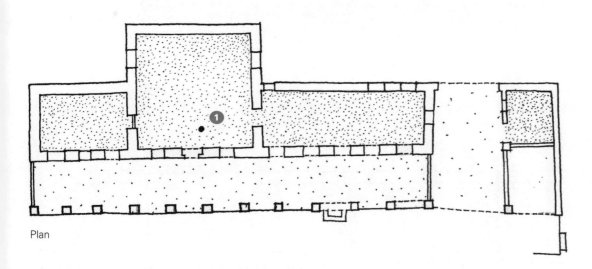

Plan

• Ground floor plan. The house consists of three main rooms different in shape and size. The rooms are all open to the *liwan*. There is no courtyard in this house. The room on the east corner could be added later. There is also a covered corridor between the two sections of the house

▨ Private room

▨ Circulation

☐ Open private space

• The view shows the inside of one of the rooms which may have been considered as main one. Typical traditional roof is utilized in this house

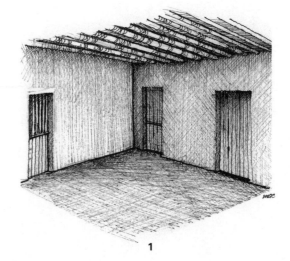

1

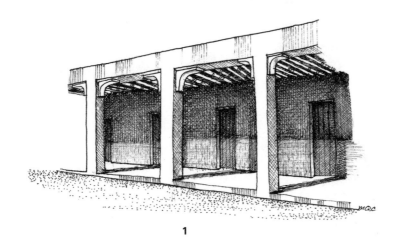

• View of the *liwan*
and decorated arches

1

East elevation

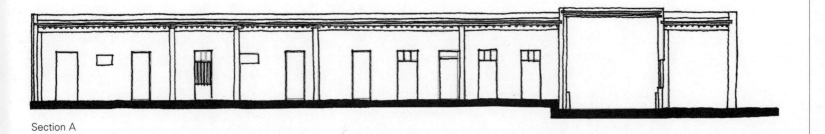

Section A

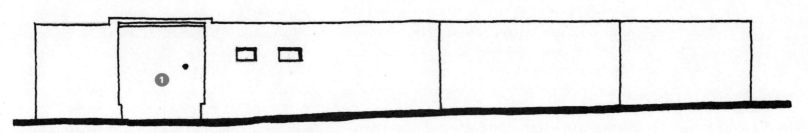

West elevation

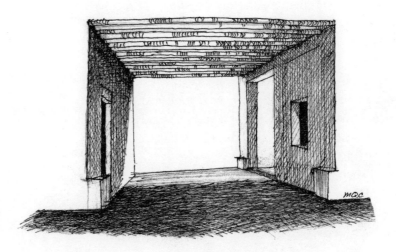

• Tradition roof is also used
for the shaded corridor
connecting the two sections
of the house

1

Al Jaber House (Al Asmakh, Doha) (1935)

Introduction

Al Jaber House is also located in the Asmakh area of Doha. The number of historic buildings in this area suggests that it should be preserved as a historic district in the centre of Doha. The house is typical of the Qatari architecture of the period, having a common courtyard for the house and L-shaped buildings around it. It appears that it was an important house in the area since it had one, possibly two wells, and an imposing entrance. The large walled courtyard also displays the importance of the house.

Architectural Description of the House

Al Jaber House is traditionally set around a large central courtyard. The courtyard is surrounded by a high wall, and features a large gate that gives onto the street. The gate is of decorative stone and has a *khokha* in its wooden door. The fence around the property has probably been replaced for most of its original length, with only the east wall and the old entrance gate seeming original. The gate exists on the street frontage but has been sealed with hollow blocks on the inside.

The architecture is plain and typical, with no relief details or decorated columns. The main house consists of eight rooms, with bathrooms and a separate room on the entrance side of the courtyard. The additional buildings are hollow block. Along the east wall of the courtyard there is evidence of buildings and entrances that have been demolished, with a stone and mud raised area still visible. In the north-east corner, an old well has been built over and is now used as a bathroom. There is also evidence here of previous buildings and entrances, as much of this area is of early construction. The well probably contains salt water.

The courtyard is the setting for a large outdoor seating area and a thriving tree that supplies well-needed shade. Beneath this tree is part of an old wall, suggesting that there was another well or washing place here also. Now, the area serves as the main washing and water tanking area.

All of the rooms open onto a raised porch that extends the length of the house. The porch floor is made of concrete and the roof is the traditional roof of *danshal* beams overlaid with *basgill* and *mangharour*. Many of the original doors and windows remain. All of the rooms have rectangular recesses in the walls and original roofs, with the exception of one small room. A staircase leads to the roof.

Much of the house appears to have been constructed at the same time, with the exception of the kitchen, outer room and bathrooms. The area that has been demolished on the east side was probably part of the original house, which was abandoned earlier and left to ruins. There are no architectural features that set this house apart from the others, except for the staircase to the roof. This staircase is one straight flight, unlike the other staircases that turn 90° with landings.

• Aerial perspective. The house is typical Qatari architecture, having a common courtyard for the house and L-shaped building. The architecture is plain and typical with no relief details or decorated columns

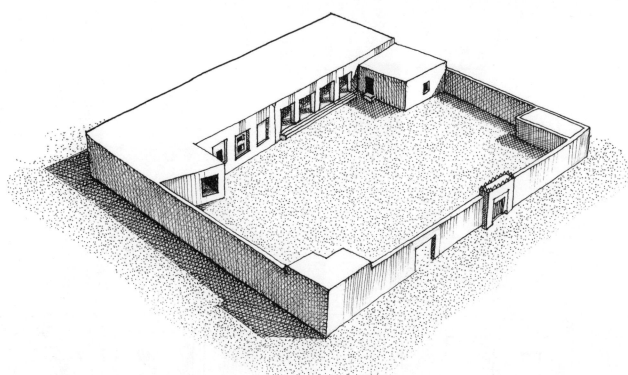

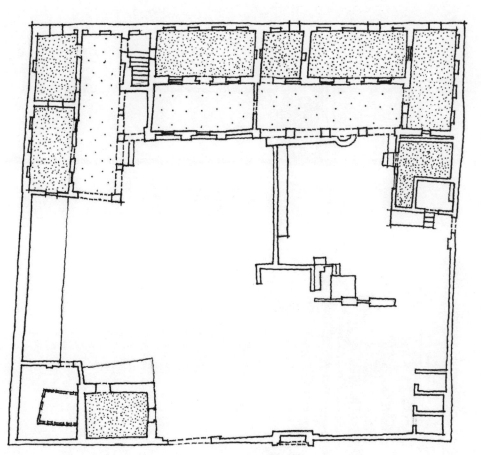

Private room

Circulation

Open private space

• Ground floor plan. Al Jaber is traditionally set around a large central courtyard. The main house consists of eight rooms, with bathrooms and a separate room on the entrance side of the courtyard

Plan

- View of windows and recesses in the walls
- The arches are simple in design and no architectural decoration have been considered

1

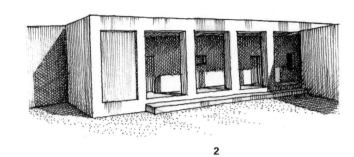

2

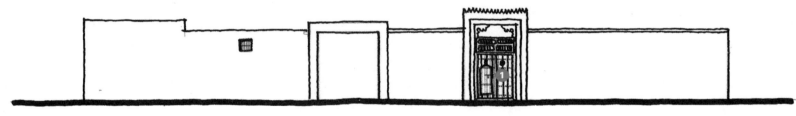

Section A

North elevation

- There are no architectural features that set this house apart from the main entrance to the house

1

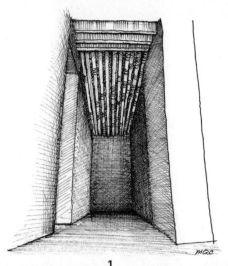

• Traditional roof is considered in the construction of this house

• View of shaded liwan

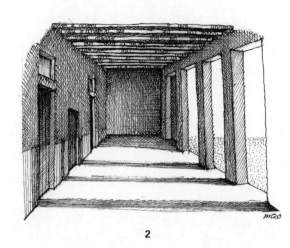

1

2

Section B

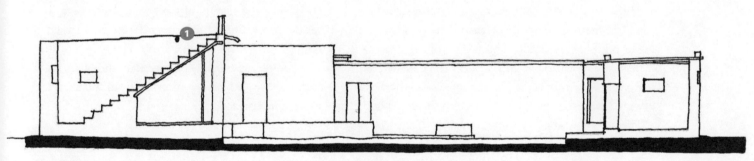

Section C

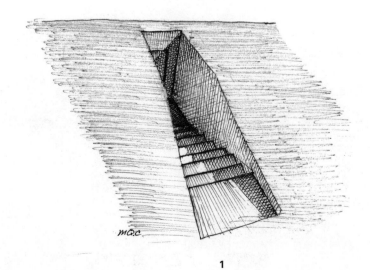

1

• View of the stair

Al Karaani House (Doha)
(1935)

Introduction

Al Karaani House is the house adjacent to Al Maarifiyya House (see pp. 140–145) on Abu Harith Street, a narrow street parallel to Maymoun Street to the north. In 1935, Abu Harith and Maymoun streets did not exist. This and evidence from aerial photographs leads to the belief that this house was not constructed until after 1952 and most probably was constructed during the same period as Al Maarifiyya House.

Architectural Description of the House

Built on a plot measuring 620 square metres, Al Karaani House is a rectangle 30 metres long and 22 metres wide. The original gate to this house was on the west façade. This is now blocked and a new gate on the north façade has been constructed. Another addition is the corridor space 2.5 metres wide that leads from the entrance to the courtyard. The corridor takes up a total area of 140 square metres and was originally part of the courtyard. The house is U-shaped in plan around a central courtyard that measures 13 by 11 metres. Except for the new block added to the entrance and some toilets inside the courtyard, the rest of the house is original.

The access to the house when it was constructed was through a beautiful gate with round columns and flower-shaped capitals located at the midway point of the west wall of the house. The gate, as such, is semi-circular, made of wood, and fitted with a *khokha*.

The only decorations other than the gate on the west façade are some high recesses and windows on the north-west corner of the house. The rectangular room to the left of the main gate is a *majlis* with windows that look onto two streets. The layout of the *majlis* at the north-west corner and its relation

to the main gate is typical of old Qatari houses since it allows guests to enter the guest area directly without passing through the private section of the house or the courtyard. Family privacy has played a major role in the planning and design of houses in Qatar.

The linear set of rooms along the west wall is also decorated with recesses on the courtyard side. A staircase leads up to the roof of the house. The bottom section of the U shape has an arcade structure of five square arches supported by square pillars with chamfered corners. Decorative elements are fitted on the corners of the pillars at the top. The remaining section of the house is simple and has no decoration. It section ends approximately 11 metres from the north façade. The height of the new two-storey block is greater than the other parts of the house and can be accessed from the corridor at the new entrance.

• Aerial perspective.
The house is of rectangular
form

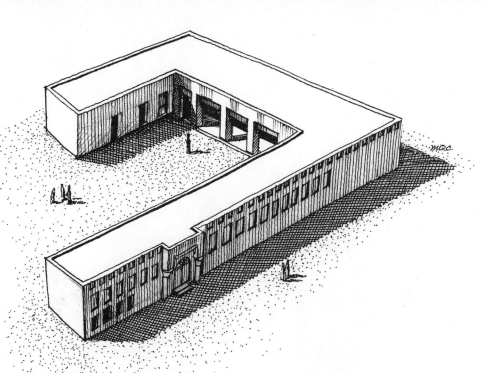

• Ground flloor plan. The
house is U-shaped in plan
around a central courtyard.
A shaded porch or *liwan* is
serving some of the rooms.
The rectangular room to the
left of the main gate is a
majlis with windows that look
onto the street. The layout of
the *majlis* or the North West
corner and its relation to the
main gate is typical of Qatari
houses since it allows guest
to enter the *majlis* (guest
area) directly without passing
through the private section
on the courtyard

• View of inside room

Main gate

Majlis

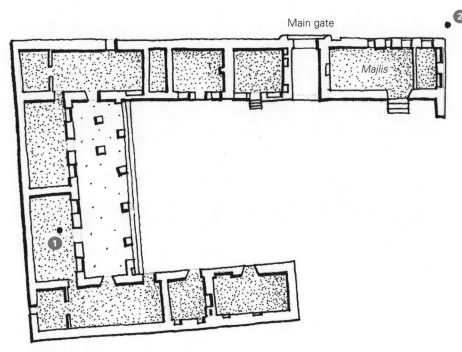

Ground floor plan

 Private room

 Circulation

  Open private space

1

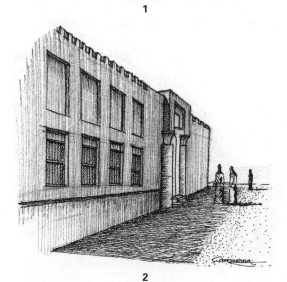

• The only decorations other
than the gate are some high
recesses and windows

2

137

1

• The main gate to the house

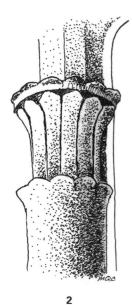

2

• Decorated columns are used for the gate

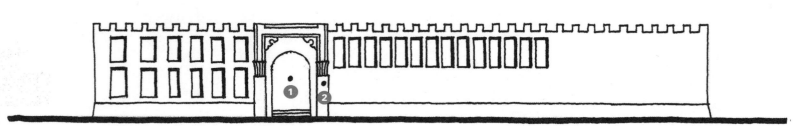

Elevation B

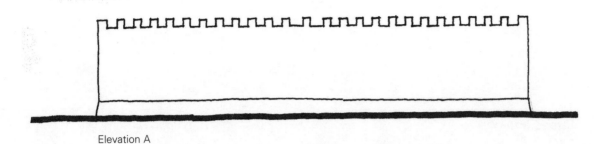

Elevation A

Section

1

• View showing the arches
and shaded porch (*liwan*)

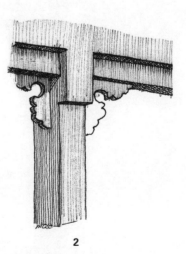

2

• Decorative element used in
the corners of the arches

Al Maarfiyya House (Abu Harith, Doha) (Post 1947)

Introduction

Located in Al-Asmakh on Abu Harith Street, a narrow street parallel to and south of Maymoun Street, Al Maarfiyya House is one of the oldest buildings in the Suq area of Doha. Once crowded with beautiful old buildings, few now remain. There is no doubt that the actual date of this house is later than 1947. Aerial photographs dating back to 1947 show evidence that Maymoun and Abu Harith Streets had not yet been defined. Other aerial photographs from 1956 show clearly both streets with urban settlements already developed and Al Maarfiyya House.

Architectural Description of the House

Al Maarfiyya House is a typical Qatari style house. It has a trapezoidal plan with an average length of 31 metres and a width of 18 metres. It consists of a series of rooms on all four sides around a central courtyard. The block can be accessed from two sides: the north and the east.

The entry from the north is through a simple modern steel gate while the entry from the east, which was probably the only entrance, is through a decorative gate with semi-circular columns and decorations inside the corners at the columns-lintel intersection.

The elevations of this house feature recesses all around the house. The parapets on the roof are *badgheers*, some of which had to be rebuilt at some stage. It is now evident that they are made from a mixture of old and new materials. On the north and south façades there are two benches each approximately 85 centimetres high.

Streets contour the building on all sides except the west, where another building is erected adjacent. The courtyard takes almost the same shape as the plot Its measurements are approximately 10 metres by 18 metres. Compared to other old houses around Doha, the rooms of this house are of medium size: the ground floor doesn't have a single large room, for example, on the scale of a *majlis*, but contains around 15 different spaces all of average size. Entering through the north gate, you see an arcade on the front wall consisting of four, equally spaced square arches, with decorative features at the corners of the columns where they meet with the beams. Three out of the four arches have been filled with concrete bricks, while the remaining one acts as a lobby for a room on the far south side of the house and another room on the south-east corner.

New rooms have been built with concrete bricks inside the courtyard, which, as a result, has lost its sense of scale. Walking into it, it is not easy to recognise the boundaries. The room on the north-west corner is totally closed from the inside and is currently used as a grocery store.

The first floor has the same plan as the ground floor. Two staircases lead to the second level, one at the north entrance and the other on the south-east side, next to the arcade of what used to be a porch.

On the first level, there are two main rooms dividing the roof into four distinct terraces. The terrace and room on the west part of the house are on a lower level than the rest of the house, while the remaining buildings are approximately on the same level.

The room on the south-west corner is impressively big. It served most probably as a *majlis*. On the south-east corner, a small bathroom occupies an area of less than 4 square metres. A small bathroom also used to stand on the same side of the east wall; now all that is left is the slab of its floor. The staircase at the entrance running up from the ground floor leads to the corner room at the north part of the roof. This room has many windows all around; it also possesses two small sheds on its west and south sides.

The composition of the roof is typical of other old buildings in Qatar, *danshal* beams covered with *basgill* and *mangharour*.

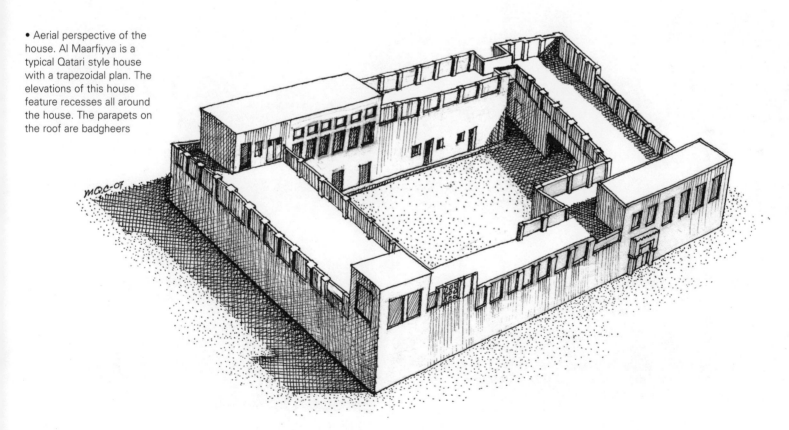

• Aerial perspective of the house. Al Maarfiyya is a typical Qatari style house with a trapezoidal plan. The elevations of this house feature recesses all around the house. The parapets on the roof are badgheers

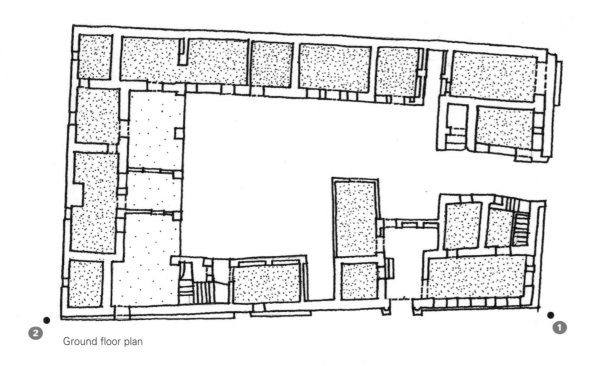

• Ground floor plan.
The house consists of series
of rooms on all four sides
around a central courtyard.
The house can be accessed
from two sides: the north
and the east. The rooms are
of medium size: the ground
floor does not have a large
room, for example on the
scale of *majlis*

Ground floor plan

	Private room
	Circulation
	Open private space

• View indicating one of the
entrances to the house,
recesses on the parapets,
and windows on the external
walls

• The higher part in this
house may have been as
wind tower but now is used
as a room

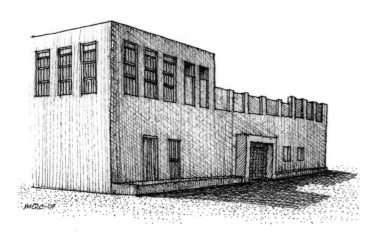

1

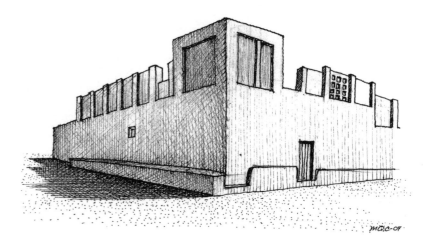

2

142

• First floor plan. This plan is the same as the ground floor. Two staircases near to this level. In this floor there are two main rooms dividing the roof into four distinct terraces

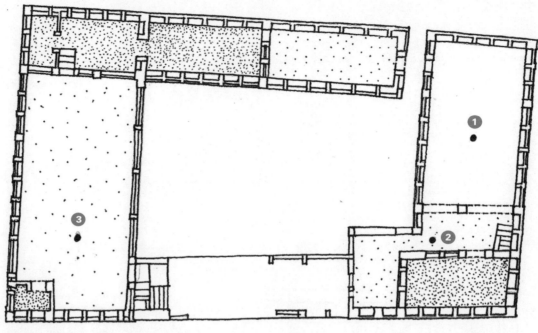

First floor plan

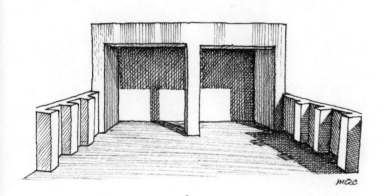

1

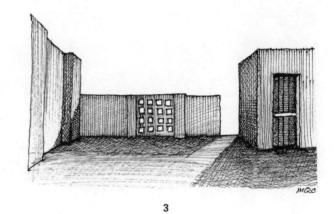

3

• Detail showing parapets on both sides and shaded area. This shaded area could be the lobby to the room inside

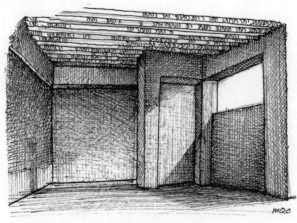

2

• The inside of the major room with traditional roof

• View showing decorative gate with semicircular columns and decorations inside the corners at the columns-lintel intersection

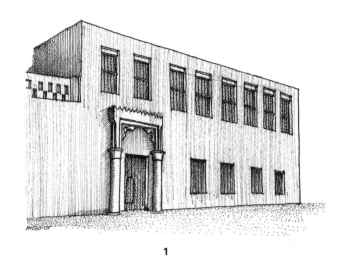

1

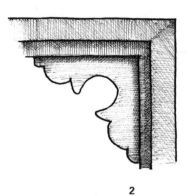

2

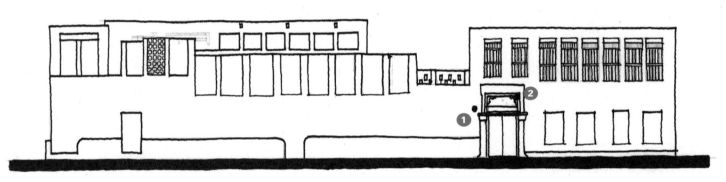

Elevation 1

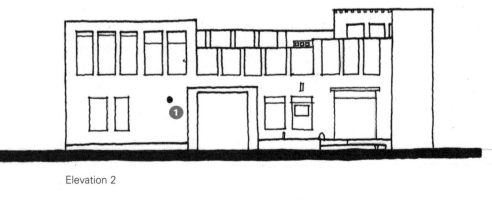

Elevation 2

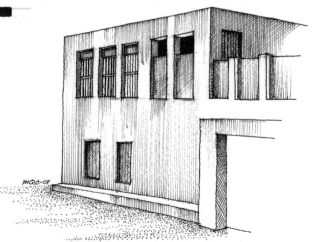

1

• View of an arcade on the front wall consisting of four equally spaced arches with decorative features at the corners of the columns where they meet with beams

1

Section A

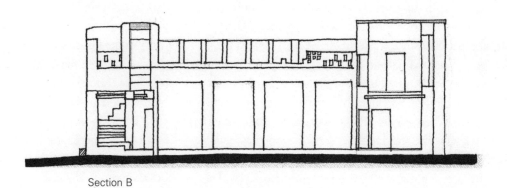

Section B

Al Asmakh House (Al Asmakh, Doha) (1930)

Introduction

According to some references, Al Asmakh house was built in 1925. It is located on Maymoun Street, to the south of the Ethnographic Museum, and less than one kilometre from Doha Corniche. The main features and architectural elements reflecting the culture and style are still present.

Architectural Description of the House

Al Asmakh house is a two storey rectangular building (34 × 15 m), rich with architectural decorations. The building can be accessed from four different entrances, which were recently installed to allow for the existing divisions. The staircase from the street is obviously new as it is constructed totally from concrete. Some of the arches that were present before the staircase was built are still visible, but totally or partly covered with the staircase structure. The original staircase ran up from the courtside, where there is now an entrance for a separate room. The second flight of the staircase still exists and can be seen behind the wall on the east side as one goes up the new staircase. Rooms on the ground floor have a certain hierarchy in size suggesting the different functions they may have served. There are five rooms that seem to be part of the old house and another nineteen rooms added later, six of which are bathrooms. In the north-west corner is the largest room, which was probably the *majlis*. The west part of that room has been cut away and used as a store for the shop on the other side of the street. The block on the south-west corner is totally new. A part of it covers three floors and it can be accessed from an opening between two rooms on the west side of the plot. The remaining part of the courtyard is divided into two separate courtyards. Bathrooms have been built inside these courts. The east section of the house has an arcade built to allow a view from the porch into the courtyard, however, the arcade is now filled and the space used as separate rooms. The arches are decorated with small saw-tooth elements running along the curve of the arch, identical to the arches of Al Mandani House, except that the latter are located in the first floor of the house.

As mentioned earlier, the original way to the upper level is blocked. The bathroom block occupies its place. The upper level rooms on the east side of the house are totally separate from the other sections and they can only be accessed from the street. The upper floor consists of four rooms. Only two rooms on the street side are original.

The walls of the other small rooms have been built on top of the original *badgheer* of the parapet. The parapet overlooking the court is made of two different materials, wood and precast units. The wooden part is the earlier of the two, so the precast units must have been added as a replacement. Moreover, a wall has been built behind the wooden parapet, thus blocking the view into the court. Most of the house walls are built of very thick stone, but today, when new walls are built, the material used is hollow concrete blocks. The staircases present are built from concrete. The original windows and doors were all made from wood, but many of them are now blocked and others have been replaced with air conditioning units. Gates to the courts on the ground floor are made of steel. All the rooms of this house still have the traditional Qatari ceiling. Basically, it consists of *danshal* wood beams overlain with *basgill* and *manharour*. But due to the bad condition of the *danshal* and some water leaks inside the room, the ceilings have been hidden by the installation of a false ceiling.

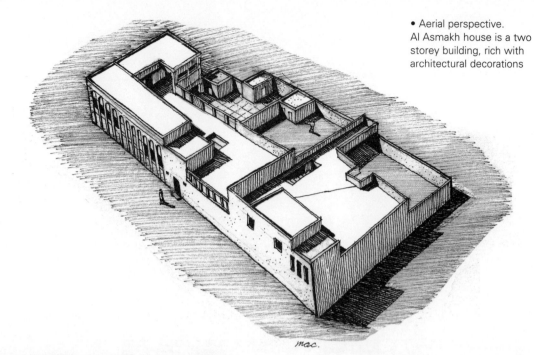

• Aerial perspective.
Al Asmakh house is a two
storey building, rich with
architectural decorations

• Ground floor plan. There are
five rooms that seem to be
part of the old house.
The other rooms maybe
added later. There is no
defined courtyard in this
house. In the north-west
corner is the largest room,
which was probably the
majlis

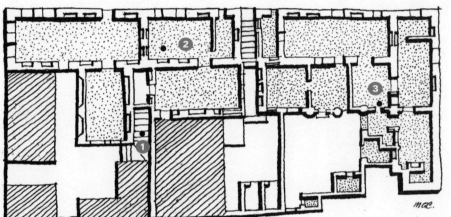

	Private room
	Circulation
	Open private space

Ground floor plan

• View of one of staircases
• Typical example of one
room. It is rich with recesses
inside
• Connecting door between
two different rooms

1

2

3

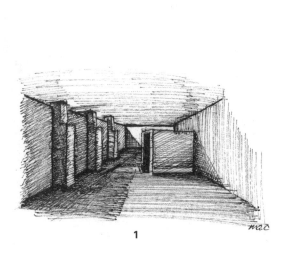

1

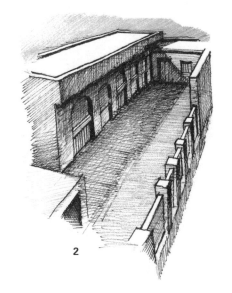

2

3

- View showing parapets and staircase
- Recesses used in the upper room in one seen in this view
- View of the stair leading to the lower floor

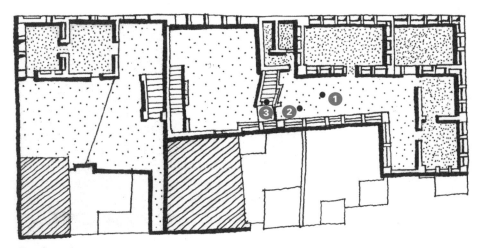

First floor plan

	Private room
	Circulation
	Open private space
	Extension

- First floor plan. The upper floor consists of four rooms. Only two rooms on the street side are original
- Detail of the main gate to the house with decorated arches

• View of windows and on the top there are recesses of arcaded walls
• Another enhance to the house maybe created later
• Here in this view the walls are recessed with openings on the top

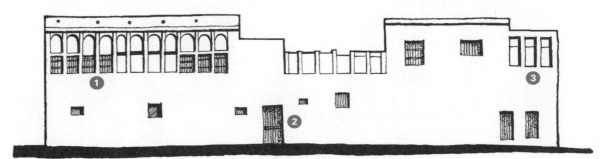

North elevation

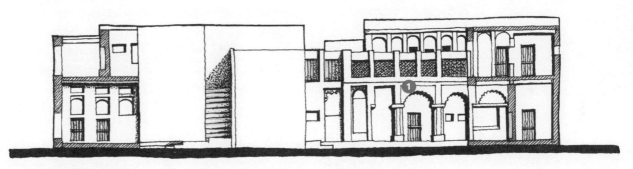

Section A-A

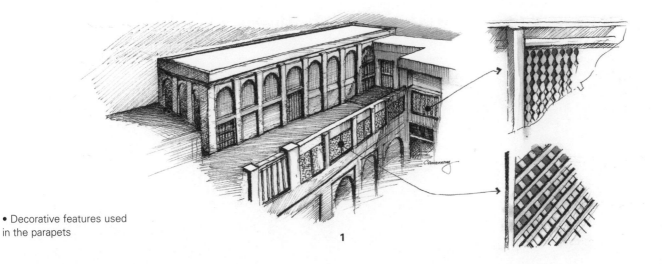

• Decorative features used in the parapets

Noura Bint Saif House (Al Asmakh, Doha) (1930)

Introduction

Noura Bint Saif House dates from 1926. The house forms part of the chain of old Qatari houses built on Maymoun Street. The style seen in the earlier Qatari houses is clearly visible in this one, especially the rows of rooms and the bounding porch.

Architectural Description of the House

Although this house has only a single storey, the courtyard is one of the largest among the remaining old houses in Doha. Probably belonging to a middle income family, the property can be accessed from two sides. On the north side, the only entrance now in use has a new steel gate. In the north-west corner, where the original wooden gate is still in place, lies the second entrance. The general layout of the house is identical to many other old residences: it is formed by two main parts – a guest area and the main family accommodation.

The main section of the house is L-shaped, containing seven rooms of which the one on the north-west corner has been recently built.

The rooms are bound by a porch approximately 3 metres deep decorated with an attractive arcade of round slender columns and corner details. The shapes of the details are unique and tailored to this house.

The west and south porches of the main building, being 40 centimetres to 60 centimetres higher than the courtyard level, are accessed down two sets of three steps. The porch provides a social space as well as a canopy of shade above the doors and windows of the rooms, sheltering the rooms from the harsh sun during the day. Five wood doors give access to the rooms. Each door is flanked by a window on each side, except for the door to the new room in the north-west corner.

The original wooden gate is perfectly located between the main house and the guest section with the *majlis*. Whenever a guest visited they would be able to access the *majlis* directly without having contact with the family section of the property. The guest section is formed of three rooms.

The width of the rooms is constant at 3.2 metres, but the length varies between 6 and 8.5 metres. The central room is now divided equally into two by a concrete block wall.

On the south-east side of the block lies what is thought to have been a garage. This structure may have been added around 1950 when cars became popular in Qatar. Adjacent to this structure, four recently constructed rooms stand in a line. The roof of the house is built in the traditional Qatari way, with *danshal* wood beams overlain with *basgill* and *mangharour*.

• Aerial perspective. Although this house has only a single storey, the courtyard is one of the largest among the remaining old houses in Doha

• Ground floor plan. The general layout of the house is identical to many other old residences. It is formed by two main parts – a guest area and the main family accommodation. The main section of the house is L-shaped, containing seven rooms

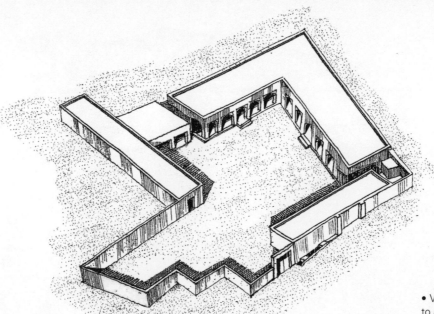

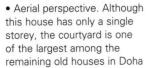

• View of an entrance to a room

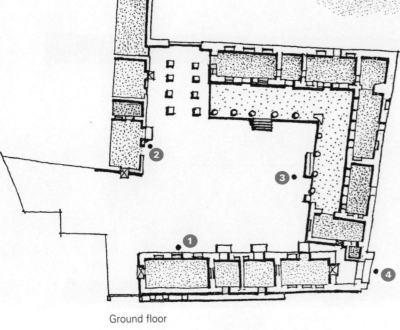

Ground floor

Private room

Circulation

Open private space

1

2

• The rooms are bound by the porch decorated with an attractive arcade of round slender columns and corner details

• The main entrance to the house

3

4

151

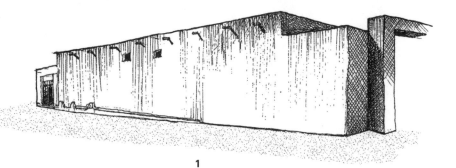

• The view in the south side of house is plain with almost no windows

1

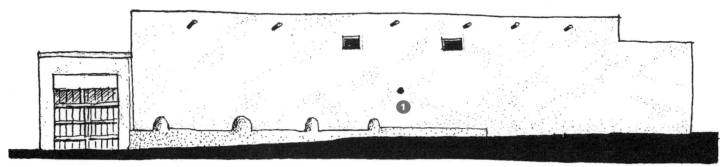

South elevation

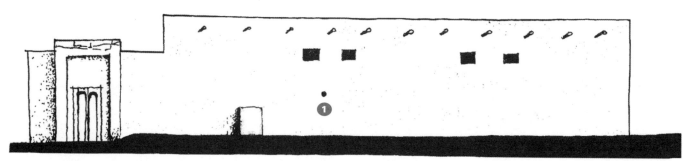

East elevation

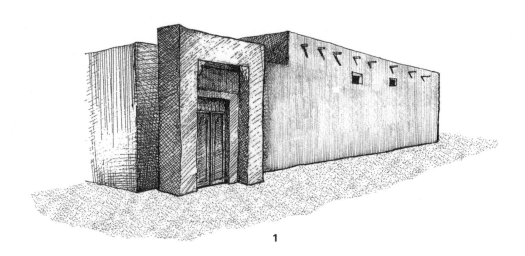

1

• Perspective showing decorative elements used in the corners of the arcades

1

Section A-A

Section B-B

• View of typical room in this house with traditional roof and recesses in the walls. These recesses are used as corners to have decorations

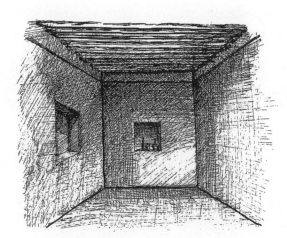

1

Ismail Mandani House (Al Asmakh, Doha) (1940)

Introduction

According to some sources the house was built in 1925. It stands in the Baharat Al Jufain area to the south of the Ethnographic Museum, less than one kilometre away from Doha's Corniche. This house is one of the few old houses in Doha rich with architectural elements that reflect the culture and wealth of its occupants.

Architectural Description of the House

Ismail Mandani House is a two-storey building exhibiting the features and details that distinguished the Qatari home from other types of houses around the Gulf Region. The Qatari house has its own language, form and function, although in general it abides by the rules dictated by the desert environment and Islamic religion. Two-storey houses were particular to the upper class, and generally upper-class families built their houses in such a way that they reflected their financial status, with many recesses and gypsum decorations internally and externally.

The entrance gate is at the south-west corner of the house. The house comprises two detached sections: the one to the left of the entrance gate most probably served as the *majlis*. The other part, a U-shaped building, runs parallel to the south-east and north walls of the block and therefore occupies most of the plot. The courtyard is trapezoidal, no more than 16 metres long and 7.5 metres wide. At the north-west end of the U-shaped building, a bathroom and a small lobby have been added. New concrete block work is used in many small places in this house, sometimes replacing the building's original walls.

The ground floor is divided into 15 different rooms, some of them are original whereas others have been added at a later date. Originally, the number of rooms on the ground floor was no more than nine and the additions and alterations that occurred over the last 70 years added six more spaces of different functions to the house. The courtyard has two separate *iwans*. One is in the front of the entrance and the other on the south block just beneath the first floor *iwan*. The south arm of the U is connected to the rest of the house via a staircase made from concrete. This staircase probably replaced the original stone staircase that led up to the first floor. Although small in terms of its footprint, this house has four rooms on the first floor, unlike other two-storey buildings that usually had only one or two rooms even though their size was larger. Having four rooms on the first floor usually suggests that more activities were present. Three of these upper-storey rooms enjoy a porch (10 × 3 m) lined by a beautiful arcade, which is one of the features that distinguishes this house. It consists of four arches, with each arch decorated with small saw-tooth elements along the curve on both the inside and outside. At 190 centimetres high, a wooden beam links the round columns, and below that a wooden parapet is fitted with wooden blinds that obstruct the view from a sitting position.

To the south-east of the upper block is a separate room (8 × 2.5 m), fenced with *badgheers*, it probably used to be an upper *majlis* with access to the roof of the east and north parts of the house. External areas such as this roof were used as sleeping areas in the summer and the *badgheers* provide both privacy and shelter while also providing the necessary airflow. All the rooms in this house still have the traditional Qatari ceiling: *danshal* wood beams overlain with *basgill* and *mangharour*.

• Aerial perspective. This house is a two-storey building exhibiting the features and details that distinguished the Qatari home from other types of houses around the Gulf region

• Ground floor. The house comprises two detached sectors. The one to the left of the entrance gate most probably served as the *majlis*. The other part is a U-shaped building. The courtyard is trapezoidal. The ground floor is divided into 15 rooms, some of which are original

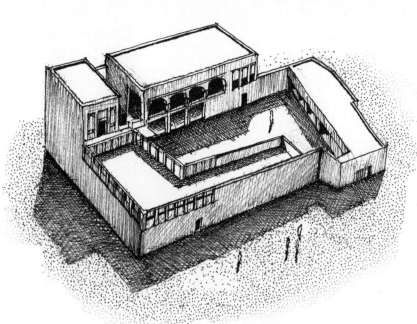

1

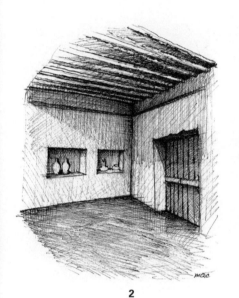

2

• View of typical room with traditional roof and recesses
• Main entrance to the house

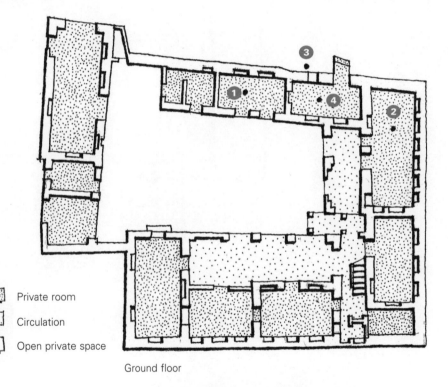

Private room

Circulation

Open private space

Ground floor

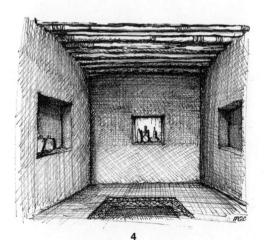

3

4

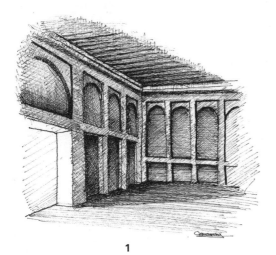

1

2

• The *majlis* is fenced with badgheers. This treatment provides both privacy and shelter while also providing the necessary ventilation

• View of the entrance to the *majlis*

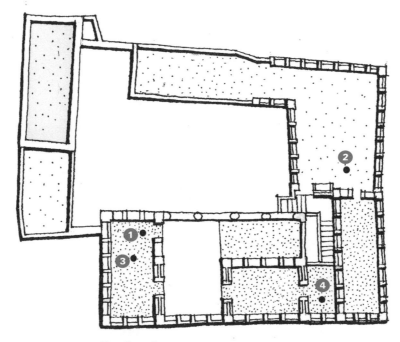

First floor plan

• First floor plan. Although small in size this house has four rooms in the upper floor

3

• Three of the upper floor rooms have a porch lined by a beautiful arcade, which is one of the features that distinguishes this house
• This view presents two different types of recesses in the walls

4

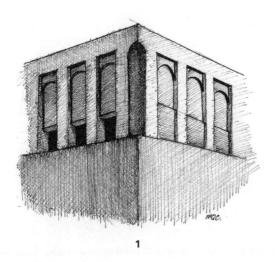

1

• This view indicates recesses and badgheers in the external walls

2

• One type of recesses arcaded on the top

North elevation

West elevation

• This perspective shows different types of arcades used in lower and upper floors
• The main entrance to the house and type of parapets are shown in this view

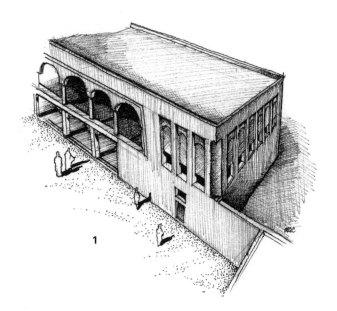

1

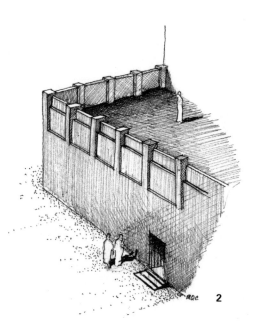

2

• Detailed view of the arcade

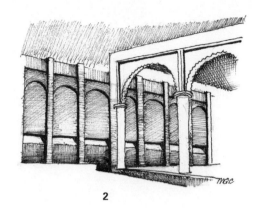

Section A-A

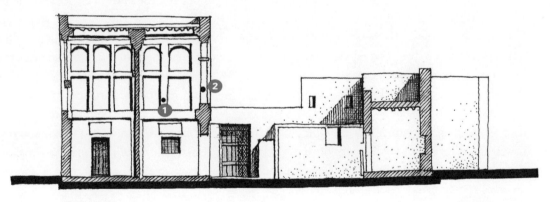

Section B-B

• View of the recesses on the walls and openings
• In this case the windows on the lower part of the wall are open to let the sunlight and air flow

Daughters of Ali Ahmadi House (Al Asmakh, Doha) (1940)

Introduction

Daughters of Ali Ahmadi House is located exactly in front of Ismael Madani House (see pp. 154–159). The entrances of the two houses face one other in the Barahat Al Jufairi area to the south of the Ethnographic Museum and less than 1 kilometre from Doha Corniche. The house dates from 1940 and is one of the most architecturally important in Qatar.

Architectural Description of the House

Built on a small piece of land, Daughters of Ali Ahmadi House has many features. The built area occupies the whole site, except for the courtyard, which covers approximately 120 square metres: the house is literally built around the courtyard.

The only access to the house is through a gate in the north-west corner. The original wooden gate has been replaced with a modern steel gate that opens directly into the courtyard. South of the gate is the main *majlis*, approximately 180 centimetres higher than the level of the courtyard, a unique feature unseen in other buildings. A series of steps go up to the *majlis*, the walls of which are decorated with recesses and *badgheers*, both externally and internally. The *majlis* itself is a rectangle measuring 8 × 3 metres. This standard width of rooms and spaces is enforced by the length of the *danshal* beam used to support the ceiling structure.

On the north wall, just at the right hand side of the entrance, two old rooms still stand but their roofs have collapsed because of the decaying wood. The larger of the old rooms is divided into two spaces by means of a hollow block wall. Two new rooms have been added adjacent, on the north-east corner of the plot. A completely new space has been added between the original building block and the old rooms at the entrance, with a slightly higher roof.

The original building is U-shaped and runs along the north, west and east walls. Five rooms are fitted into this layout. The depth of these rooms is approximately 3 metres and an arcaded porch separates the rooms from the courtyard. The square arcades are supported by square columns and decorated at the corner with details measuring approximately 90 × 90 centimetres. The west part of the arcade consists of three arches and the south part as well, making these parts of the arcade almost equal in length.

Besides the staircase that leads to the *majlis* on the split level floor, there are two staircases that link the courtyard with the roof. The first staircase is directly opposite the entrance gate and the other runs adjacent and parallel to the west wall of the *majlis*. A first floor room stands alone on the south-west corner of the house, with terraces running along both east and north sides. The roof is surrounded with *badgheers* along its parapet. Although part of the parapet has been restored with concrete hollow blocks, some parts of the original *badgheers* still exist. All the ceilings are made using *danshal* wood beams overlain with *basgill* and *mangharour*.

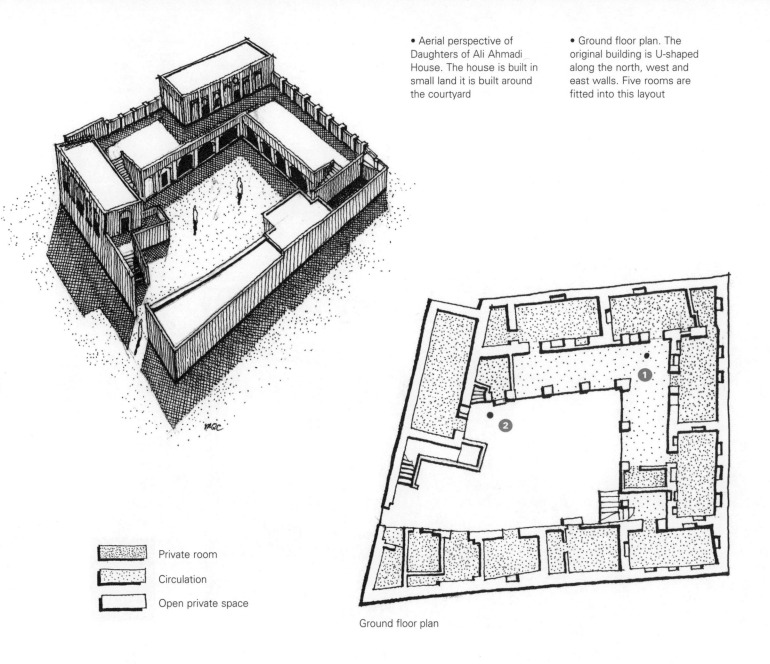

• Aerial perspective of Daughters of Ali Ahmadi House. The house is built in small land it is built around the courtyard

• Ground floor plan. The original building is U-shaped along the north, west and east walls. Five rooms are fitted into this layout

Private room

Circulation

Open private space

Ground floor plan

• View of shaded porch
• The type of recesses used in this house is long if compared with other old houses

1

2

161

1

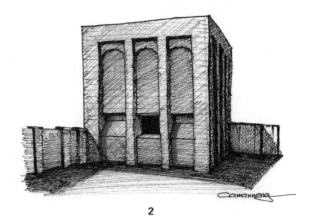

2

• First floor plan. There are two staircases that lead to the *majlis*. A first floor room stands alone on the south west of the house

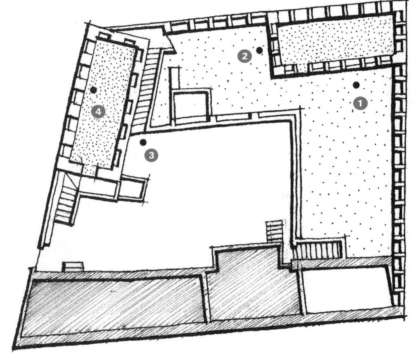

First floor plan

4

3

• The *majlis* is surrounded with recesses on the walls and badgheers
• View of one of the stairs leading to the *majlis*

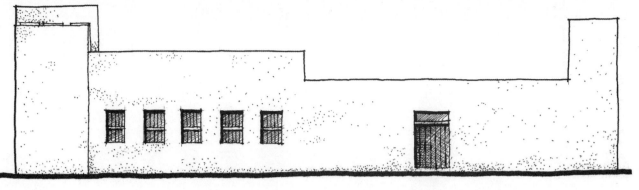

Elevation

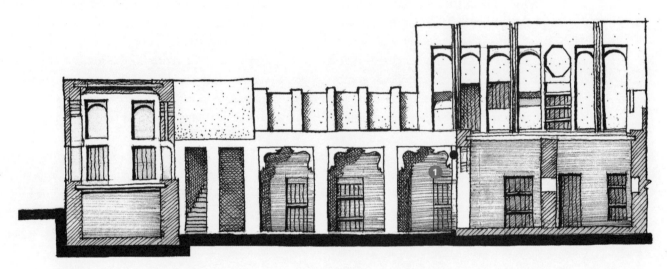

Section

• The arcaded porch separates the rooms from the courtyard. The square arcades are supported by square columns and decorated elements in the corners

1

Khaled Yousuf House (Al Jasra, Doha) (1935)

Introduction

The Khaled Yousuf House is in the old part of Doha, close to where the *suqs* and port were before the addition of the Corniche. Now, the house sits further from the Corniche, but still in the heart of Doha City. Khaled Yousuf House is somewhat hidden with a large modern building covering the main façade. This building removes much of the old character of the house, and may have been built over the top of some of the original buildings.

Architectural Description of the House

Khaled Yousuf House is a small rectangle measuring 14.5 by 18 metres. The rooms are built around a small courtyard, although previously it may have been that the courtyard was larger as it appears the new structure has taken some of this land. The architecture is simple with few decorations, large square columns and a few recesses in the walls. The house is two storeys high, plus it has a small room on the roof that was probably used for storage or as a summer bedroom. Access to the roof is via a staircase in the centre of the south wall that traverses the two floors to the roof. There appears to be no main gate in the wall. Access is via a small door that was added later, where you enter through one of the ground floor rooms.

All of the rooms are in a good condition and have their traditional *danshal* wood beams overlain with *basgill* and *mangharour*. There are few new additions to the structure, which is rare for many of the houses in Doha. On the second floor, there is a large area that has no access.

• Aerial perspective. Khaled Yousuf house is a small rectangular building. The architecture is simple with few decorations
• Ground floor plan. In this plan the rooms are built around a small courtyard
• First floor plan. The house is two-storeys high, plus it has a room on the roof
• Recesses in the walls used decorative elements
• Another type of recesses on the internal walls of a typical Qatari room

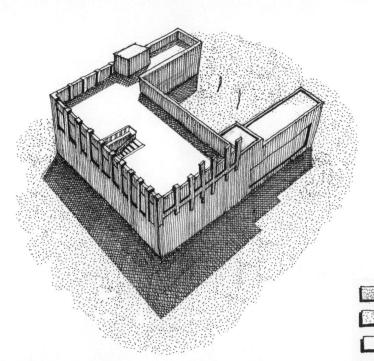

Private room	
Circulation	
Open private space	

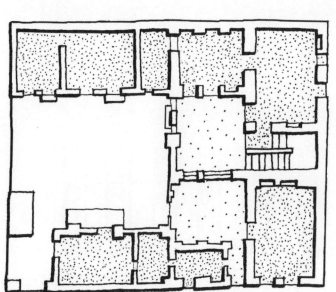

Ground floor plan

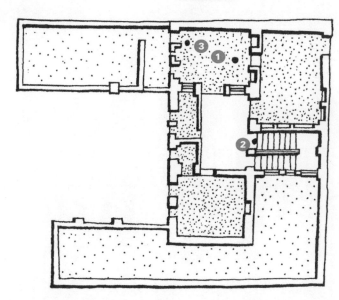

First floor plan

1

2

3

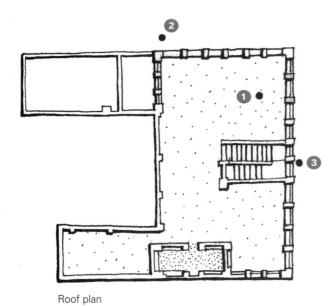

Roof plan

• View of the parapets from the roof
• View of the parapets on external walls

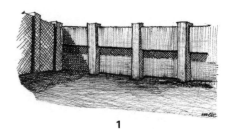

1

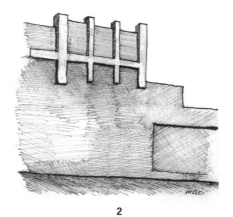

2

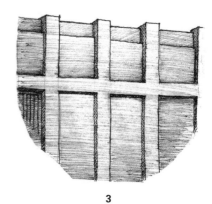

3

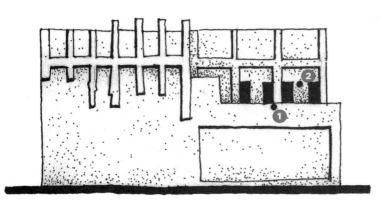

North elevation

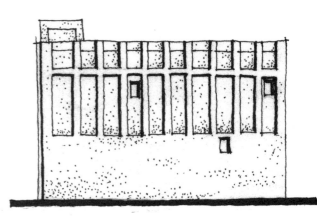

East elevation

• View showing recesses on the walls and parapets. These type of parapets allow ventilation

1

2

166

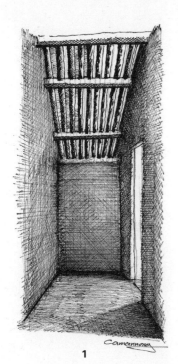

1

• Traditional roof used below the stair
• Decorative element on the roof

2

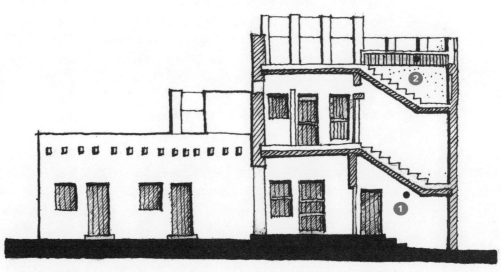

Section A-A

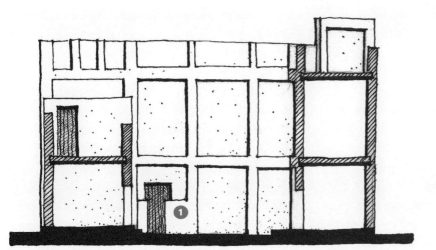

Section B-B

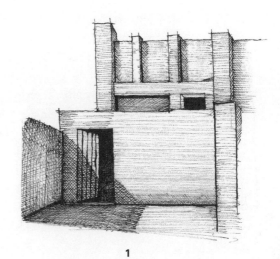

1

Sheikh Jassim Al Thani House (Al Jasra, Doha) (1935)

Introduction

Sheikh Jassim Al Thani House stands half a kilometre from the Corniche and 200 metres from Abdullah Bin Thani roundabout, on a plot approximately covering 3400 square metres. The house dates to 1935. At that time Doha's urban sprawl did not exceed the Al Asmakh area, therefore this house was literally on the outskirts of Doha.

Architectural Description of the House

The plot on which Sheikh Jassim Al Thani House was built is irregular in shape, probably dictated by the two buildings on its east side. The irregular outline of the boundary affected the layout of the buildings inside the plot as well. The house actually has four separate blocks, one each in the north-east, north-west and south-west corners, and the fourth at the south edge of the plot. Two small rooms are also built separately on the south-east edge. This layout made the inner courtyard look like a plaza, a very large open space between the building blocks.

The south block is totally separated from the house; it even has a separate entrance on the south wall, it consists of two building blocks on the east and west sides, both of which have two storeys. Another small building on the south side has only one storey.

This part of the building had *badgheers* on the roof, which means that the roof may also have been used as a living space. The main entrance from Ukaz Street leads directly into the large courtyard. Immediately after entering the main gate, and on the west side is the main *majlis* of the compound, a rather simple rectangle (18.85 × 9.45 m) cut into two parallel spaces. The front space may have been a porch to the other: it features an arcade supported on round columns.

The parapet of this part of the house is a metal grill overlooking the courtyard and a *badgheer* on the other sides. This section of the building is linked to the north-west corner by a linear stretch 27.75 metres long and 4.35 metres wide; it has no specific features of its own. The north-west section of the house is also arcaded on the east and south sides. The east side has five arches, three of which are of equal width and two that are narrow and long. This part of the house is also linked to the part on the north-east corner by a rather simple rectangle measuring 28.20 × 4.60 metres.

This block forms a separate corner within the compound; it has its own boundary wall, suggesting that probably it was used as a separate house for one of the sons of the owner. The layout consists of a main house on the west edge of the block with seven square arches decorated at the corner and equally spaced. This block measures 23.40 × 21.30 metres and overlaps the linear building that runs east-west on the north edge. The former block is higher than the latter by 140 centimetres. An entrance gate serves the block from the street on the north side and another gate gives access from the east side. This latter gate penetrates the east block and divides it into two main parts, north and south. These two parts have recesses on their walls on both the outside and inside. The south part measures 10.65 × 4.40 metres, while the north part is only 17.50 × 3.75 metres. There is one staircase that leads to the roof of the compound. The ceiling is made of the traditional layers of typical old houses and buildings of Qatar which consists of *danshal* wood beams overlain with *basgill* and *mangharour*.

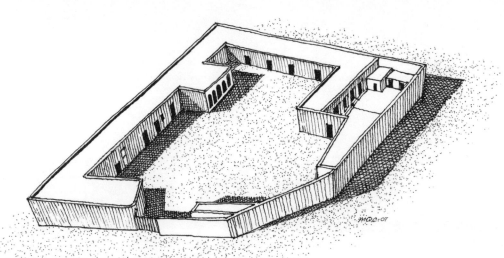

• Aerial perspective.
The house seems to have
been built in irregular shape,
probably dictated by the two
buildings on its east side
• Ground floor plan.
The irregular outline of the
boundary affected the layout
of building inside the plot.
Two small rooms are also
built separately on the south
east edge. This layout made
the inner courtyard look like a
plaza, a very large open
space between the building
blocks

 Private room

 Circulation

 Open private space

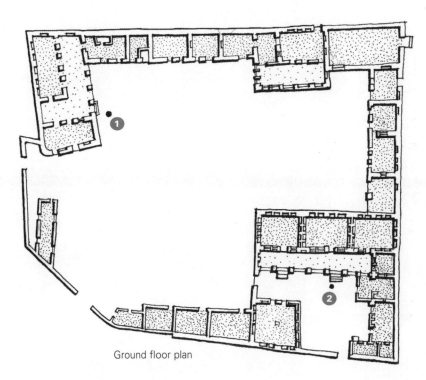

Ground floor plan

• This space represents an
arcaded porch between the
courtyard and the *majlis*
• Another type of arcaded
porch leading to the rooms

1

2

Section C-C

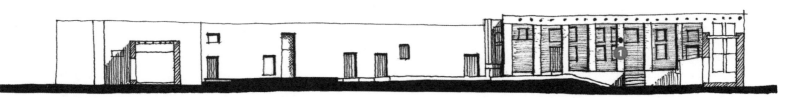

Section D-D

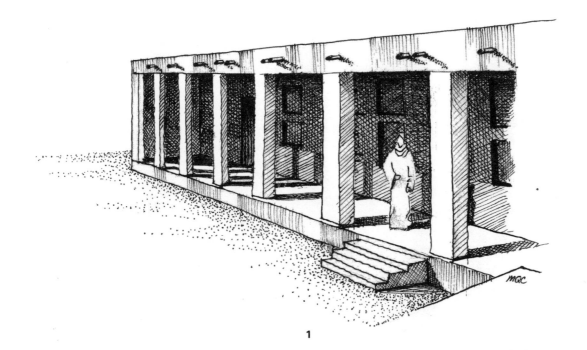

• This view shows another different type of arcaded porch leading to the rooms

1

• View of the porch from
inside. It is built using
traditional roof

1

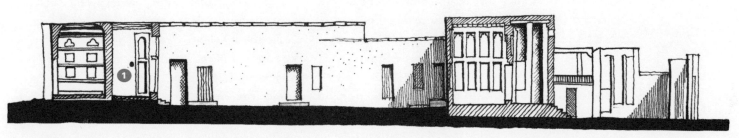

Section A-A

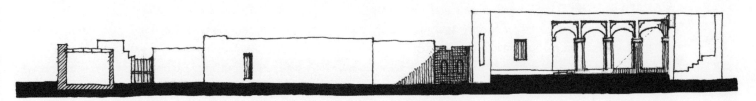

Section B-B

• The main gate to the house
with a small door. The small
door is usually used in order
to preserve privacy

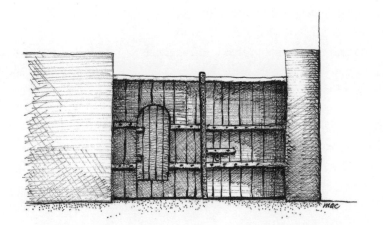

Abdullah Abdul Rahman Obaidan House (Ukaz Street, Doha) (1950)

Introduction

This house stands on Ukaz Street at the Abdullah Bin Thani roundabout. It belongs to the Obaidan family. Located half a kilometre away from the Corniche, the house was built after 1952 during the construction boom that lasted between 1947 and 1956. Before that time, when Ukaz Street was on the outskirts of Doha, none of the buildings that now line that street existed.

Architectural Description of the House

Abdullah Abdul Rahman Obaidan House is a large square, occupying the whole plot and measuring approximately 38 × 32 metres.

The actual structure is built around a central court measuring 22 × 17 metres. The only entrance to the house is through a gate in the south wall, which is blocked by another linear structure overlooking Ukaz Street. This linear building acts as a buffer zone between the street and the main house and has a *majlis*. The entrance is a large wooden gate with a *khokha*. Inside the entrance lobby on the west side, a small porch with three square arches supported by four columns, provides a sort of lobby for the *majlis*. The interior of the court is filled with recent additions, consisting of bathrooms and bedrooms, all built with hollow concrete blocks. The arcade of the porch runs the whole length of three sides: the south, west, and north. The arcade of the south porch has six square arches supported on hexagonal columns decorated at the corners with the tile beams. All the columns on this side are equidistant and have capitals below the decorations. The arcade on the west side of the court comprises seven arches and six columns that are also hexagonal, and decorated with the same details as the previous columns. The north arcade is the longest, with nine square arches equally spaced and detailed like the above. All the columns of the arcade have square bases no longer than 45 centimetres on each side. Many sets of steps have been added to give access to the separate spaces inside the porch and main building. The depth of the court is not more than 3 metres. The main building has an average height of 4.80 metres while the *majlis* on the south side is 4 metres in height.

The east part of the building is the only section not provided with an arcade. Instead a wall blocks it entirely from the courtyard, probably because it served a different function.

The main building comprises 10 rooms. Some of them are subdivided into smaller spaces and in most of them there is a bathroom inside the main structure. All the rooms are rectangular, and are fitted with traditional windows and wooden doors. The windows are fitted with a vertical metal grill typical of old windows in Qatar. The ceiling is constructed in the traditional manner, with *danshal* wood beams overlain with *basgill* and *mangharour*. A staircase is built for each sectioned of the arcaded house, which are placed approximately in the middle of the long side of each building.

• Aerial perspective. Obaidan house is a large square with a plain elevation

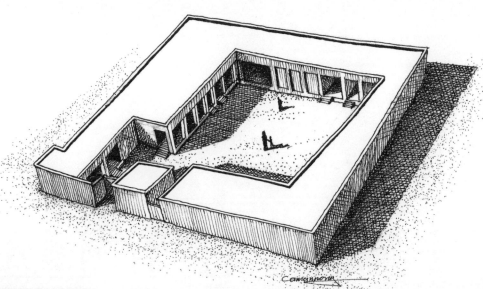

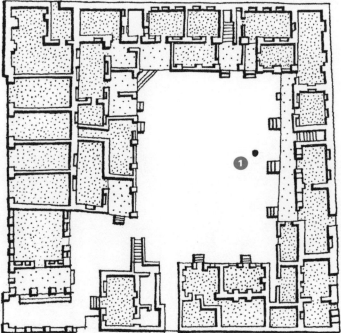

Ground floor plan

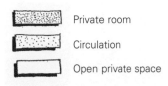

Private room

Circulation

Open private space

• Ground floor plan.
The actual house is built around a central courtyard. Inside the entrance lobby on the west side, a small porch with three square arches supported by four columns, provides a sort of a lobby for the *majlis*

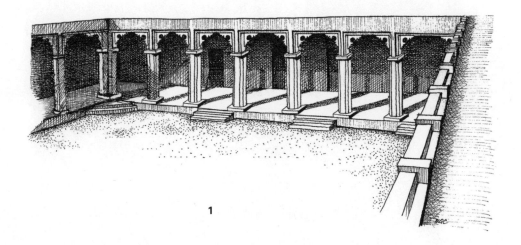

• This perspective shows multiple arcades forming a porch to the rooms

1

Elevation A-A

• The entrance is a large
wooden gate with a small
door known as "Khokha"
• Types of windows

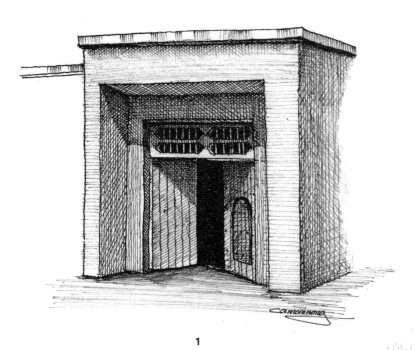

1

2

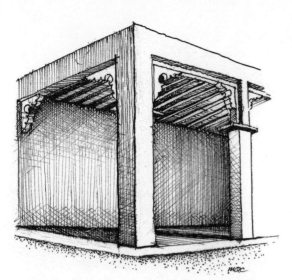

• Traditional roof used to build the porch
• This detail shows decorated arches

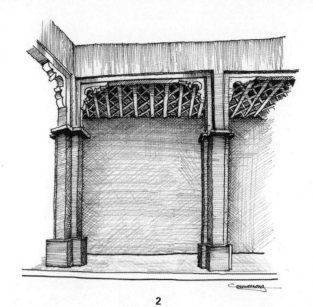

1

2

Section A-A

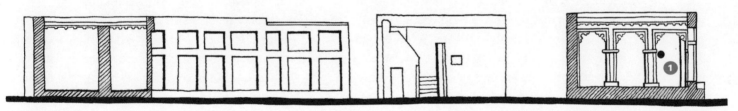

Section B-B

• Another view of the arcade

1

Ali Akbar Ahmed Housing (Ukaz Street, Doha) (1940)

Introduction

Ali Akbar Ahmed Housing was built in or around 1940. It is now in the centre of the old district of Doha. The area was much less densely populated when the house was built, whereas now, the street frontage is occupied by shops.

Architectural Description of the House

Ali Akbar Ahmed Housing is built around three separate courtyards, however, the three areas have similar construction and architectural details, hinting that they were all built at the same time. This notion is supported by examination of the aerial photographs taken in 1956, which reveal that all three areas of the compound existed at that time. There are four entrances to the compound, all from a long *sikka* that comes to a dead-end at the last door. The architectural details are typical of houses of this type and era. Taking the first and largest area as an example, the house is built around a central courtyard, and is single storey. The roof was lined with *badgheers*, however many of these have fallen or been removed. Stairs access the roof, which would have been used in the warmer months for sleeping and entertaining. The courtyard edge of the roof is ringed with a stone and concrete fence, a typical feature of the era.

Entrance to all areas of the compound is through plain steel gateways, not the ornate style of many of the more important families, where the main gate and door contains a *khokha*. The internal structure in all three areas is made from stone, with the roofs being constructed from the traditional materials of *danshal* wood beams overlain with *basgill* and *mangharour*. However, in many of the rooms a modern plywood false ceiling is found.

The second area consists of three rooms and is L-shaped. Its entrance is through a simple steel gate from the secondary street. There is one porch area, but this does not have cement details in the corners.

• Aerial perspective. Ali Akbar house is of rectangular form. The house probably consisted of two separated buildings or more
• Ground floor plan. The house was built around three separate courtyards. The largest part of the house was built around central courtyard, and is single storey

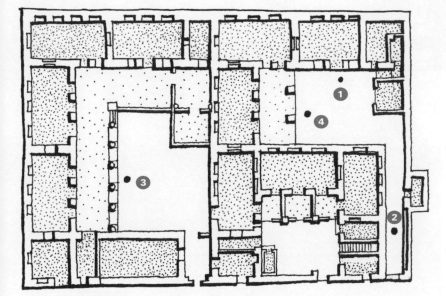

 Private room

 Circulation

 Open private space

Ground floor plan

1

• Narrow entrance to the house
• View of the porch with its simple arcades
• On the other side of the house the arches are decorated in the corners

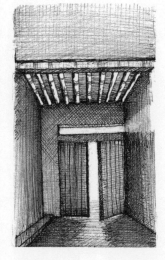
2

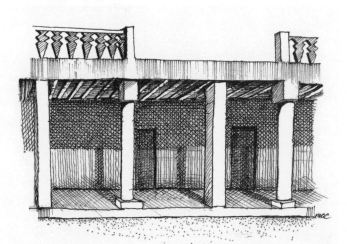
3

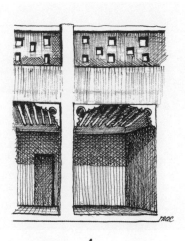
4

• One of the main entrances
to the house

1

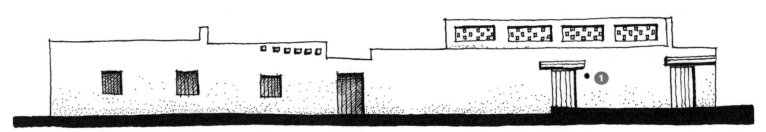

Front elevation

• Decorations used in the parapets

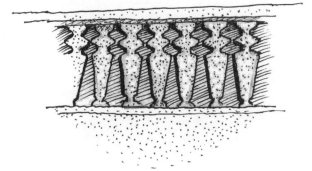

1

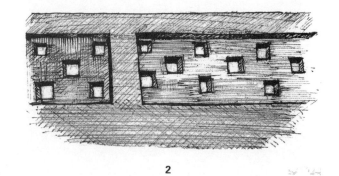

2

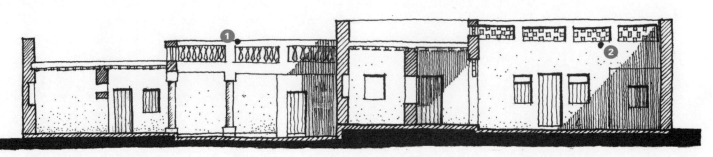

Section A-A

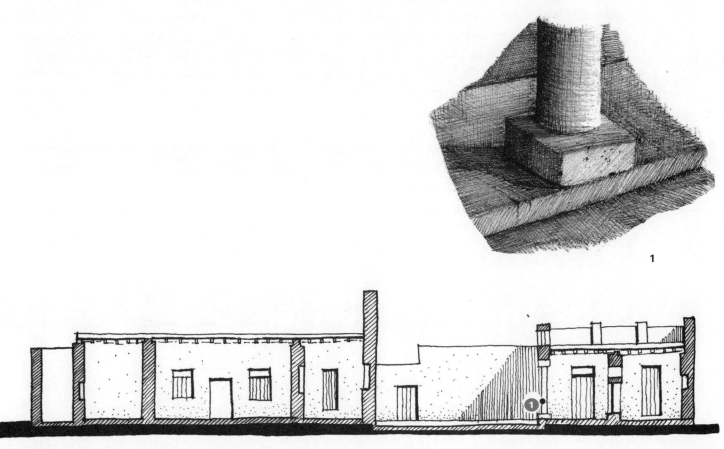

1

Section B-B

Al Othman House (Al Murjan Street, Doha)
(Pre 1950)

Introduction

This house is on Al Murjan Street at the Abdullah Bin Thani roundabout. It belongs to the Al Othman family. This house, located half a kilometre away from the Corniche, was built prior to 1950. Before that time, this area was on the outskirts of Doha and none of the buildings that now line the streets existed.

Architectural Description of the House

Al Othman House is a large rectangular property that occupies the entire plot between Abdullah Bin Thani Roundabout, Murjan Street and two *sikkas* in the west and the south. The actual structure is built around a central court and has many entrances, the majority of which are not original. The house has been modified to allow easy access from the *sikkas*. The original entrance to the house is through a gate in the east wall. There is some evidence that this gate has been moved forward from its original position, as the east façade has been built over. There are shops on the east façade that are not part of the original house. Despite this, the house has retained its structure, meaning that the first room inside the entrance gate used to be the *majlis* where meetings and social activities for the men took place.

In some houses, there was a second, more private, entrance that allowed the women access without mixing with the guests. This was probably the gate in the north-west corner that has since been blocked with hollow blocks. The gate, however still remains. Both of the gates have a *khoka*, but are in poor condition. The latter gate leads to stairs at the rear of the house that climb to the roof. This was also common, as it gave private access to the ladies *majlis*.

The three visible elevations of the house show varying architecture, which suggests there have been additions and alterations to the building over time, but much of the structure is traditional. In the east rooms the roof has been replaced, most likely during the construction of the additions. The porch areas along the inside of the court have been filled with either hollow block or aluminium windows, thereby creating nine rooms. At the south-west corner there is an open area with a shade. This is used as a garage and working area but it may have been a part of the house in the past. It is possible that there was some traditional structure here that has since been demolished. The condition of the wall and its alignment with the rest of the house suggest that this was either an older section or an early addition.

• Aerial perspective.
Al Othman house is a large
rectangular building that
occupies the entire plot.
It has two main gates

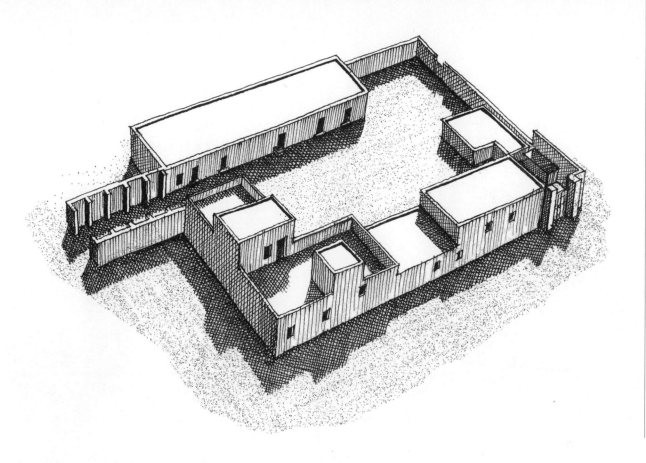

Entrance gate

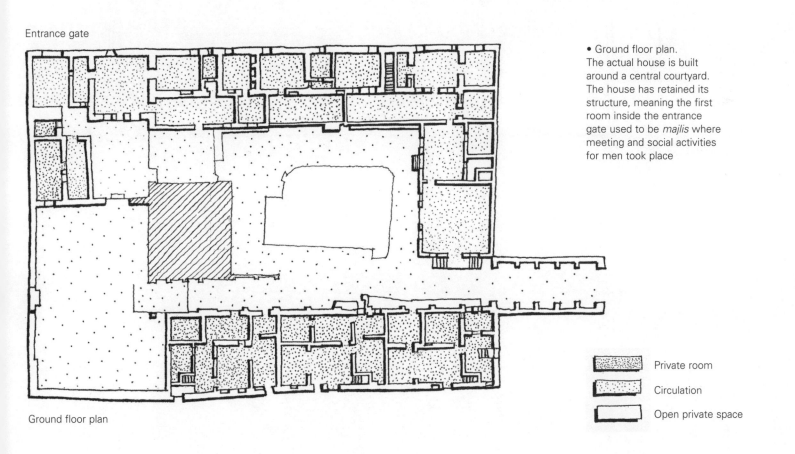

• Ground floor plan.
The actual house is built
around a central courtyard.
The house has retained its
structure, meaning the first
room inside the entrance
gate used to be *majlis* where
meeting and social activities
for men took place

Ground floor plan

Private room

Circulation

Open private space

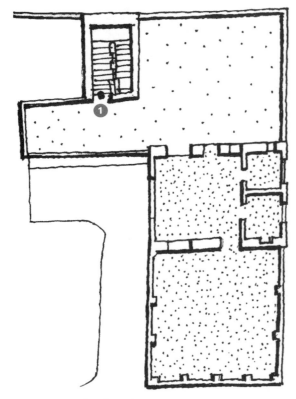

First floor plan

1

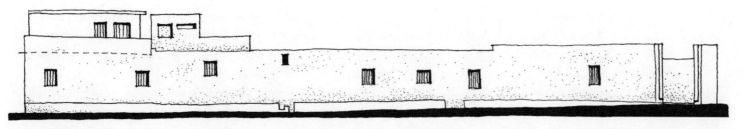

Elevation

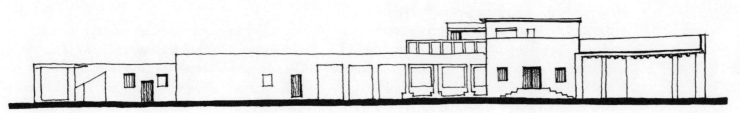

Section A-A

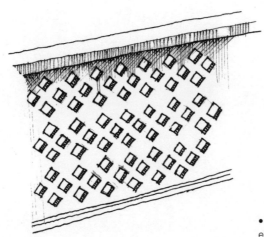

• Detail of a decorative
element used for the parapet

Sheikh Hamad Bin Abdullah House
(Al Jasra, Doha)
(1930)

Introduction

Sheikh Hamad Bin Abdullah house is located very near to the Corniche in a complex that includes the Amiri Diwan and the Diwan Mosque. It is a large house typical of a ruling family. Built in 1930, it was undergoing major renovation. A feature of this house was the extensive use of gypsum decorations both inside and outside, the mark of a home of an important family.

Architectural Description of the House

The house is built around a central courtyard with both upper and ground floors. There are two entrances to this courtyard, one in the west wall and one in the south wall. The entrance on the west side has a large wooden gate that has been restored with a *khokha* and is perfectly detailed. The entrance in the west wall gives access to the lobby of the building, which was probably the *majlis* in earlier times. The second gate in the south wall is less ornate and probably served as a secondary entrance for staff or as a private entrance.

The interior of the court has been redesigned in a more modern style, with concrete and brick paved paths. The buildings around the courtyard all have an arched arcade with octagonal columns on square bases and with square capitals decorated with gypsum inlays.

The courtyard and house do not appear to have been altered, with the latter totally constructed from the traditional materials of limestone, mud and gypsum plaster, albeit recently restored. The gypsum decorations may also have been replaced or repaired. Once again, the exterior is heavily decorated with many recesses in the walls and *badgheers* around the roof parapets, as was common. All of these have been restored, though cracking is evident in some roof details.

Internally, the rooms have been adapted for use as offices and are well restored and renovated. The original roof construction consists of *danshal* wood beams overlain with *basgill* and *mangharour*. It has been renovated in all parts, including the colours and decorations that adorned the wooden false ceilings. The many elaborate gypsum details and colouring are a feature of this property. Upstairs, there appears to be a winter *majlis*, which is still under restoration.

• Aerial perspective. Sheikh Hamad Bin Abdullah house is a typical large building. It has witnessed many renovation works
• Ground floor plan. The house is built around a central courtyard with both upper and ground floors

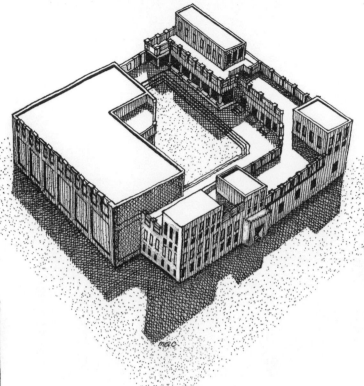

 Private room

 Circulation

 Open private space

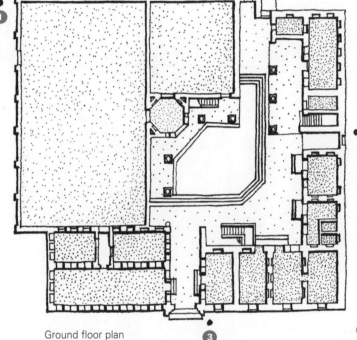

Ground floor plan

• The recesses on the external walls are large in size, maybe because of the big size of the room
• Perspective showing recesses on the walls and badgheers
• The main entrance to the house
• Another gate to the house

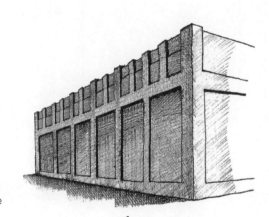

1

2

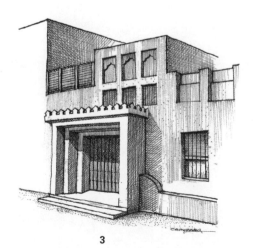

3

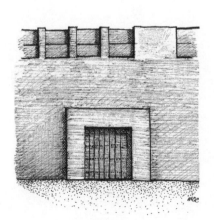

4

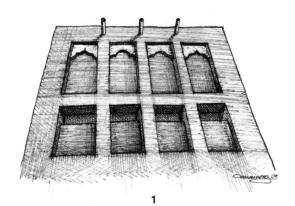

• Perspective showing recesses on the external walls decorated with arches

1

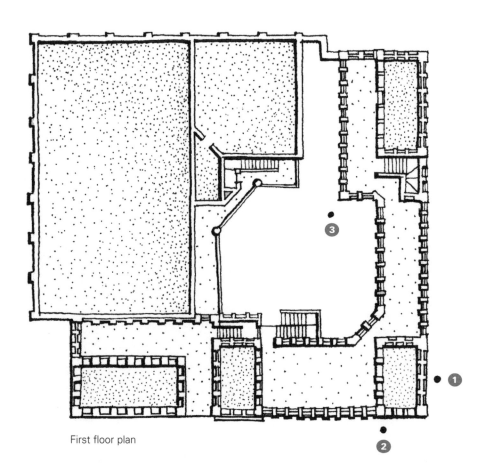

First floor plan

2

• This view shows shaded porch and decorated arcades

3

• Decorative element on the top of the main gate
• Parapets
• North elevation.
This elevation represents a module of three windows and three recessed windows. They are symmetrically arranged

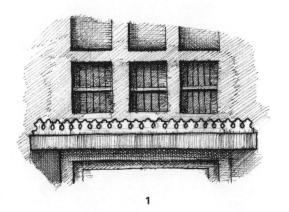

1

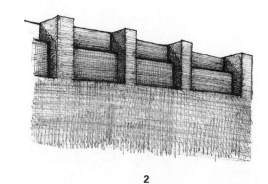

2

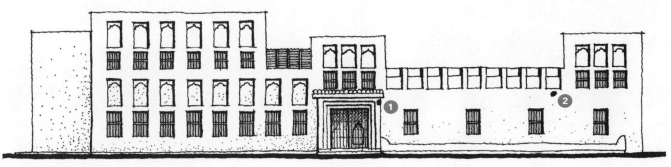

North elevation

East elevation

• The module of three windows recesses and parapets is indicated here
• The module of three can be arranged in many ways

1

2

3

• View showing the stair
taking onto upper floor
• Decorative element used
for opening

1

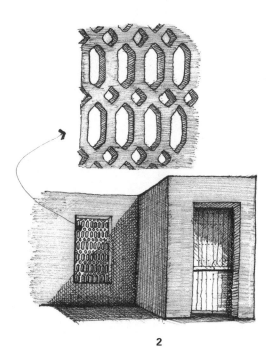

2

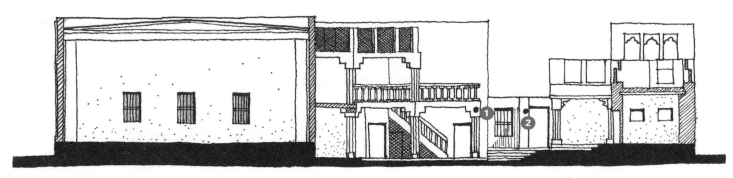

Section A-A

• Detail showing the parapets
on the upper floor

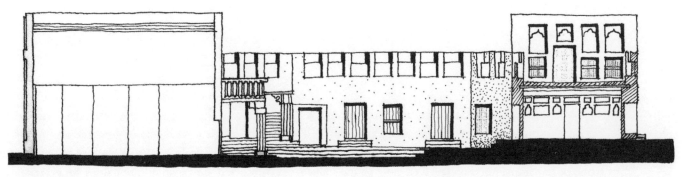

Section B-B

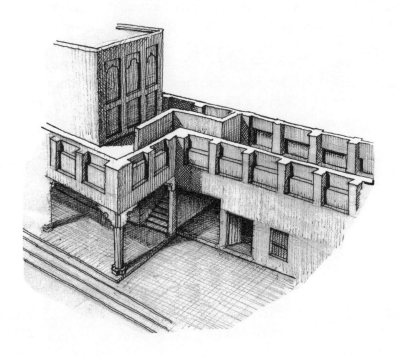

• Detail showing the entrance
to the upper room.
The entrance is decorated
with recesses on the walls

Al Khulaifi House (Off the Corniche, Doha) (1940)

Introduction

Al Khulaifi House is a compound built at the north end of the Corniche in Doha. At the time of its construction, it would have been one of few houses in the area, and close to the Palace of Sheikh Abdullah Bin Hamad Al Thani, which is now the National Museum. The urban areas of Doha have now been extended to this area, and the house is surrounded by developments such as hotels, the Doha Club, and the popular coffee shops.

Architectural Description of the House

Al Khulaifi House is a walled compound built in 1940. It is unusual in that only one building shares the wall of the compound, this being the entrance. The original gate may have been built over during the restoration, as modern materials are now used. There is a large entrance gate on the east wall that appears to be original. This gate has the hallmarks of the main entrance, with a *khoka*. The new entrance gives access to an area that could have been the *majlis* as it is close to the compound's main entrance. The layout of the house is strangely fragmented and not the usual Qatari architecture. Not all of the rooms are connected, and many do not share an external wall, which suggests that the house was built in stages. The internal structure of all the areas is in stone, with roofs constructed from the traditional materials of *danshal* wood beams overlain with *basgill* and *mangharour*; however, some of the rooms have been fitted with a modern plywood false ceiling. The architecture is basically simple, with large square columns and simple arcades. The fence around the property may have been replaced or rebuilt, as it appears to be more modern than the house.

One room of the compound has no white paint finish and has been left the traditional gypsum tan colour. This is also the most heavily recessed building in the plot, having simple square recesses externally and internally on each wall.

• Aerial perspective.
Al Khulaifi house is a walled
compound built in 1910. It is
not common that only one
building shares the wall of
the compound, this being
entrance
• Ground floor plan.
The layout of this house is
fragmented and not all rooms
are connected and many do
not share wall, which
suggests that the house was
built in stages

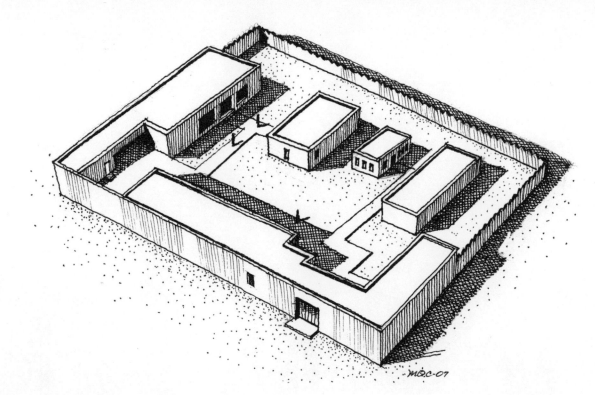

 Private room

 Circulation

 Open private space

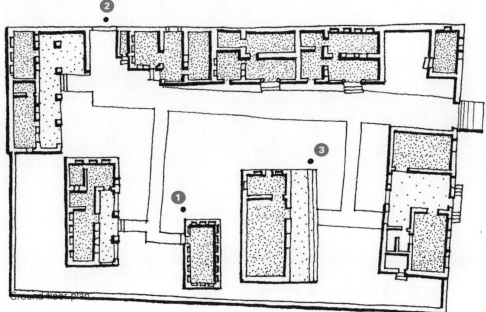

Ground floor plan

• The main gate to the house

2

• These perspectives shows
separate rooms inside the
house

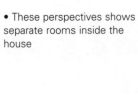

1

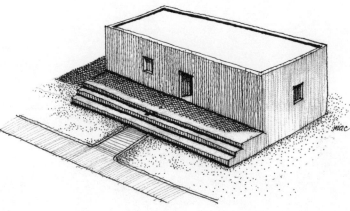

3

• The main gate entrance
to the house which is leading
to the *majlis*

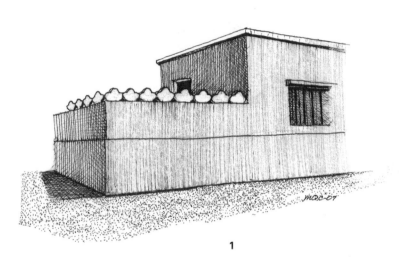

1

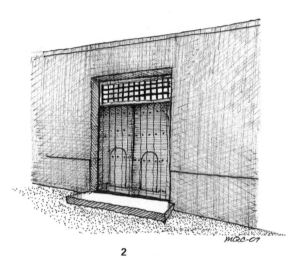

2

Front elevation

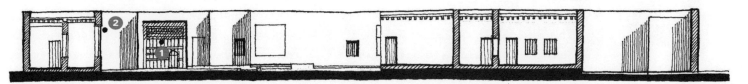

Section A-A

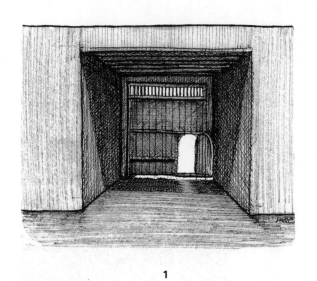

1

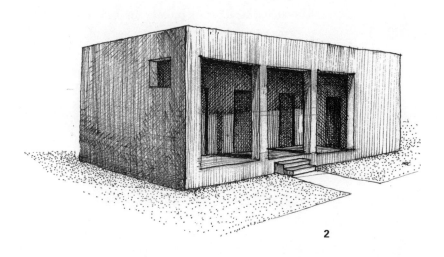

2

• The porch is simple with no decorated arches

Al Sulaiti House (Al Refaa, Doha) (Post 1940)

Introduction

The house is located in Old Al Salata. This area of Doha was named after the Sulaiti family that seems to have owned many pieces of land here. This house is located half a kilometre from the Corniche and was built after 1940. At the time it was built, the only other building of any size was Sheikh Abdullah Bin Jassim Bin Hamad Al Thani Palace, which is now the Qatar National Museum. The House of Al Sulaiti is now used as a home for the Qatar Folkloric Troupe.

Architectural Description of the House

Sulaiti House has a large rectangular shape and occupies a plot between three minor streets and a *sikka*.

The actual structure is built around a central courtyard. There are two entrances to the house, one from the front street through a gate located on the south wall. This entrance has a large wooden gate that has been restored without a *khokha*, but is perfectly detailed. The second gate is also in the south wall and gives easy access to the ornate corner room, which was most probably used as the *majlis*. This entrance is most likely to be the original one in the property, with the other being added during the restoration.

The interior of the court has since been redesigned in a more modern style with concrete paving and brick paved paths. The buildings around the courtyard all have an arcade of simple square columns and beams. The east and north wings seem to have been completely restored from hollow blocks. The *majlis* and south wings appear more original and well restored.

Internally, the rooms have been adapted as club rooms and offices, and are also well restored and renovated. The original roof construction consists of *danshal* wood beams overlain with *basgill* and *mangharour* and has been renovated in the older parts of the house. In the newer sections, a modern concrete roof replaces the traditional one.

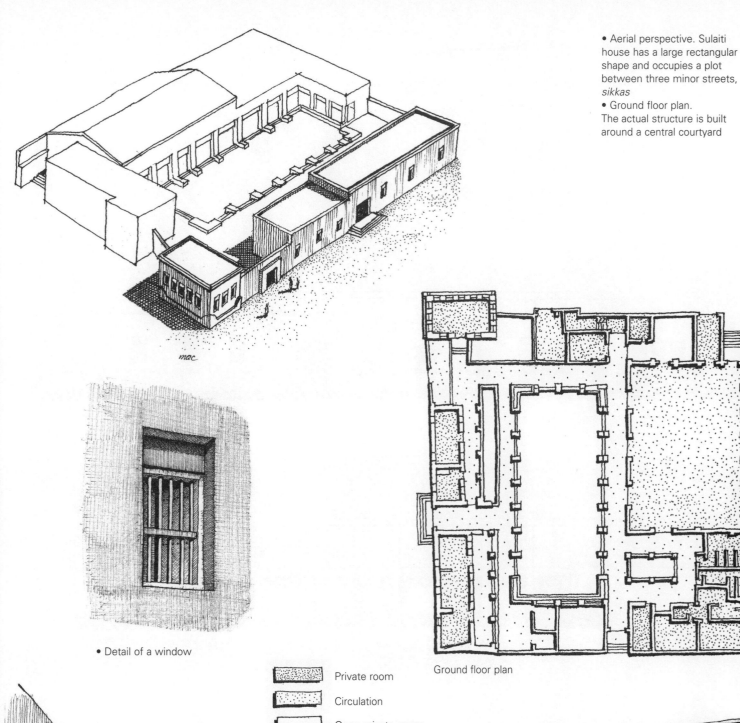

• Aerial perspective. Sulaiti house has a large rectangular shape and occupies a plot between three minor streets, *sikkas*

• Ground floor plan. The actual structure is built around a central courtyard

Ground floor plan

• Detail of a window

Private room

Circulation

Open private space

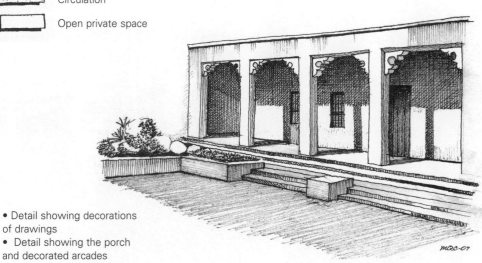

• Detail showing decorations of drawings

• Detail showing the porch and decorated arcades

• Secondary gate to the
house

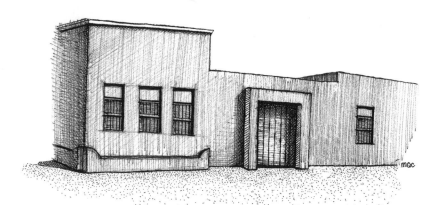

1

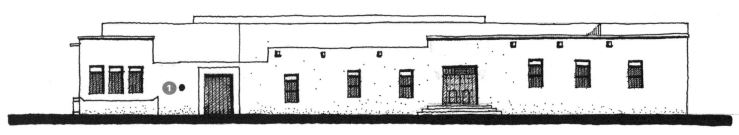

Section B-B

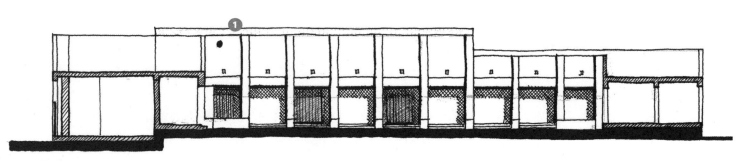

Section A-A

• View of the parapets

1

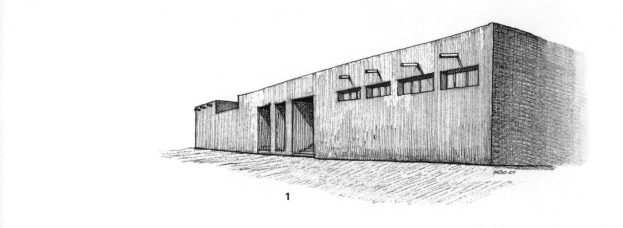

1

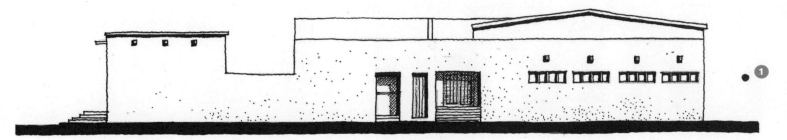

South elevation

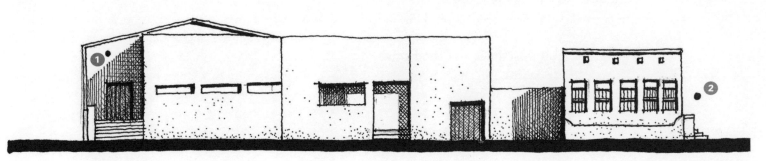

North elevation

1

2

Al Ansari Property (Al Khor) (1930)

Brief Description and History

Al Khor is the second largest town in Qatar north of Greater Doha. It was once a thriving fishing port and pearling centre. Today, it is a quiet town best known for its attractive Corniche. The old section of Al Khor is built on a low rise overlooking the Corniche. The Al Ansari property, consisting of two old houses, is located in a residential neighbourhood close to the centre of the old part of Al Khor, close to the town's principal east-west street (Al Khor Main Street). The houses date from 1930 and were built by the locally prominent Al Ansari family, who probably also owned the adjacent Old Al Khor Suq (see pp. 318–321) well.

Architectural Description of the Houses

It appears the original Al-Ansari property encompassed the north-east quadrant of the city block upon which it now stands, but was progressively subdivided over the years, accommodating the two houses one sees today plus the adjoining suq along the north side of the property. The Old Suq shares a rear wall with the two houses.

The Old Suq was built in 1910. The first of what later became two houses was probably built next, around 1930, on the west side of the property behind the market, with shops on either side. The house was gradually expanded, so that eventually the rooms were built around two small courtyards, probably to accommodate different parts of an extended family.

The east part of the property was then walled off entirely, creating a large separate open courtyard with rooms of a small house built at the south-west corner of the courtyard. This house has only three rooms, all of which give onto the court, plus a fourth much smaller room accessed through one of the larger rooms. Two rooms have doorways that open onto a covered porch that looks onto the courtyard. This portion of the property is in extremely poor condition, in various stages of collapse.

The west section of the property contains two small but separate houses connected by a narrow corridor that runs along the houses' east walls. Each house is built around a small courtyard lined by several rooms. These two houses are internal buildings, meaning that they have no windows or entrances facing outside the property. The houses were occupied by members of the same extended family. The main entrance for the two internal houses is a portal that runs through the middle of the Old Suq on the north side of the property. It occupies a space approximately the same size as the adjacent shops on either side. There is a secondary entrance in the south wall of the property, at the end of the long, narrow passageway that runs through the two internal houses.

All three houses (the two internal ones and the house on the west side of the property) were built in the traditional manner using local materials common to most buildings constructed during the early 1900s. Walls were built of layered rock held in place with thick mud plaster. Roofs were constructed of *danshal* beams overlain with *basgill* and *mangharour*, and covered with a layer of mud on top. Though in poor condition, the underside of these roofs can be seen inside most of the rooms. In some, the old ceilings have been covered over with plywood, which itself is unsightly and falling off in many places. The original woodwork, such as doors, windows, shutters and their frames, is mostly long gone. The large double metal gate in the east wall of the property is old and weathered, but probably not original. That would likely have been made of wood imported from India. In the middle of the suq there is a wooden double door with a *khokha* as the main entrance to the internal houses. However, this has been blocked by a wall constructed on the inside. There are no exterior windows in any of the rooms, but this was not uncommon among traditional Qatari houses. Two of the houses are built on an interior parcel of land completely hemmed in by the other houses on three sides and by the suq on the fourth.

• Aerial perspective. Al Ansari property consists of two old houses. It is located in a residential area near the centre of the old part of Al Khor town

• Ground floor plan. The house was gradually expanded, so that the rooms were built around two small courtyards, probably to accommodate different parts of extended family

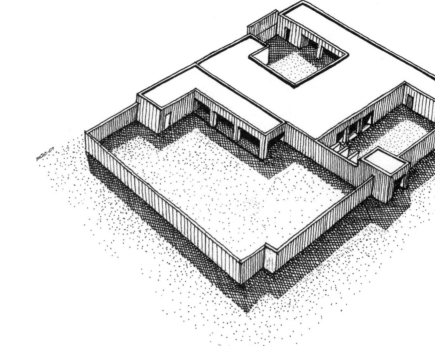

 Private room

 Circulation

 Open private space

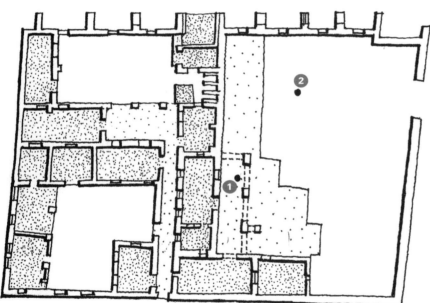

Ground floor plan

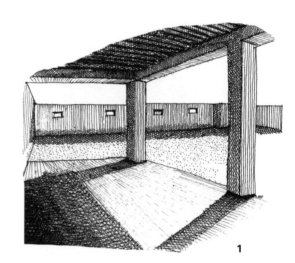

• View from the shaded porch

1

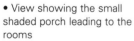
• View showing the small shaded porch leading to the rooms

2

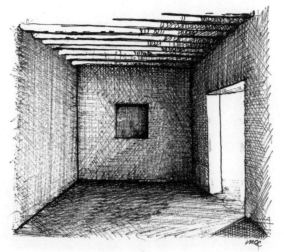

• View from the inside room

1

Section A

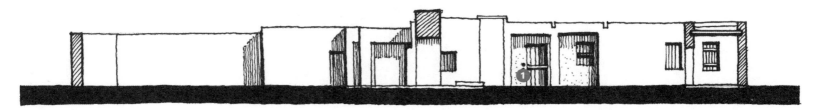

Section B

• Detail of traditional roof

1

• Some decorative elements used for the parapets

1

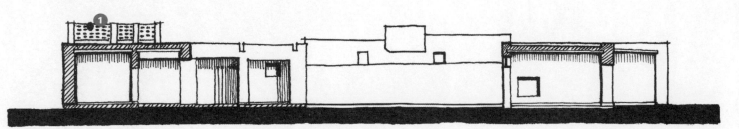

Section C

Section D

• Openings on the wall

1

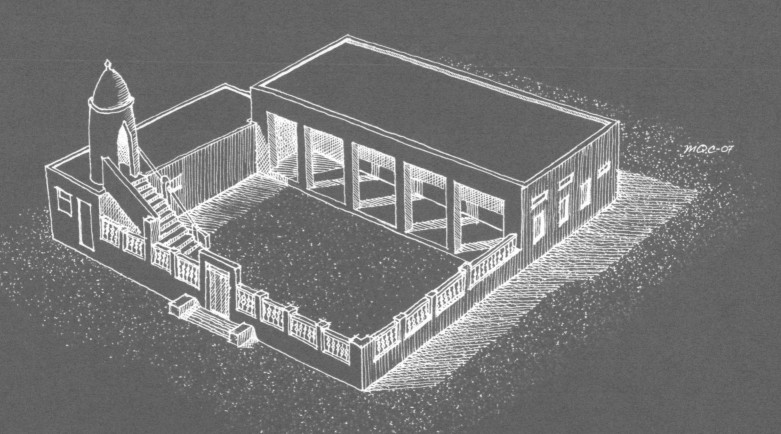

MOSQUES

Al Ayouni Mosque
(1935)

Brief Description and History

Al Ayouni is the largest mosque in Wakrah, itself the largest town south of Doha. The building dates from 1935 and, like many mosques in the town, is built close to the shoreline. This is because the town's main activities, such as fishing and trading, took place here. In consequence, it was close to the sea that the original settlements developed. This mosque was continuously maintained and heavily used before the new larger mosque on the Wakrah main road was built. This eventually led to Al Ayouni being abandoned.

Architectural Description of the Mosque

The mosque has an almost square plan, measuring approximately 17 by 16 metres, and is distinguished by having a base 67 centimetres above street level. Three concrete steps lead through the single entrance on the east wall to a shallow rectangular courtyard 13 metres by 6 metres, which has recently been paved with cement screed. Both the *meda* (ablution fountain) and the minaret of the mosque lie outside the courtyard boundary on the south side, only the staircase leading up to the minaret is inside the courtyard.

The Courtyard

The only entrance to the courtyard is in the east wall, which makes Al Ayouni one of the rare mosques to have a single entrance. Most Qatari mosques have three entrances, one on the east wall and two on the north and south walls of the courtyard. The *meda* and the minaret, both of which are on the south-east wall, can be accessed from the courtyard. The minaret, also one of a few of its kind, stands on the roof of the ablution area. An *imam*'s room, constructed from concrete hollow blocks, has been added between the ablution area and the open *iwan*.

The Minaret

Eighteen steps lead up to the minaret that stands above the ablution block. The handrails of the staircase are not similar; the east one is solid and made of stone while the west one is hollow with a wooden handrail, though it is thought that the wooden one replaced an earlier stone handrail. The body of the minaret is conical with four openings: one door and three windows. All the openings are pointed and in the shape of a triangle. The inside of the minaret is circular and very small with a 90-centimetre diameter and barely 2.4 metres of clear height.

The Open Prayer Area

The external prayer hall or *iwan* can be accessed through five newly built portals that probably replaced the original ones when this part of the roof was replaced. The new concrete columns that define these portals are square with sides measuring 22 centimetres. The north wall of the open *iwan* has two wooden windows and two rectangular openings on top of them, while the windows on the south wall were blocked when the *imam*'s room was built. Square wooden beams run across the concrete ceiling of the open *iwan*.

The Prayer Hall

The *iwan* Al Kebla can be accessed through three doors on the wall that separates the open *iwan* from the inner one. This wall is fitted with four window openings that allow the light and wind to penetrate the *iwan*. All the windows on this wall are fitted with six vertical metal bar inserts; similar to many other mosques, the windows have four wooden leafs: two lower ones and two upper ones. The original side walls of the inner *iwan* have been altered, with both windows of the south wall filled in and replaced with an opening for an air conditioning unit. One window in the north wall has been left intact while the other has been replaced by an opening for an air conditioner.

The *kebla* wall is void of any windows, instead it is fitted with four recesses used as shelves for prayer books, two on each side of the *mihrab*. The *mihrab* is a very simple semi-circular feature with thick stone walls that support a domed roof, and a decorative pointed arch at its entrance. From the outside, the *mihrab* protrudes some 1.5 metres from the *kebla* wall. The inner *iwan* has a roof built in the traditional manner, consisting of *danshal* wood beams with *basgill* laid perpendicular to the beam, and then *mangharour* placed above. Finally, a thick layer of mud plaster mixed with straw is applied on top.

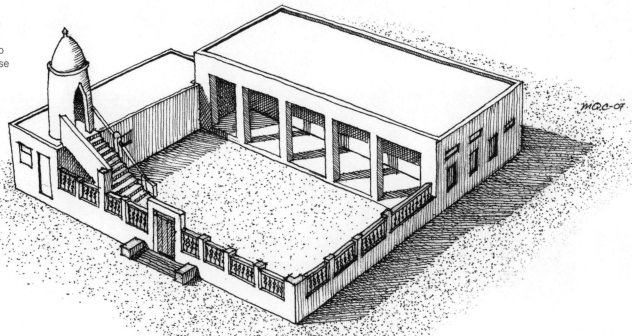

• Aerial perspective of the mosque. Al Ayouni Mosque is the largest mosque in Wakrah. It was built close to the shoreline. This is because the town's main activities, such as fishing and trading, took place here

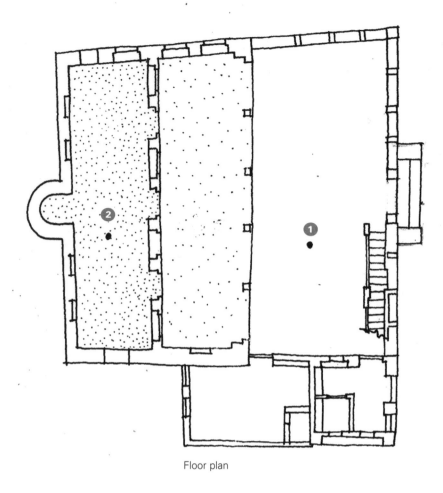

• Floor plan. The mosque has an almost square plan. Both ablution fountain and the minaret of the mosque lie outside the courtyard boundary on the south side

Floor plan

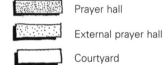

Prayer hall

External prayer hall

Courtyard

• Staircase leading up to the minaret is inside the courtyard

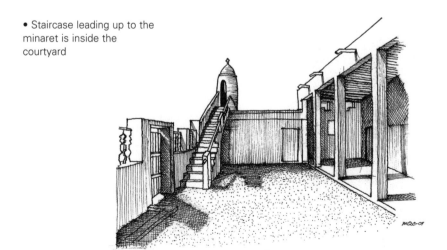

1

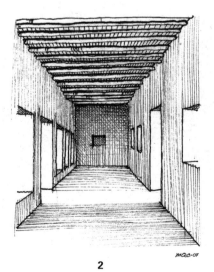

2

• The minaret is conical with four openings. All openings are of triangular shape

• Windows of the mosque

1

2

3

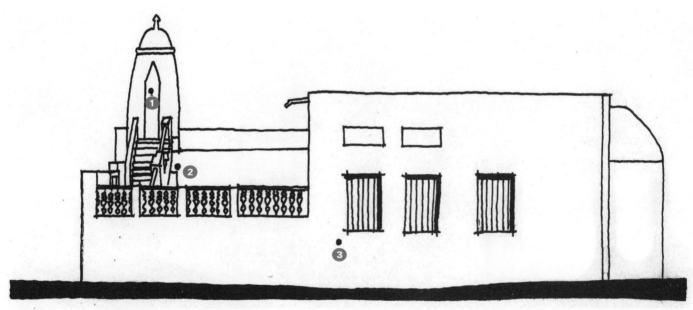

North elevation

209

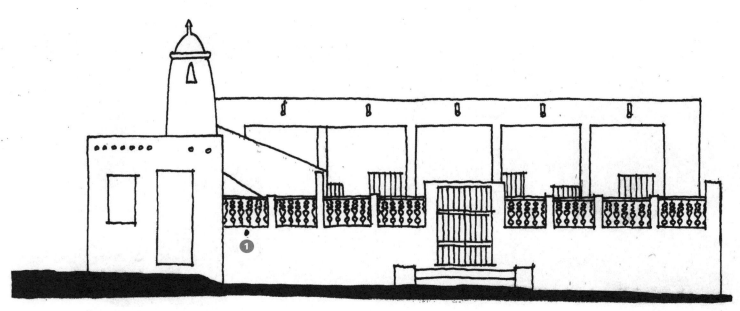

East elevation

• Perspective of the entrance
to the mosque

1

- View from the mosque hall
- External prayer hall
- Detail of boundary wall designed for the mosque

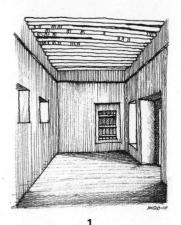

1

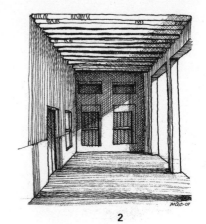

2

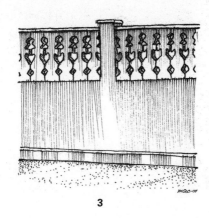

3

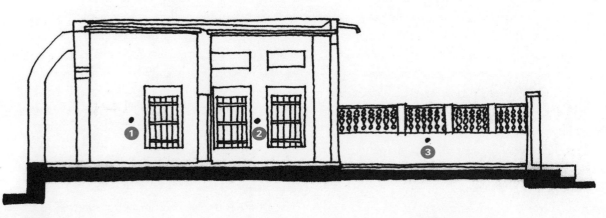

Section A-A

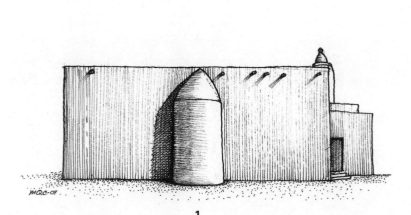

West elevation

1

• The west façade is decorated with a wall forming the same shape of the minaret

2

• The minaret

Abu Manaratain Mosque (Al Wakrah) (1940)

Brief Description and History

Abu Manaratain is a mosque still in use that was constructed near the coastline in Wakrah in 1940. Compared to other old mosques in Wakrah and all around Qatar, it is very small and shallow in terms of the depth of its footprint. The name of the mosque, Abu Manaratain (The Mosque with Two Minarets) suggests that it had twin minarets at an earlier stage. The mosque is one of several built near the coast. Abu Manaratain mosque has been continuously maintained, renovated and is still in very good shape.

Architectural Description of the Mosque

Abu Manaratain is unique in several ways. For example, the courtyard is located on the south side of the prayer hall instead of the east side, giving it a longitudinal layout across the north-south axis. In size it does not exceed 27 metres in length by 8 metres in width, while the mosque itself consists of a single *iwan* measuring 12 by 3 metres. At one time another mosque stood adjacent to Abu Manaratain on the west side but it has since been demolished.

The Courtyard

The mosque can be accessed through at least five different entrances, three of which have staircases. A fourth staircase descends from the west wall of the courtyard to an enclosed space that may have served as a *meda*. A new ablution area has been built out of hollow concrete blocks on the south wall. Part of the courtyard is paved with mosaic tiles to provide a clean walkway from the ablution block. The original section is still simple earth. A saltwater well three metres deep lies on the south-east corner of the prayer hall.

The Minaret

The top of the 9 metre high minaret on the north-west corner of the building block is reached via a flight of forty steps. The overall shape of the minaret is conical on a square base and ends in a small space for the *muezzin* that stands 160 centimetres high inside and 130 centimetres in diameter. It has four openings, one on each side. There are no window openings in the body of the minaret. Stone is the main building material.

The Prayer Hall

The external prayer hall or open *iwan* does not exist in this mosque; instead, the front entrance leads directly to the 3-metre deep space outside the closed *iwan*. A corrugated metal sheet has been installed to cover this space which can be considered part of the courtyard.

The east wall of the prayer hall is the façade of the building. It stands almost 4 metres in height, and features four wooden windows and a wooden door in the middle. Another door on the south side used to be a working door before it was blocked with plywood from the inside. The north side wall has two windows, whereas the *kebla* wall has no signs of openings, just four recesses, two on each side of the *mihrab*, which are used as book shelves. The interior of the prayer hall was entirely changed at a certain date; plywood sheets now cover the surfaces of the walls and the interior of the *mihrab*. The original ceiling of both the hall and the *mihrab* has been covered with gypsum board fitted with fluorescent lights. The *mihrab* is a 120 × 88 centimetre rectangle chamfered on both corners of its west wall.

• Aerial perspective.
Abu Manaratain is a unique mosque in several ways. The courtyard is located on the south side of the south side of the prayer hall instead of east side, giving it a longitudinal layout across the north-south axis

• Ground floor plan. The mosque can be accessed through at least five different entrances. In this mosque the external prayer hall does not exist

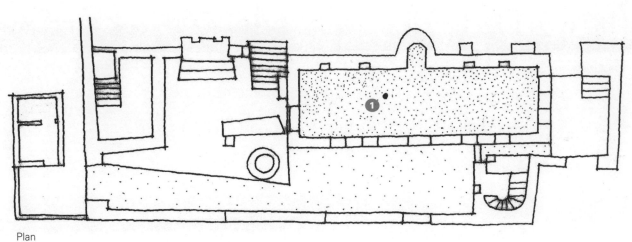

Plan

• View of the prayer hall

Prayer hall

Circulation

Courtyard

1

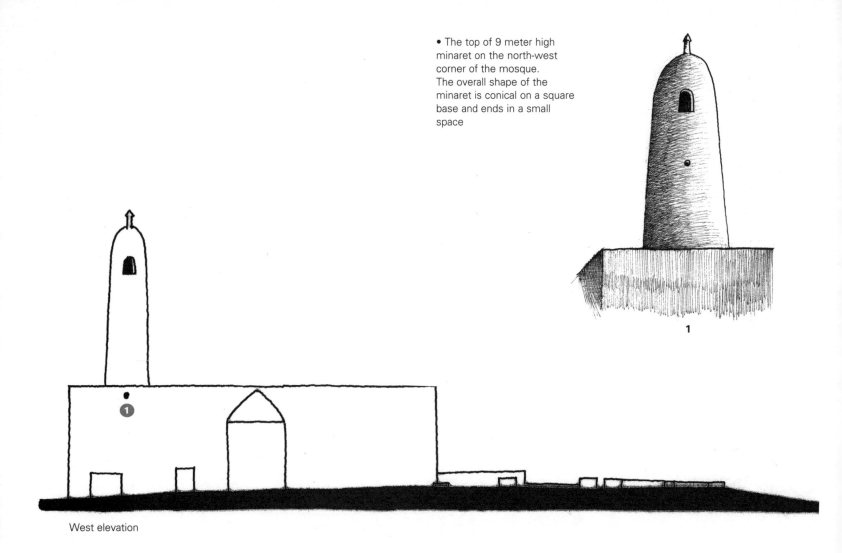

• The top of 9 meter high minaret on the north-west corner of the mosque. The overall shape of the minaret is conical on a square base and ends in a small space

1

West elevation

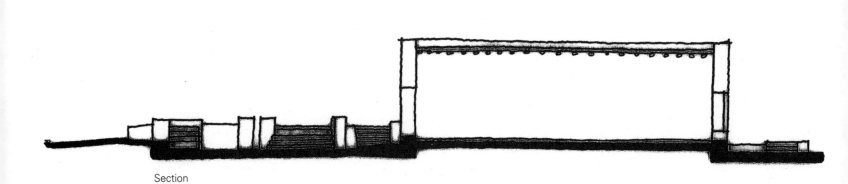

Section

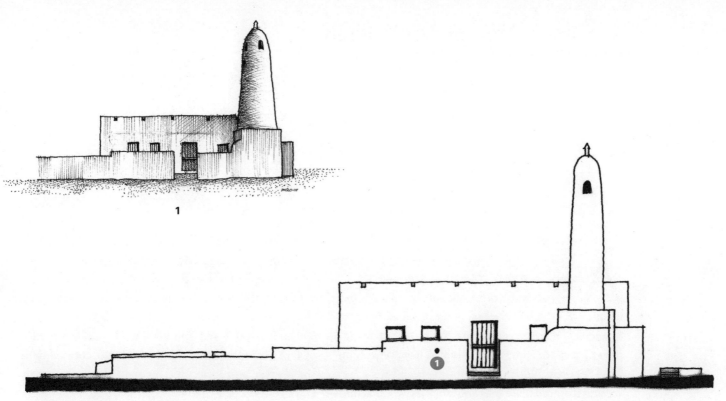

1

East elevation

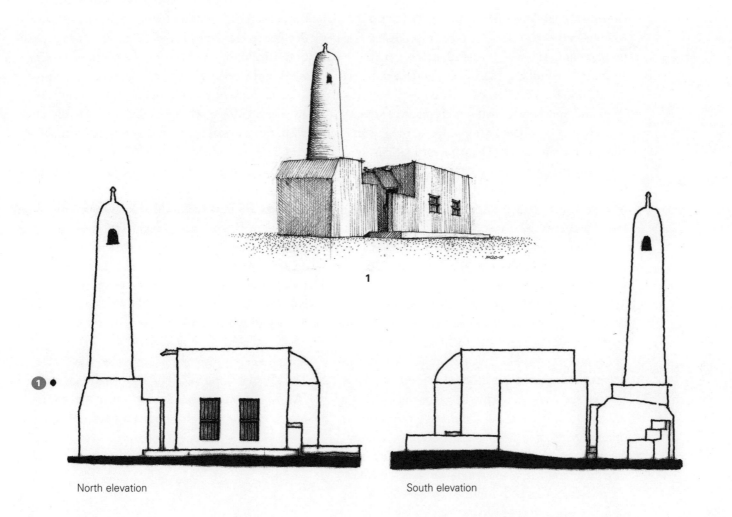

1

North elevation

South elevation

Al Subaiei Mosque (Al Wakrah) (1940)

Brief Description and History

Al Subaiei is the third in the series of mosques close to Wakrah Museum. Although it appears to be of recent construction, it dates from 1940. Much of the layout has been entirely replaced. The courtyard *meda*, the *imam*'s room and the minaret are all new, all of which have been built from concrete blocks. This mosque is an active one, serving its immediate neighbourhood, which is one of the reasons why it has been continuously maintained.

Architectural Description of the Mosque

Al Subaiei is bigger than the other two mosques near the shoreline. It is a rectangle 22 metres long by 13 wide. The building can be divided into two parts, the old and the new. The old section comprises the inner and outer prayer halls and is made of stone; the new part consists of the courtyard, the minaret and the ablution block. The courtyard, originally a square open space measuring 12 by 12 metres, has been reduced in size by the addition of the *imam*'s house and the *meda*. Now it is a rectangle (12 × 8 m) paved with mosaic tiles and fenced with a steel grill on the north and south sides.

The Minaret

The minaret was accessed directly from the courtyard and was very close to the entrance on the north wall of the court. After adding the *imam*'s house and the small kitchen next to it, the original entry to the minaret was blocked and can now only be accessed through the kitchen. The minaret has a modern look, but still has the characteristics seen in other minarets around Qatar. It has a square body 5.5 metres tall standing on a square base. Each side of the minaret has a long window installed inside a rectangular recess with rounded corners. At the top of the tower, a square balcony is bounded by an aluminium handrail octagonal in plan. Although the balcony was originally added as a space for the *muezzin* to stand so the call to prayer would reach farther, this is not the method used anymore but has remained part of the architectural language. The balcony is reached via a steel spiral staircase. The dome on top of the minaret is decorated with a cornice and supported on eight slender columns.

The Open Prayer Area

The open *iwan* has five archways, each rounded at the corners. The two archways at the sides have decorative handrails made of gypsum. The external prayer hall is 3 metres deep. The north and south walls of the open *iwan* had openings that are now filled in, but one remains open on the north wall, and the window itself is aluminium. From the open *iwan*, the internal prayer hall is reached through a door in the middle of the wall. Three windows on each side of the door provide the *iwan* with light and ventilation. Looking from the inside of the prayer hall, the windows sit inside wall recesses with sills no more than 10 centimetres high. The openings in the south side wall have been blocked and replaced with an opening for an air conditioning unit. The north wall is fitted with two aluminium windows. No windows can be seen on the *kebla* wall; instead, it has four recesses, two on each side of the *mihrab*, which are used as book shelves. The *mihrab* is semicircular in plan and has a domed roof. The original wooden ceiling has been renovated. *Danshal* beams are painted for protection and the roof is treated with an external waterproofing layer.

• Aerial perspective.
Al Subaiei Mosque is bigger
than the other two mosques
near the shore line
• Ground floor plan.
The courtyard, originally
a square open space,
has been reduced by
the addition of imman house
and the meda

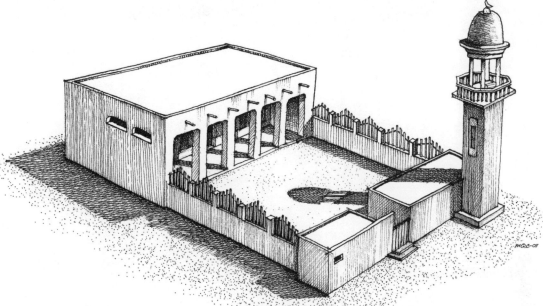

• View of the prayer hall

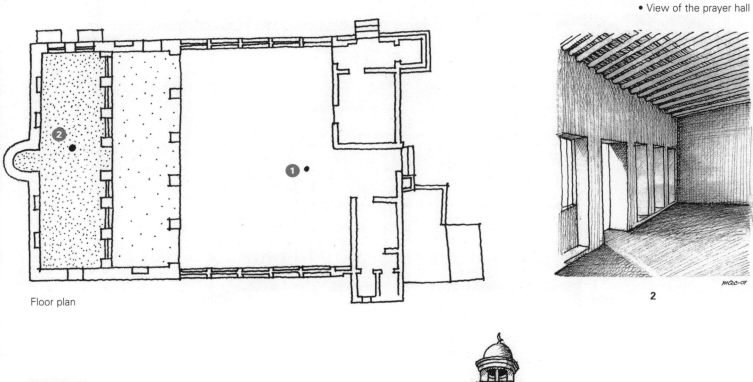

2

Floor plan

 Prayer hall

 External prayer hall

 Courtyard

1

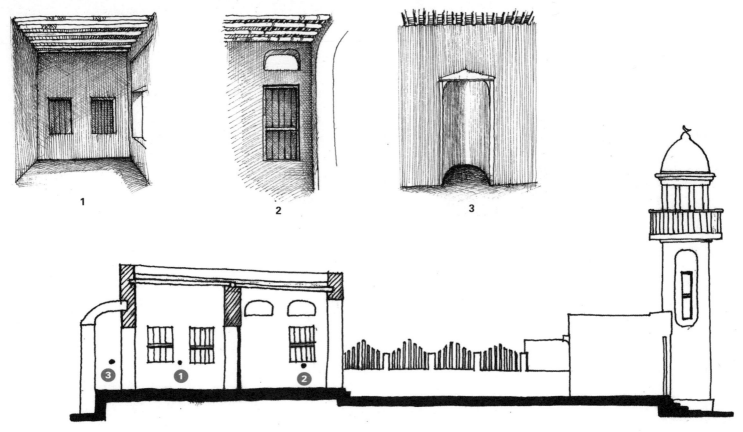

1

2

3

Longitudinal section

Transversal section

• The open *iwan* has five archways, each rounded at the corners. The two archways at the sides have decorative handrails made of gypsum

1

218

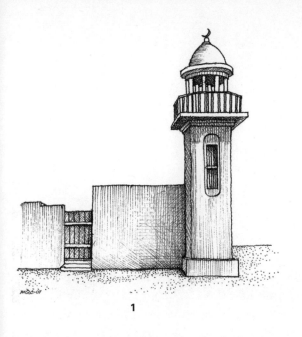

1

• The minaret has a modern look, but still has the characteristics seen in other minarets around Qatar. It has square body and stands on a square base

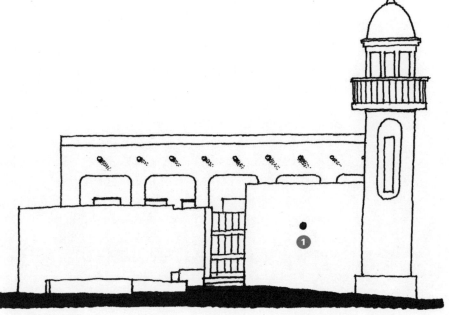

East elevation

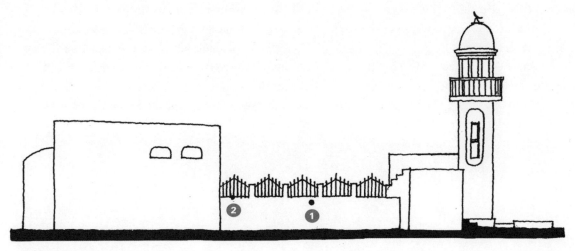

South elevation

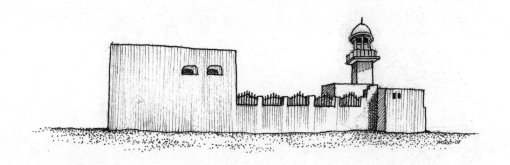

1

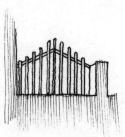

2

Al Sana Mosque (Al Sana Village) (1950)

Brief Description and History

The mosque is located on a small rise in the desert in Al Sana village approximately 60 kilometres north-west of Doha. The history of Al Sana mosque goes back to the year 1950. The area surrounding the mosque has been through a lot of changes. The village has become much smaller as the population has abandoned the smaller villages throughout Qatar during the past few decades and moved to Greater Doha.

Architectural Description of the Mosque

The mosque has one entrance to the courtyard, which is located in the north external wall. The adjoining north façade has four window openings to the *iwans*. The minaret stands at the north-east corner of the mosque. The courtyard has five arches which form the first *iwan*. Another five arches form the *iwan* of the *kebla*, which is also an open *iwan*. The two *iwans* are not separated by any walls or doors. In this way, the Al Sana mosque differs from many other mosques, which contain one or more open *iwans* as well as a closed *iwan* for the *kebla*.

The *mihrab* of the *kebla* that protrudes from the external façade of the west wall is semicircular. On the inside the *mihrab* faces the *iwan* through a square arch decorated at the corners. Three steps inside the *mihrab* lead to the *minbar*, which can be seen through another smaller square arch, right beside the other arch.

The Minaret

The minaret is built on a square base with a door leading to the stairs. The tower of the minaret has collapsed, with debris strewn down the minaret stairwell and piled up around the minaret base. The cylindrical shaft, which still remains, only rises 1.5 metres above the square base. Adjacent to the base of the minaret, a door leads to a newer building that was not an important section of the original mosque.

• Aerial perspective. Al Sana Mosque differs from many other mosques, which contain one or more *iwans* as well as a close *iwan* for the *kebla*

• Ground floor plan. The mosque has one entrance to the courtyard, which is located in the north external wall. The minaret stands at the north-east corner of the mosque

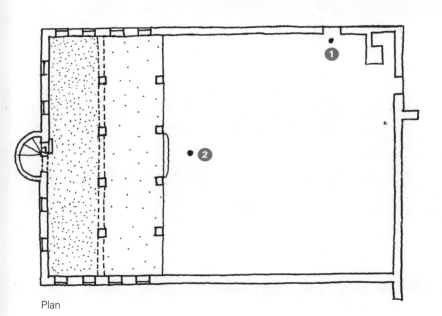

Plan

1 • Entrance to the mosque

 Prayer hall

 External prayer hall

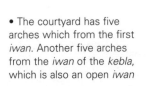 Courtyard

• The courtyard has five arches which from the first *iwan*. Another five arches from the *iwan* of the *kebla*, which is also an open *iwan*

2

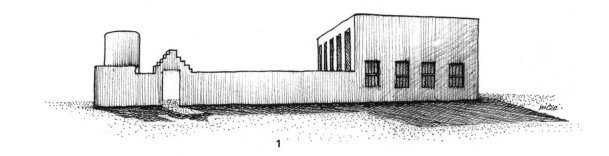

1

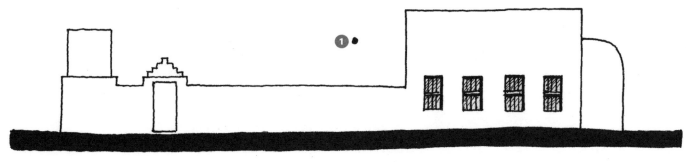

North elevation

South elevation

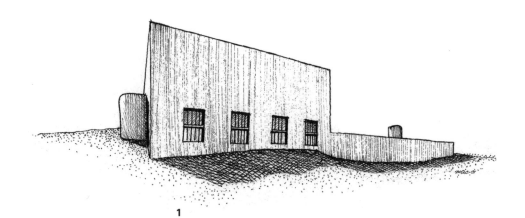

1

• The minaret is built on square base with a door to the stairs

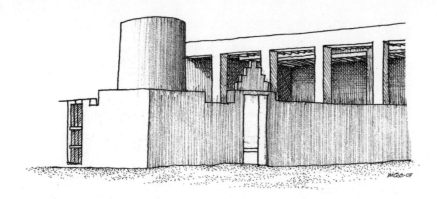

1

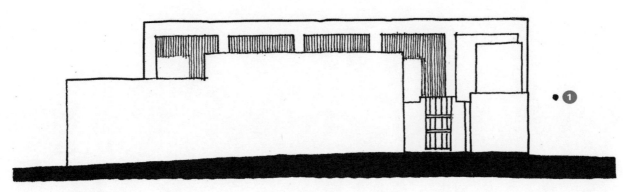

East elevation

West elevation

• The shape of the *kebla* from the external wall

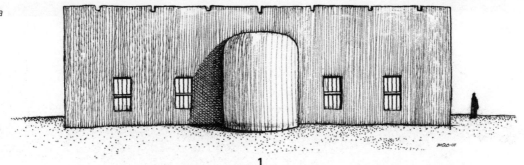

1

• View of the stairs

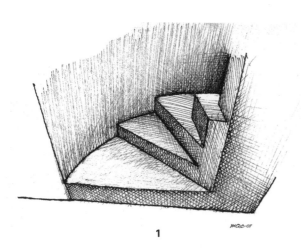

1

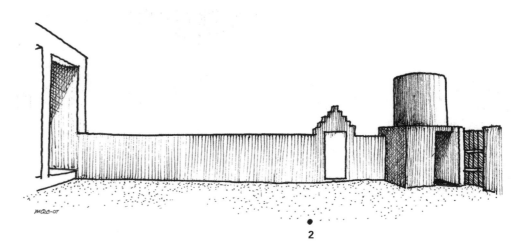

2

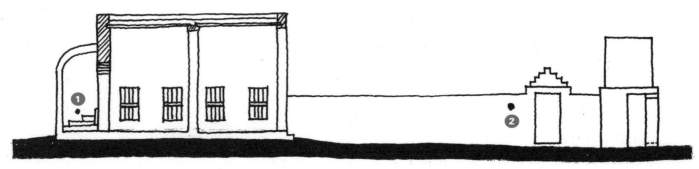

Longitudinal section

224

• Decorated arches

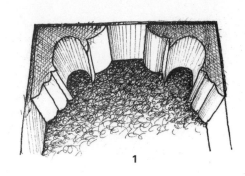

1

Transversal section 2

2

Transversal section 1

• View of the arches

1

Umm Al Qahab Mosque (Um Al Qahab Village) (1945)

Brief Description and History

Umm Al Qahab is a much used mosque which serves in old rural. The original building was constructed in 1945 when more people were living in the area than today. Numerous alterations have been made to the mosque, such as roofing the open *iwan*, carpeting the floor, and modernising the area used for ablution, with the result that the mosque has lost much of its original architectural appearance.

Architectural Description of the Mosque

The mosque measures 10 × 14.28 metres. The entrance is in the east wall, close to the surrounding houses. An open *iwan*, with an iron frame, has been added to the right of the entrance. A large part of the courtyard and the originally open *iwan* (3.40 × 9.36 m) has been made into a closed *iwan* (5.40 × 9.60 m) with a corrugated metal roof. The cement floor has been covered with carpets. The *kebla* is situated at the north-east corner of the mosque to the left of the entrance. The ablution area and the toilets are located at the end of the courtyard, which has now been reduced to a two-metre wide passage at the south-east corner due to the construction of the closed *iwan*.

The wall, which precedes the *iwan* of the *kebla*, is painted white. The doors have been removed and the openings squared. All the *iwan*'s vents have been closed, and the walls painted white. The roof has also been replaced with corrugated metal sheeting. The *mihrab* is semicircular, with an opening for light on each side, and a semicircular dome. The external façade of the *iwan* of the *kebla* has two openings, both now closed. The concrete that covers portions of the external wall is clearly visible.

The minaret is the oldest part of the mosque and has not undergone many changes since its construction. It stands on a square base and has a door leading to the staircase. The square base rises as high as the outer wall of the mosque. The minaret has a rounded vertical shaft, with a dome resting on six pillars, each 2.39 metres high. The dome and the pillars represent a skeleton built in a traditional way. The pillars are coated with traditional mortar. The stairs leading to the minaret are also built in the traditional manner, but the exterior of the tower has been covered with a layer of cement.

• Aerial perspective. The mosque has a lot of its original architectural appearance
• Ground floor plan. A large part of the courtyard and the originally open *iwan* has been made into a closed *iwan*

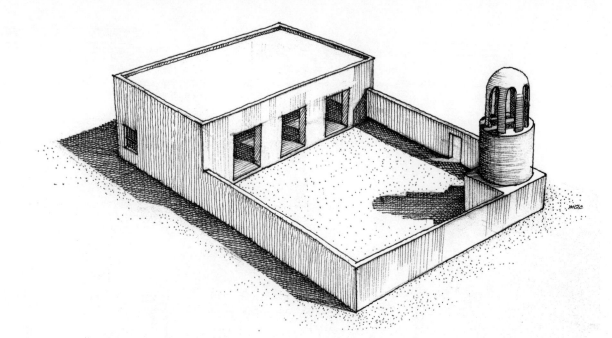

 Prayer hall

Courtyard

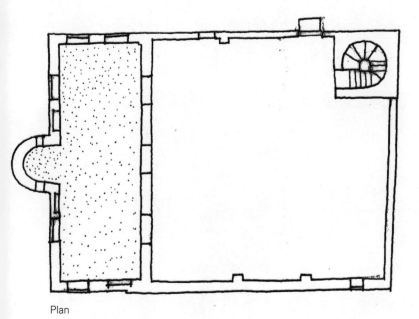

Plan

1

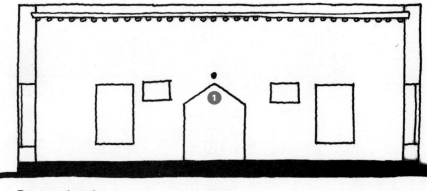

Transversal section

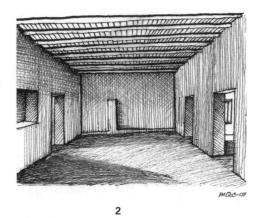

2

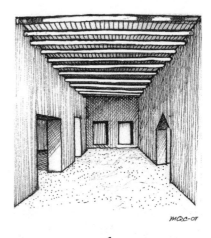

1

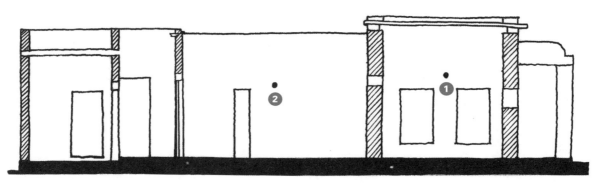

Longitudinal section

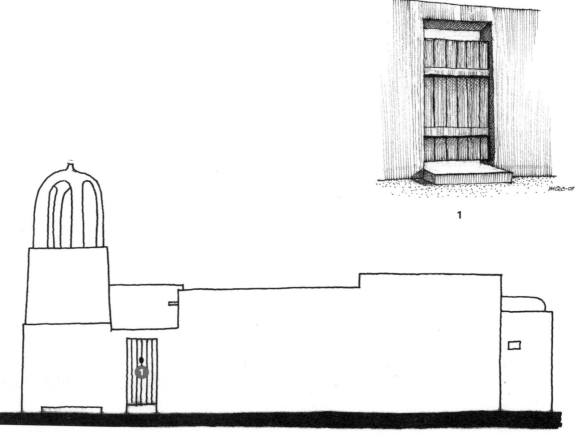

1

North elevation

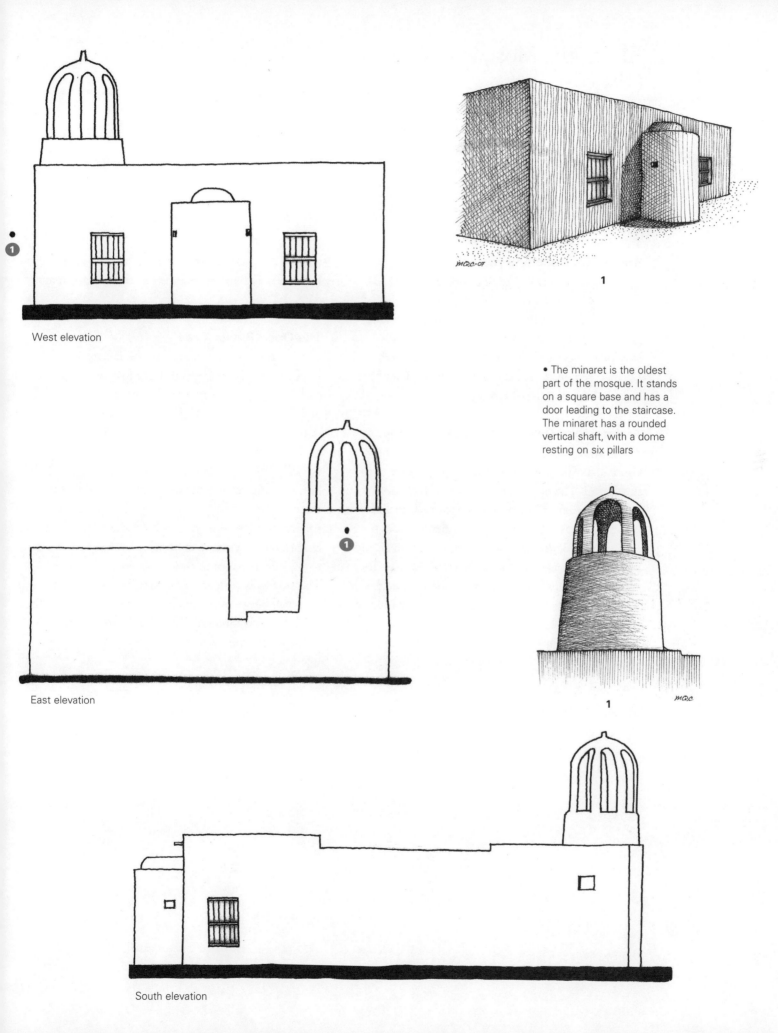

West elevation

1

• The minaret is the oldest part of the mosque. It stands on a square base and has a door leading to the staircase. The minaret has a rounded vertical shaft, with a dome resting on six pillars

East elevation

1

South elevation

Al Khotba Mosque (Dukhan)
(1943)

Brief Description and History

Oil deposits were discovered in Dukhan in 1938 and soon after plans for the construction of a mosque began to take place. Al Khotba mosque was completed in 1942. It is located close to the main road leading to the Dukhan reqion. Al Khotba is considered one of the most beautiful of the old mosques.

Architectural Description of the Mosque

The entrance on the south façade leads into the courtyard. There is a corresponding entrance in the north wall. The original south façade has four window openings, one of which is sealed up with concrete blocks. The other three openings still have traditional wooden windows with wood frames and iron bars. The western façade of the *kebla* has the *mihrab* in the middle, with one window on each side. There are gutters for rainwater along the top of the west-facing wall.

The minaret stands at the north-east corner of the courtyard. The *meda* is at the opposite corner but outside the original boundaries of the mosque. It appears to have been added to the site at a later date.

The Open Prayer Area

The open *iwan* is connected to the courtyard through six squared portals built in a simple post and lintel style. The roof of the open *iwan* is made of wood that rests on the horizontal lintel, which in turn, lies on five square columns above the ends of the exterior walls.

Basgill sections are laid perpendicular to the horizontal lintel and the top of the wall separating the inner and outer *iwans*. The presence of these square wooden poles differs from the usual *danshal* beams, which was the material most frequently used to support the roof in these buildings.

The sidewalls contain two openings on each side. The wall between the open *iwan* and the *iwan* of the *kebla* has two modern doors that have replaced the old wooden ones. Between the doors are two windows.

The Prayer Hall

The *iwan* of the *kebla* is formed by two *iwans*. The first is roofed in a similar way to that of the open *iwan*. It is connected to the second *iwan*, which contains the *kebla*, by three square openings. One of these square openings is located opposite the *kebla* and the others on each side of the *iwan*. The *kebla* is semicircular with a buttress in the middle. It has steps on the left leading to the *imam*'s bench on the right. There were two openings in the wall of the *kebla*, which now are closed. Near each of them, there is a small rectangular vent that could have been a *badgheer*.

The mosque was apparently built in two phases. During the first phase, the *iwan* of the *kebla* was built and an open *iwan*. In the second phase, the open *iwan* was closed and another open *iwan* was added in front of it in the courtyard. Because of the two phases of construction, the main supporting poles of the roof are squared and not made of *danshal* wood, as is the case inside the *iwan* of the *kebla*.

The Minaret

The minaret is one of the oldest parts of the mosque. It was constructed at the same time as the *iwan* of the *kebla*. The minaret stands on a square base and is cylindrical in form. It ends with six circular arches that enclose the place of the *muezzin*. The simple and beautiful minaret with its rounded top echoes the rounded exterior of the *mihrab* of the *kebla*. They both have the same proportions and the same splendour.

The minaret's spiral stairway is constructed of *danshal* wood bound together with ropes and *basgill*. The stairs are covered with painted mud plaster. The courtyard doors leading into the mosque have some ancient wooden details, whereas modern ones exist between the closed and opened parts of the *iwan*.

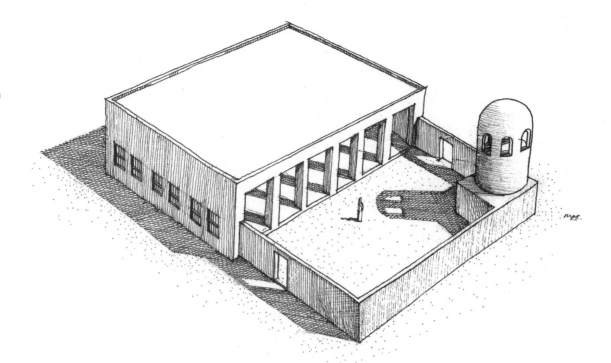

• Aerial perspective.
Al Khotba Mosque is
considered one of the most
beautiful among the old
mosques
• Ground floor plan. The open
iwan is connected to the
courtyard through six square
portals built in a simple post
and lintel style. The minaret
stands at the north-east
corner of the courtyard

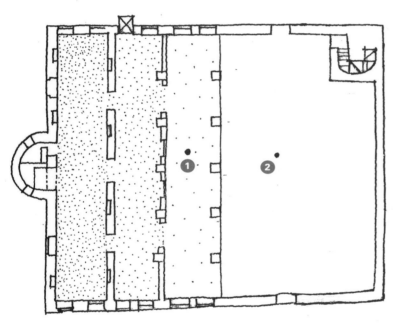

Plan

1

 Prayer hall

 External prayer hall

 Courtyard

2

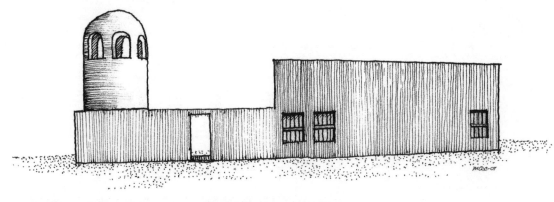

2

1

• The minaret stands on a square base and is cylindrical in form. It ends with six circular arches that enclose the place of the muezzin

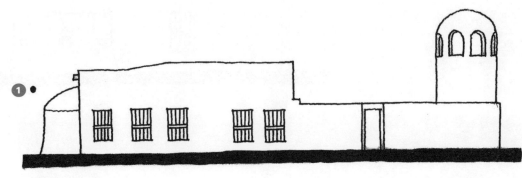

North elevation

South elevation

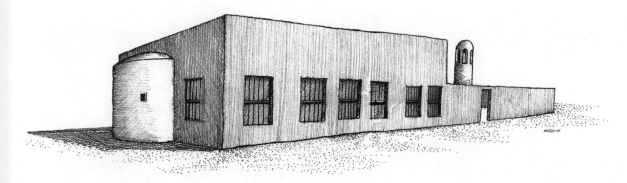

1

1

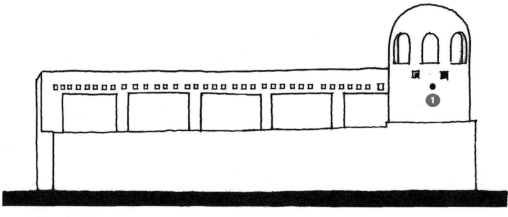

East elevation

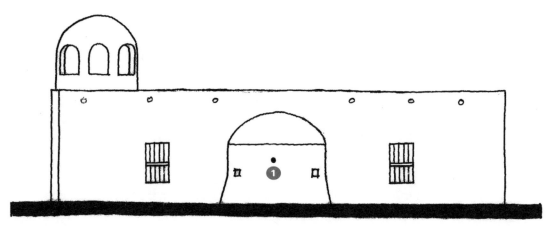

West elevation

• Detail of the *kebla* on the external wall

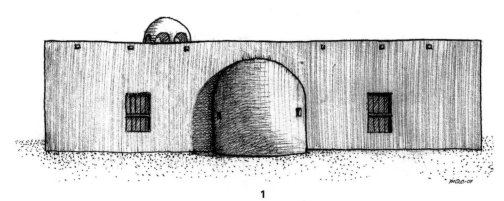

1

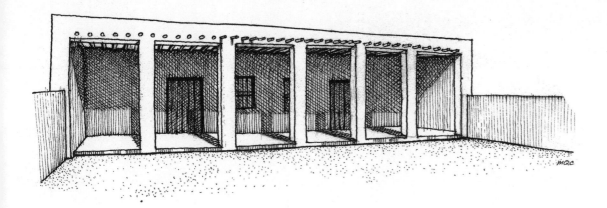

• The roof of the open *iwan* is made of wood that rests in the horizontal lintel, which in turn lies on five square columns above the ends of the exterior walls

1

Transversal section

1

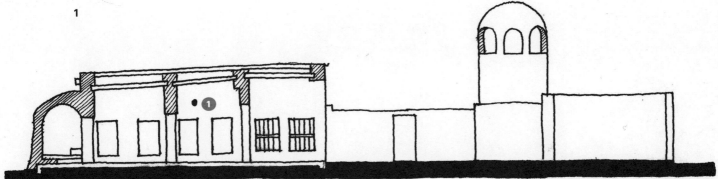

Longitudinal section

Zekreet Mosque (Madinat Zekreet) (1940)

Brief Description and History

Zekreet mosque dates from 1940. It has entrances along the north and the south external walls. The entrance to the *iwan* of the *kebla* faces towards the east. Two window openings in the mosque's *iwans* are located on the north and south-facing external walls. There is a new area for ablution at the south-east corner of the courtyard. This is most probably the place where the old well was located.

The Minaret

The courtyard measures 10.24 by 15.90 metres. The minaret stands in the north-east corner of the courtyard on a small square base. A step leads up to the arched door, which opens to a spiral staircase that climbs to the top of the minaret. The minaret is cylindrical in shape with a low circular dome at the top resting on six pillars.

The Open Prayer Area

The open *iwan* is connected to the courtyard through seven square arches. The *iwan* is 3.17 metres wide, with an opening on each side. The wall separating the *iwan* from the *iwan* of the *kebla* has three doors. The door in the middle faces the *kebla*. All the *badgheers* of the *iwan* have been closed and the old doors have been replaced with metal ones. The roof has been covered with plates of corrugated sheet metal.

The Prayer Hall

The area of the closed *iwan* is nearly equal to that of the open *iwan*. The *kebla* is located directly opposite the exterior door that leads into the closed *iwan*. The *kebla* is semicircular in shape and has two arches. One of the arches is square with steps leading to the *imam*'s bench on the right. New decorations have been recently added to this arch. The interior *iwan* has a hung ceiling of laminated plywood panelling and metal battens, which is totally out of character with the original architecture of the building.

The *badgheers* in the wall of the *kebla* have been sealed up and so have the windows that were on the other side of the *kebla* (one on each side). There is an opening (*derisha*) on each of the sidewalls. The mosque has six rainwater drains on the roof on the outside of the *kebla*.

• Aerial perspective
• Ground floor plan.
The minaret stands in the
north-east corner of the
courtyard on a small square
base. The open *iwan* is
connected to the courtyard
through seven square arches.
The *kebla* is located directly
open to the exterior door
that leads into the closed
iwan

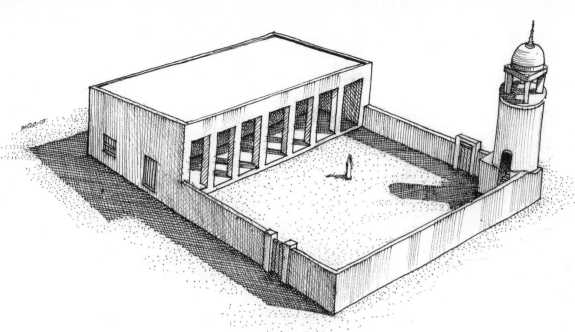

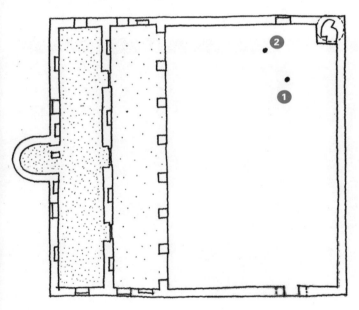

Floor plan

 Prayer hall

 External prayer hall

 Courtyard

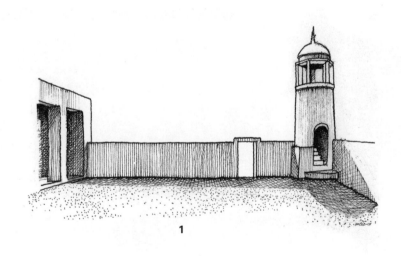

1

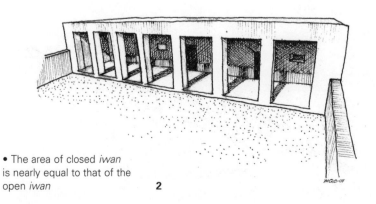

• The area of closed *iwan*
is nearly equal to that of the
open *iwan*

2

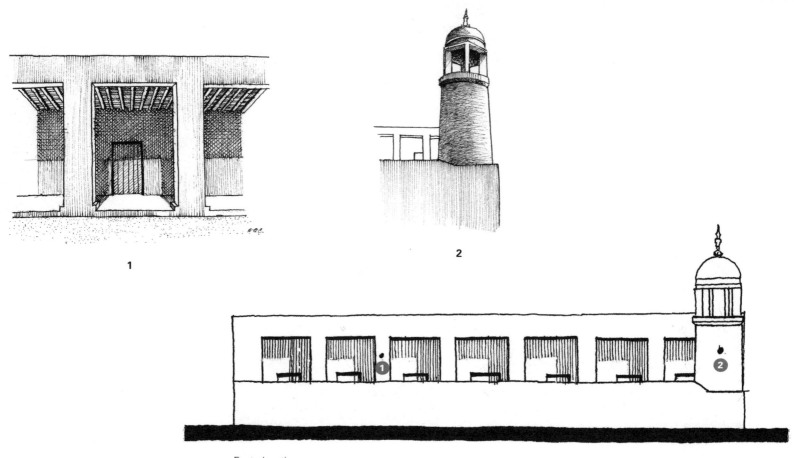

1

2

East elevation

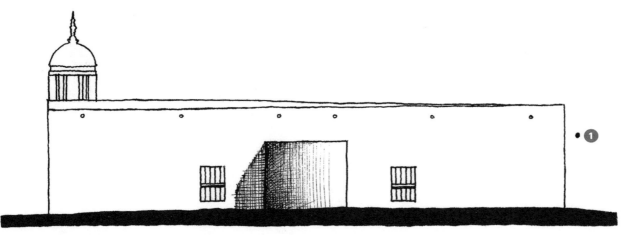

West elevation

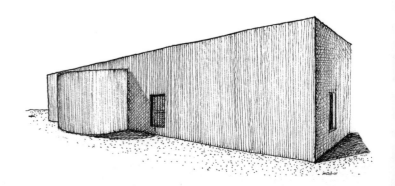

1

• The minaret is cylindrical in shape with a low circular dome at the top resting on six pillars

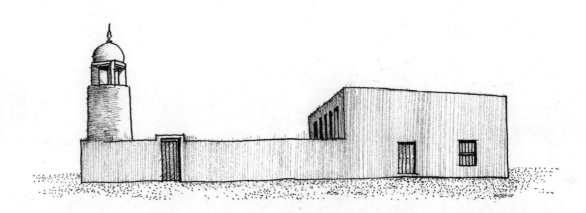

2

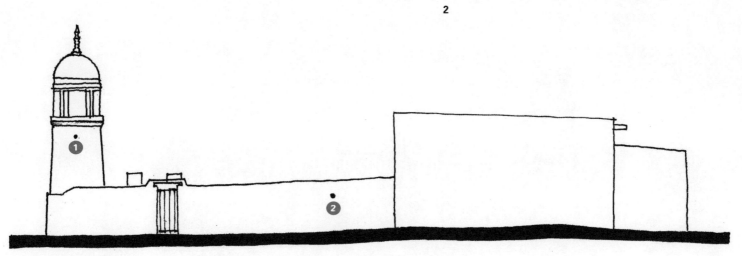

North elevation

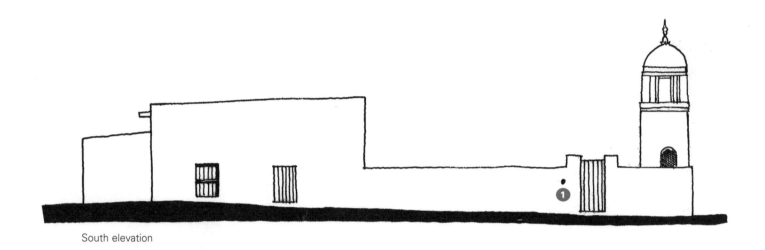

South elevation

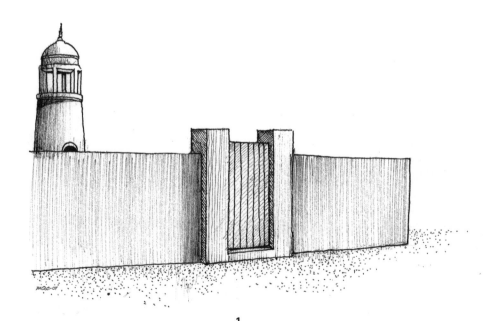

1

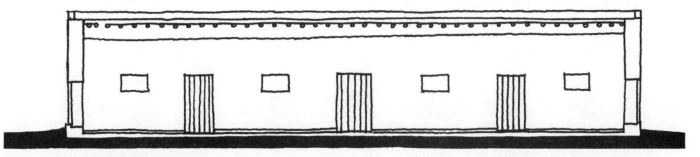

Transversal section 1

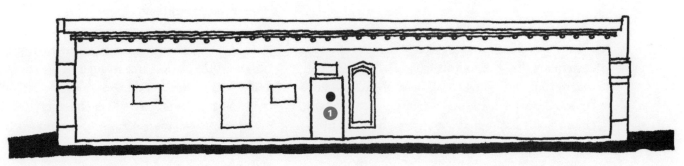

Transversal section 2

1

Al Owaynah Mosque (Al Owaynah Village) (1945)

Brief Description and History

Al Owaynah mosque was constructed in 1945. It is located in a small village just off the south side of the main highway to Dukhan, about 60 kilometres west of Doha. There is not much left of the surrounding village, which, like many others in isolated areas of Qatar, has seen much of its population move away. Al Owaynah mosque remains open however, and is still used.

Architectural Description of the Mosque

The mosque has entrances along the north and south external walls of the outside courtyard, though the south courtyard entrance has been obscured and blocked by the new house belonging to the *imam* that adjoins it. Covered with square concrete tiles, the courtyard is in the shape of a slightly skewed square, measuring approximately 12 metres square. The entire mosque, and all the rooms and areas within, are slightly skewed owing to the fact that the north façade of the mosque is slightly longer than the south façade.

The Minaret

The minaret stands in the north-east corner of the courtyard on a skewed square base the same height as the adjoining courtyard walls. A wooden door, painted blue, opens to a spiral staircase leading up to the inside of the minaret. The cylindrical tower has a long circular cone-shaped roof that rests on six square pillars that form a hexagon in plain view. Each of the pillars is approximately 1 metre in height and together they provide six window-like openings for the muezzin to call out prayers.

The Imam's House

The original *imam*'s house occupies the south-east corner of the courtyard and is now used as the ablution area. A new, much larger house has been built that extends from the south courtyard wall. The house, its courtyard and enclosed car parking space covers an area as large as the mosque itself. In fact, the new *imam* facility rather overwhelms the mosque.

The Open Prayer Area

The outer *iwan* is open to the courtyard through five rectangular portals built in simple post and lintel style, commonly used in many of the old mosques throughout Qatar that date from the 1930s and 1940s. On either end of the outer *iwan* are two windows in the north and south façade walls respectively. There is no evidence that there were any *badgheers* over any of the windows. Three doors, spaced evenly apart, lead from the outer *iwan* into the enclosed *iwan* of the *mihrab*. The door in the middle faces directly toward the *mihrab*. All the wooden doors are of later vintage than the original building.

The Prayer Hall

The area of the closed *iwan* is slightly wider than that of the open *iwan*. The *kebla* is square in shape, with two openings separated by a square pillar in the middle. The *imam*'s bench occupies the right opening. The interior *iwan* has a hung ceiling of painted plywood panelling crudely nailed to the old *danshal* beams above (now hidden). This plywood ceiling is unattractive and totally out of character with the original architecture.

The enclosed *iwan* has six windows, one on either end on the north and south walls, and four along the rear, west-facing wall. There are a further two windows on either side of the *mihrab*. The four rear windows are covered with metal shutters added later, plain on the inside and decorated with a pattern of six squares on the outside. The end windows on the north and south walls have been sealed with concrete blocks with openings for air conditioning units which protrude through to the exterior façade. The shutters have been painted blue. The blue paint, which is seen on most windows and doors in the mosque, is cracking or flaking away in many places. The roof of the *iwans* is constructed in the usual traditional way, with *danshal* beams overlain with *basgill* and *mangharour*, topped with a thick layer of mud. The roof is slightly pitched from the centre, allowing water to drain towards openings in the front and rear parapets walls that have been fitted with wooden drain spouts.

• Aerial perspective.
Al Owaynah Mosque remains open, and is still used
• Ground floor plan.
The minaret stands in the north-east corner of the courtyard. The outer *iwan* is open to the courtyard through five rectangular portals. The area of the closed *iwan* is slightly wider than the open *iwan*. The kebla is square in shape

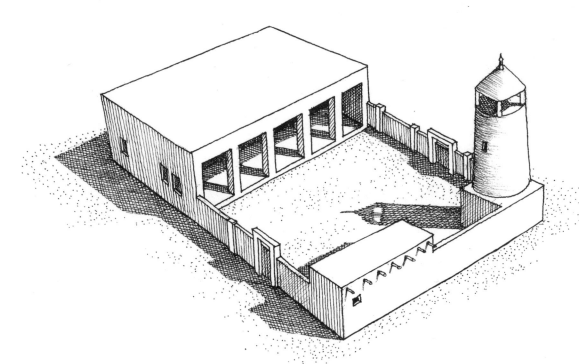

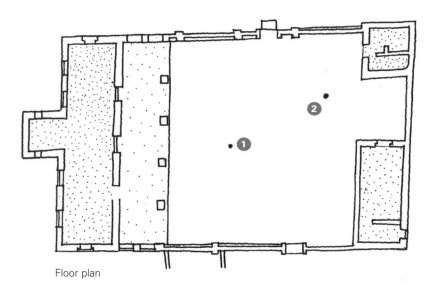

Floor plan

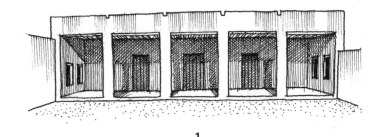

1

Prayer hall

External prayer hall

Courtyard

2

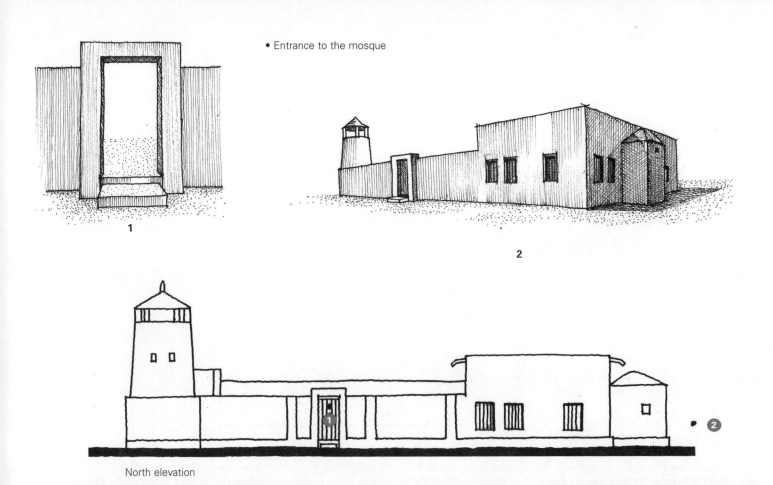

• Entrance to the mosque

1

2

North elevation

West elevation

1

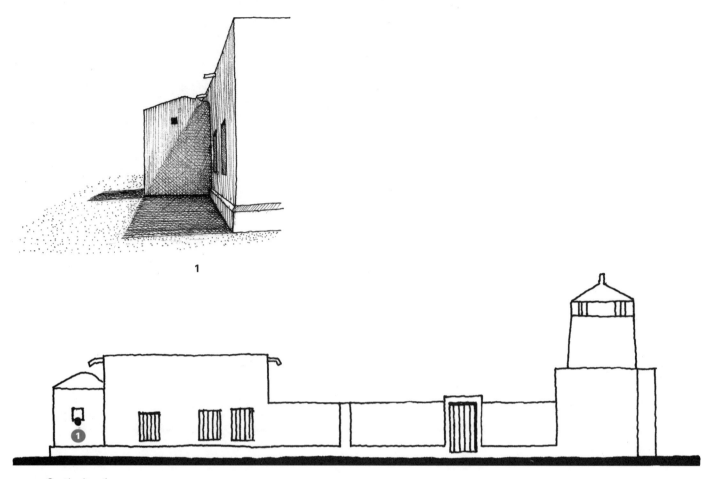

South elevation

East elevation

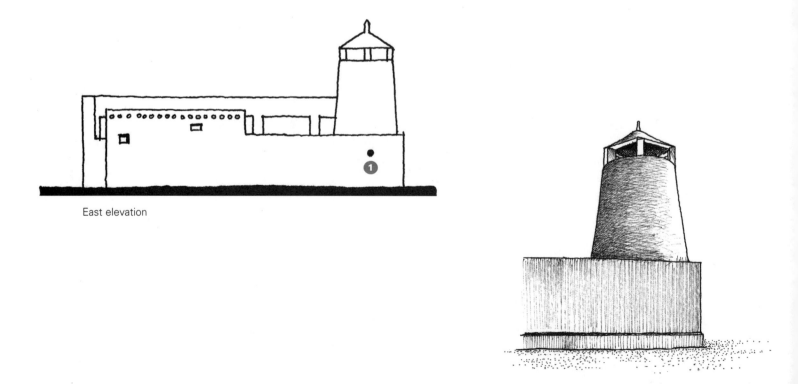

1

• Open *iwan*

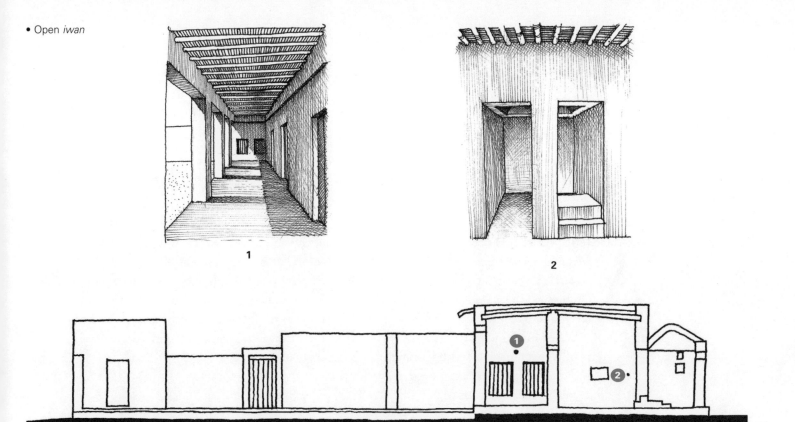

1

2

Longitudinal section

Transversal section

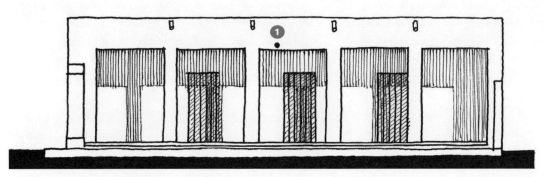

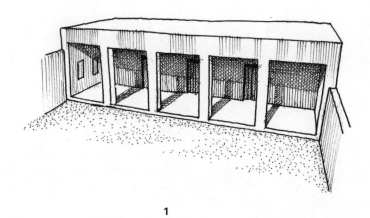

1

Arfeeq Mosque (Umm Al Ghab Village) (1945)

Brief Description and History

Arfeeq mosque was built in 1945. It sits on a low rise in the small desert village of Umm Al Ghab, off the main road and approximately midway between Dukhan and Al Jemailiyah. The surrounding village is still populated but, as with many other small rural villages, much of its population has moved away. Arfeeq mosque has been abandoned but a small makeshift mosque has been erected directly in front of the old one.

Architectural Description of the Mosque

The mosque, mainly distinguished by its relatively tall minaret, has entrances along the north and the south external walls of the outside courtyard. Each entrance has decorative steel double gate doors, all badly rusted. The sandy earth courtyard is in the shape of a long rectangle, measuring approximately 13 × 8 metres. No trace of the ablution area exists.

The Minaret

In the south-east corner of the courtyard, where the courtyard walls intersect, stands the minaret, a cylindrical shaft that rises 7.5 metres straight from the ground. It is topped with a rounded cupola that rises a metre more. Below the rounded top of the cupola are six arched openings for the *muezzin*. A narrow spiral staircase, built in the usual style of wood covered in concrete mortar, leads up inside the minaret.

The Open Prayer Area

The outer, open *iwan* opens to the courtyard through three rectangular portals built in simple post and lintel style, similar to other mosques constructed in Qatar during the 1930s and 1940s. On either end of the outer *iwan* are two windows in the north and south façade wall respectively, with decorative metal shutters painted light green but now rusting. Two evenly spaced doors lead from the outer *iwan* into the enclosed *iwan* of the *kebla*. The doors and their frames are made of wood and probably original.

The Prayer Hall

The closed *iwan* is slightly wider than the open *iwan*. The *mihrab* is roughly square, tapering inward slightly toward the rear wall. There are small rectangular openings in the external wall on either side of the *mihrab*. The original ceiling of *danshal* beams overlain with *basgill* and *mangharour* is still intact and in good condition. The ceiling over the open and closed *iwans* is the only part of this mosque constructed from traditional materials. The mud plaster covered roof over the *iwans* is entirely flat with four notched cuts in the rear parapet wall to allow for drainage.

The enclosed *iwan* originally had two windows on either end (along the north and the south walls), but one window on either end has been blocked up leaving small rectangular openings in the walls for air conditioning units. There are also two windows along the rear (west-facing) wall, one on either side of the *mihrab*. All remaining six windows have decorative metal shutters, similar to the ones in the open *iwan*. All the window shutters are painted light green, now faded and rusting in many places.

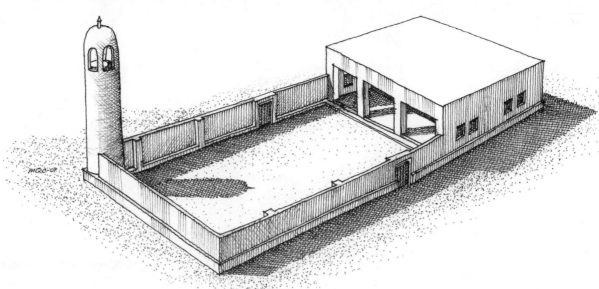

• Aerial perspective. The mosque, mainly distinguished by its relatively tall minaret, has entrances along the north and the south external walls of the outside courtyard

• Ground floor plan. The outer, open *iwan* (open prayer hall) opens to the courtyard through three rectangular portals built in simple post and lintel style. The closed *iwan* is slightly wider that open *iwan*. The *mihrab* is roughly square

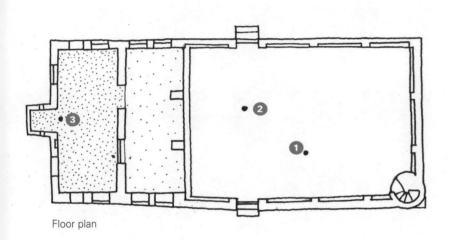

Floor plan

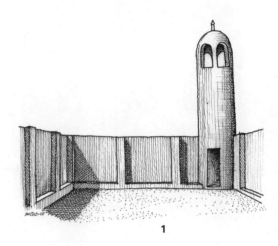

1

 Prayer hall

 External prayer hall

 Courtyard

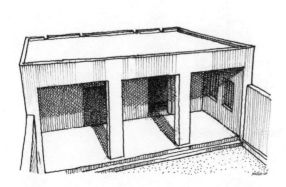

2

3

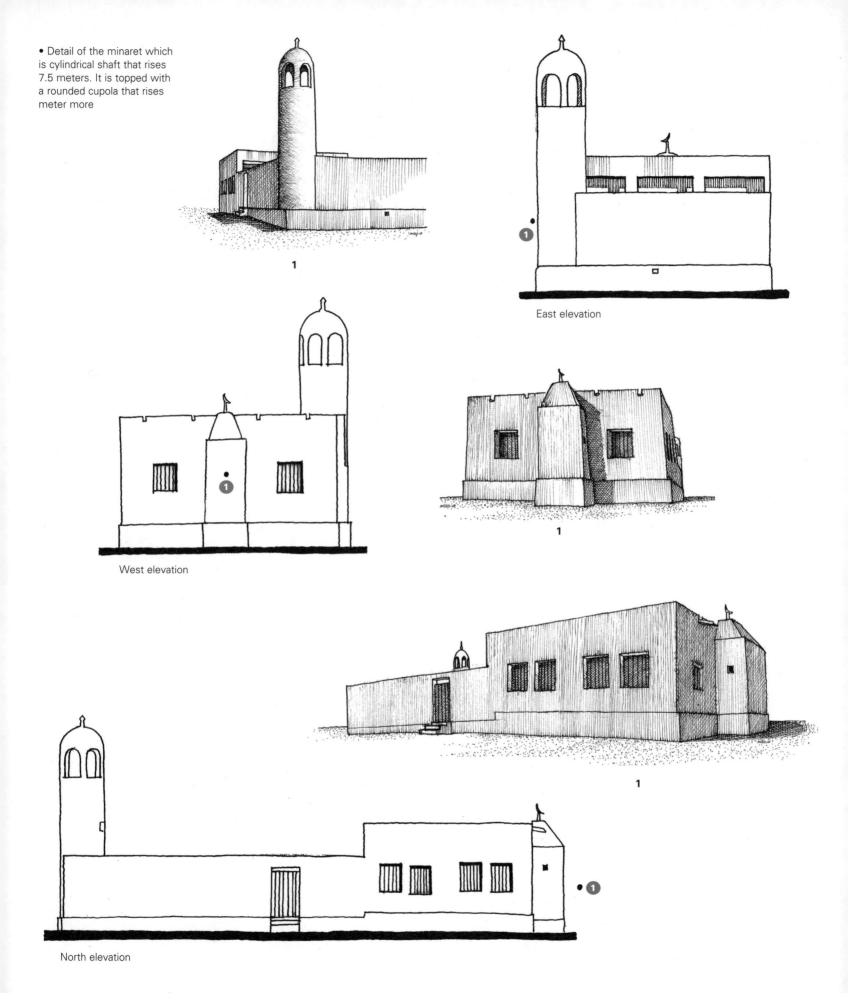

• Detail of the minaret which is cylindrical shaft that rises 7.5 meters. It is topped with a rounded cupola that rises meter more

1

East elevation

West elevation

1

1

North elevation

250

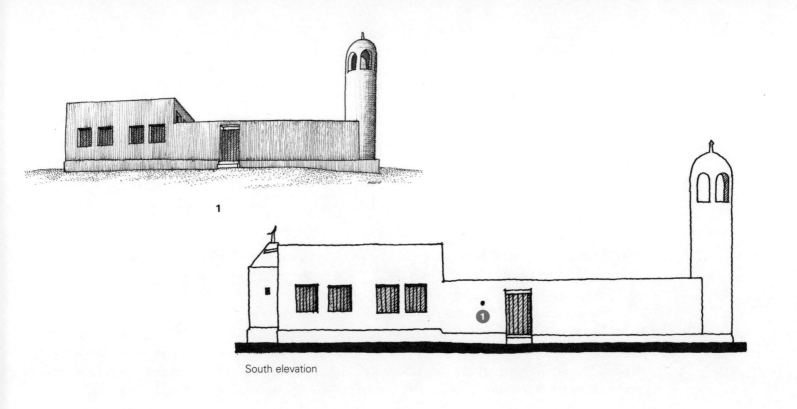

South elevation

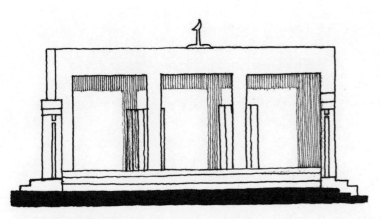

Transversal section

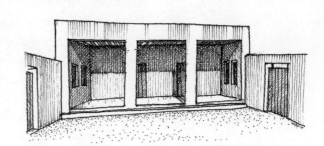

• Detail of open *iwan*

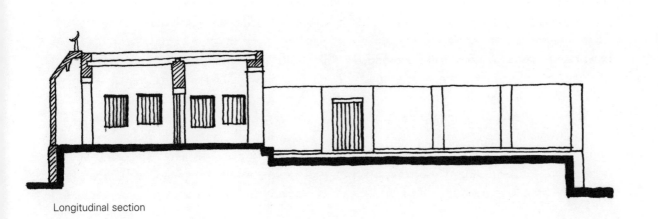

Longitudinal section

• Detail of inside open *iwan*

Bin Duham Mosque (Al Jumailiyah) (1940)

Brief Description and History

Bin Duham mosque is one of several old mosques near the village of Al Jumailiyah, approximately 65 kilometres north-west of Doha. The mosque was completed in 1942. The presence of several other old mosques in this small village, all dating from the same period, is a clear indication that considerably more people lived here sixty years ago. All but one of the old mosques in Al Jumailiyah are now abandoned as there is no longer sufficient population in the village to support more than the one.

Architectural Description of the Mosque

The mosque has opposing entrances on the north and south external walls that lead into an open courtyard. Three window openings along both the north and south façades of the *iwan*.

Two of these windows open into the outer *iwan* and one window opens into the enclosed *iwan* along both the north and south façades respectively. The wooden window frames, divided into three horizontal sections, are intact in all six windows. Each window has seven vertical round metal bars, all intact. All the windows are typical for mosques of this period.

The west façade of the *kebla* has a rounded *mihrab* in the middle, with one window on each side. All of these windows have their wooden frames and vertical bars intact. There is a small, square opening for light and ventilation at the centre of the rounded *mihrab*, about 1.5 metres above the outside ground level. The top of the rear parapet wall has six notches in the stonework, spaced regularly to allow water to drain from the roof.

The wooden drain spouts, which likely were once set into these notches, are missing. The east façade that encloses the outside courtyard is a blank wall,

with some major cracks and localised deterioration of the underlying stonework.

The Minaret

The minaret is located at the north-east corner of the courtyard. It is round, with a squat, slightly tapering base. The *meda* no longer exists though, given the configuration of the courtyard, it was probably located at the south-east corner. The minaret's narrow spiral stairway is constructed of *danshal* wood bound together with ropes, and covered with painted mud plaster.

The Open and Enclosed Prayer Areas

The open *iwan* is connected to the courtyard through four squared portals, built in a simple post and lintel style. The roof of the open *iwan* is made of *danshal* beams that rest on the horizontal lintel, which in turn rest on three square columns and the tops of the external walls.

The roof over the open and enclosed *iwan* is constructed in the traditional manner, with *danshal* beams overlain with *basgill*, which in turn is covered with a layer of plaited reed mats, called *mangharour*. A thick layer of mud mixed with straw is then laid on top. Much of this top layer of mud has been washed away to expose portions of the *iwans* below. There are three doors from the outside *iwan* to the inner, enclosed *iwan*. The old wooden doors are partially intact. Inside the closed *iwan*, the *mihrab* is a narrow semicircular recess in the middle of the west-facing wall. Two small rectangular niches are set into the wall on either side of the *mihrab*. These served as shelves for prayer books.

The only natural light coming into the *mihrab* is from a small square opening at the rear of the curved wall approximately 1 metre above the floor. This could have contained a small *badgheer* at one time.

• Aerial perspective.
The mosque has opposing
entrances on the north and
south external walls that lead
into an open courtyard
• Ground floor plan. The open
iwan is connected to the
courtyard through four
squared portals

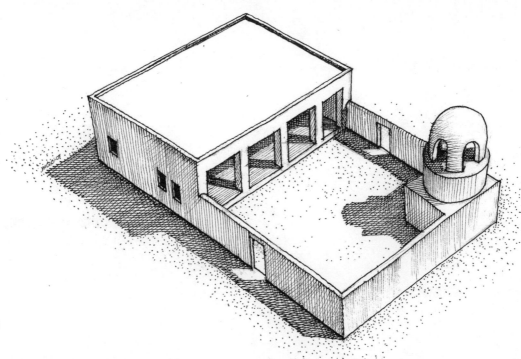

 Prayer hall

 External prayer hall

Courtyard

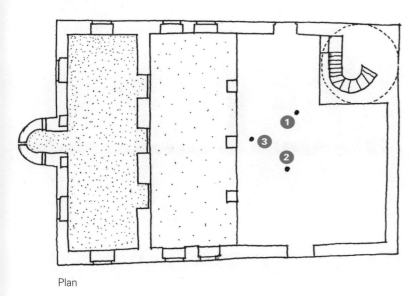

Plan

• Detail of the minaret

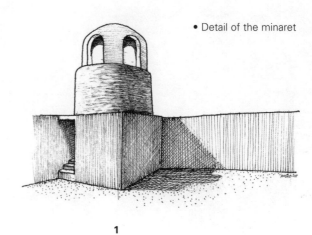

1

• Detail of open *iwan*

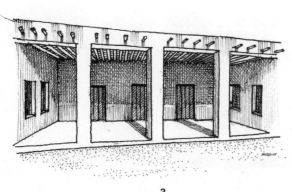

3

• View of the entrance to the
mosque

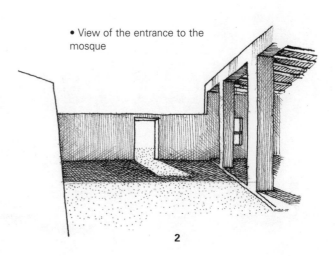

2

253

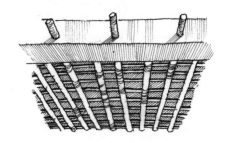

• Traditional roof used
in the mosque

1

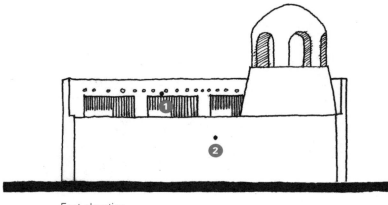

East elevation

2

1

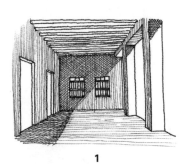

West elevation

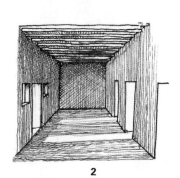

• View of the open *iwan*

1

2

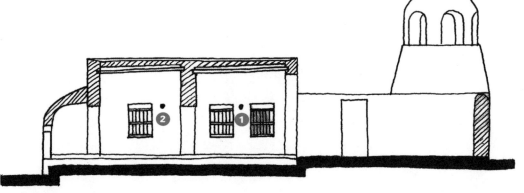

Longitudinal section

254

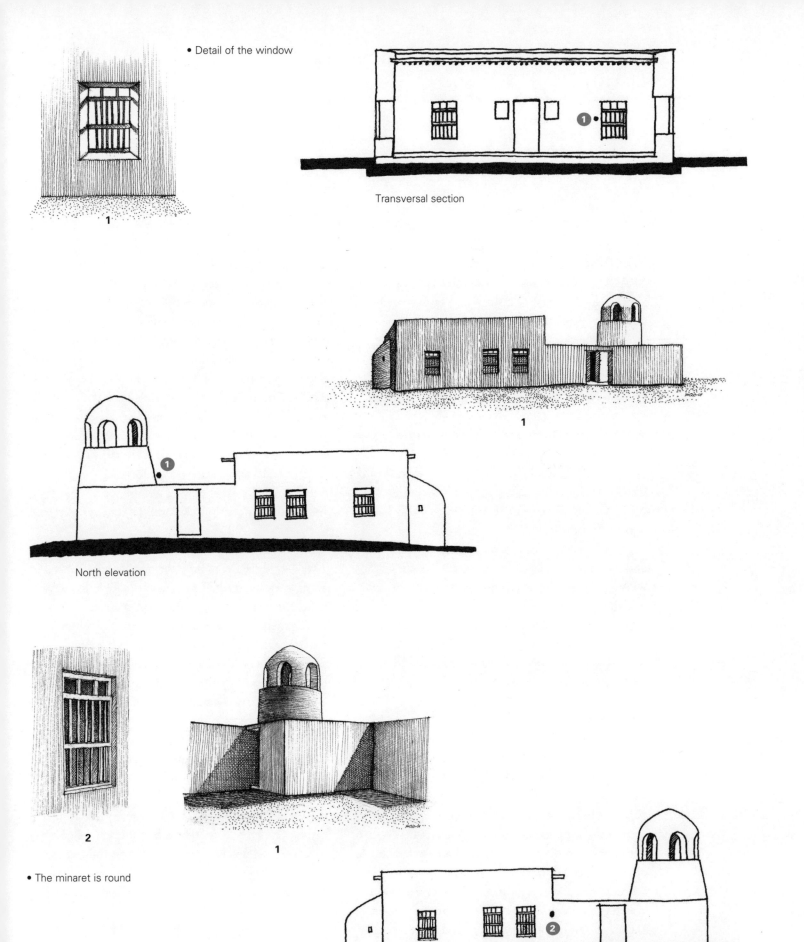

• Detail of the window

Transversal section

1

North elevation

2

• The minaret is round

1

South elevation

Al Suwaheet Mosque (Al Jumailiyah) (1940)

Brief Description and History

Al Suwaheet is one of several old mosques located in or near the village of Al Jumailiyah, approximately 65 kilometres north-west of Doha. The mosque was built in 1940. Much of the population has now left this village, in fact, directly behind Al Suwaheet Mosque are the ruins of several abandoned houses.

Architectural Description of the Mosque

The mosque has entrances in the east and south external walls that lead into an open, sandy courtyard. The *meda* no longer exists, though given the configuration of the courtyard, it was probably located at the south-east corner.

There are four window openings along both the north and the south façades of the iwans. Two of these windows open into the outer *iwan* and the other two into the enclosed inner *iwan*. The wooden window frames, each with one horizontal wood divider and seven round vertical metal bars, are intact in all eight windows and are typical of the window style in other mosques built during the same period.

The Minaret

The minaret is located at the north-east corner of the courtyard. It stands 7.3m high and is divided into three approximately equal sections. The round, squat, middle section sits on top of a square base the same height as the adjoining courtyard walls. The top section of the minaret, smaller in diameter than the base upon which it rests, consists of a rounded cupola above a space for the *muezzin* created by six open arches. The cupola is made of wedge-shaped pre-cast concrete sections. The minaret's narrow spiral stairway is constructed of *danshal* wood bound together with ropes and covered with painted mud plaster.

The Open Prayer Area

The open *iwan* is connected to the courtyard through five tall rectangular portals built in simple post and lintel style. The roof of the open *iwan* is made of *danshal* wood beams that rest on the horizontal lintel, which in turn, rests on the tops of four square columns and on the top ends of the external walls on either side. The roof over the open and enclosed *iwan* is constructed in the traditional manner of *danshal* beams overlain with *basgill*, which in turn is covered with a layer of plaited reed mats called *mangharour*. A thick layer of mud mixed with straw is then laid on top. Some of this top layer of mud has washed away over time, causing water to leak down into the *iwan* below.

The Prayer Hall

There are three doors from the outside *iwan* to the inner, enclosed *iwan*. The original wooden doors are gone, the plain-looking hollow-core wooden replacement doors are also gone. Only the middle replacement door still exists, though it has been partially torn off its hinges, however it is inappropriate to the architecture of the mosque. Inside the enclosed *iwan*, the *mihrab* is a shallow rectangular recess with chamfered corners in the middle of the west-facing wall, divided by a square pillar at the centre.

There are three small rectangular openings, one on each exterior side. The two side openings have been crudely covered over with the lids of large metal paint cans. The rounded top of the *mihrab* is made from pre-cast concrete units. The top of the rear parapet wall has eight notches in the stonework, four on each side of the *mihrab*, to allow water to drain from the roof, however, the wooden drain spouts are missing.

• Aerial perspective. The mosque has entrances in the east and south external walls that lead into open courtyard

• Ground floor plan. There are three doors from the outside *iwan* to the inner, enclosed *iwan*. Inside the enclosed *iwan*, the *mihrab* is a shallow rectangular recess

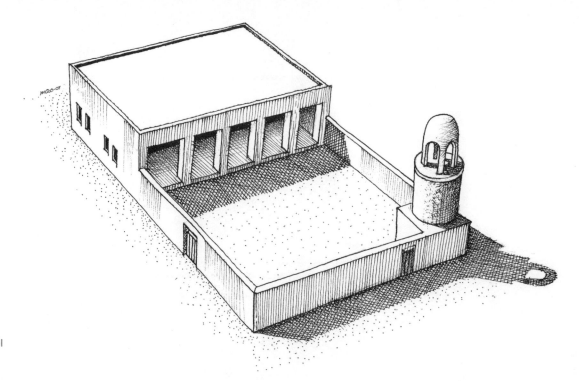

 Prayer hall

 External prayer hall

Courtyard

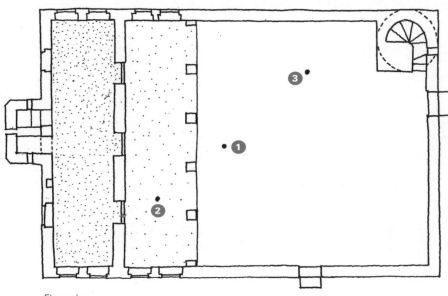

Floor plan

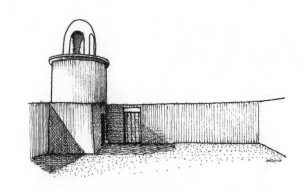

3

• View of the open *iwan*

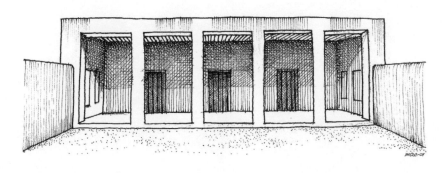

1

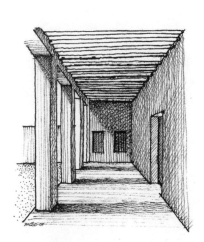

2

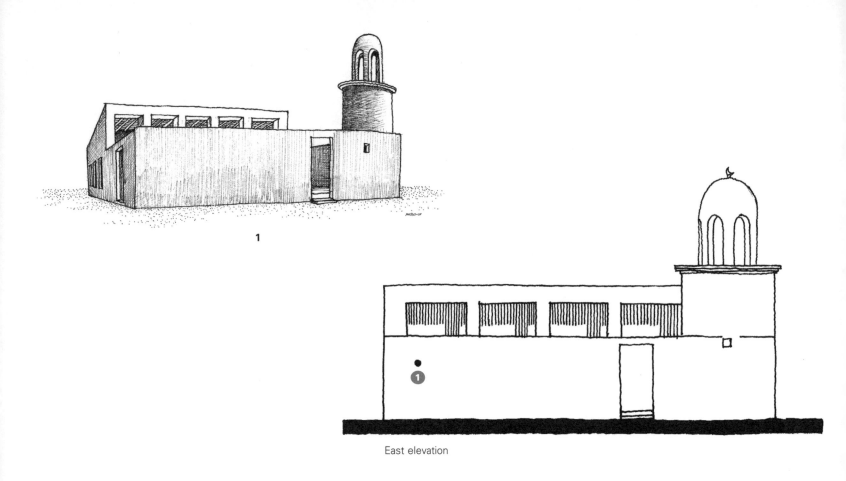

1

East elevation

North elevation

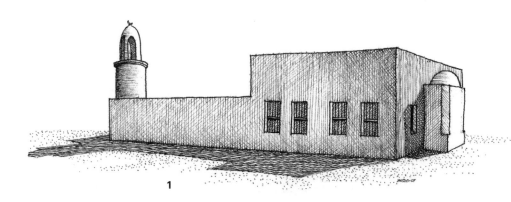

1

• View of the *mihrab*
on the external wall

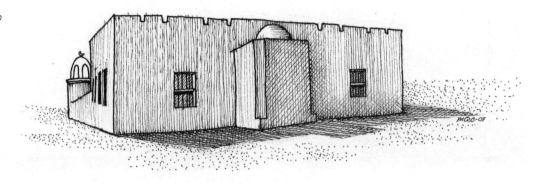

1

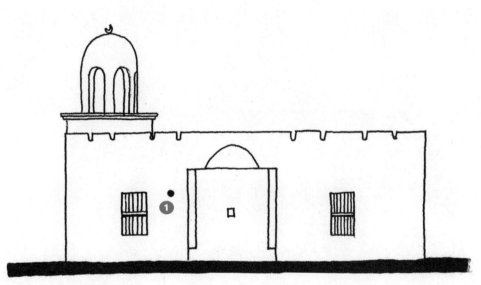

West elevation

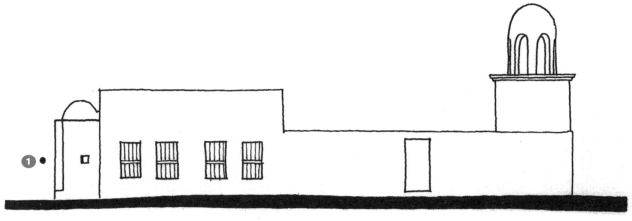

South elevation

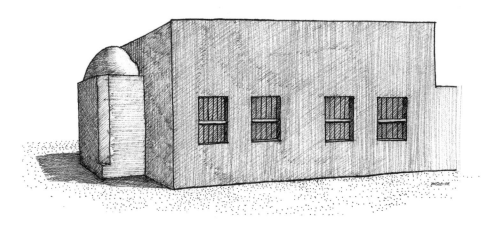

1

• The minaret is divided into three equal sections. The top section of the minaret consists of a round cupola above a space for the muezzin created by six open arches

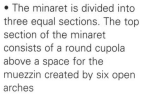

1

2

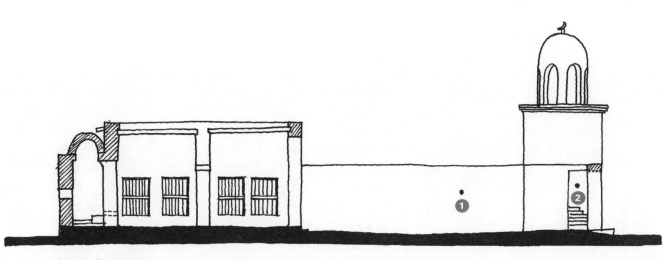

Longitudinal section

Transversal section

Al Amiri Mosque (Al Jumailiyah) (1939)

Brief Description and History

Al Amiri is one of several old mosques located in or near the village of Al Jumailiyah, approximately 65 kilometres north-west of Doha. The mosque was built in 1939, making it the oldest in the village. Al Amiri, the smallest of the Jumailiyah mosques, is the only one that remains open and active today.

Architectural Description of the Mosque

This very small mosque has opposing entrances in the north and south external walls that lead into an open, concrete tiled courtyard. The minaret is located at the north-east corner of the court. It is round, squat, slightly tapering and devoid of ornamentation or other distinguishing architectural details. The minaret's narrow spiral stairway is constructed of *danshal* wood bound together with ropes and covered with painted mud plaster. Next to the minaret is a small toilet and adjacent to that along the east courtyard wall is the ablution area.

The Open Prayer Area

Originally, there was an open *iwan*, connected to the courtyard through three squared portals, built in a simple post and lintel style. These open portals have been blocked up with concrete blocks, covered with plaster and painted, thereby creating, in effect, two enclosed *iwans* within. The roof over the enclosed and (formerly) open *iwans* is constructed in the traditional manner with *danshal* beams overlain with *basgill* and covered with *mangharour*. A thick layer of mud mixed with straw is then laid on top. The entire roof has been overlain with a corrugated metal roof, presumably in response to water leakage through the original roof. The traditional ceiling is still visible from the inside of the *iwans*, however.

There is one double door leading from the courtyard into the outer *iwan*. Leading from the outer *iwan* into the inner *iwan* are three double doors, all made of wood veneer and none of which is original. The semicircular *mihrab* opens to the *iwan* with no dividing column, as is usually the case. There is a small bench for the *imam* on the right side of the *mihrab*.

Originally, there were four windows along the south wall of the *iwans*, two in each *iwan*. Two of these windows have been plugged up entirely with new smaller openings having been made for air conditioners that now protrude through the wall. The remaining windows have also been blocked with plywood and painted white. There is a similar arrangement along the north wall of the *iwans*, except that one window remains in the outer *iwan*. This differs in that though it has been covered from the inside, the traditional wood frame and vertical iron bars remain on the exterior. There are no windows along the rear, west-facing *kebla* wall. In other words, all the windows in the mosque have been sealed up in one way or another.

The west (rear) façade of the *kebla* has a rounded *mihrab* in the middle of the wall. Originally there were three very small openings on each side and one in the centre, however, one of these openings has been blocked up entirely. There are no windows along the rear wall of the *iwan*. The top of its rear parapet wall has four notches in the stonework, two on either side of the *mihrab* to allow for water to drain from the original roof which, however, has been covered over with corrugated metal. The rough wooden drain spouts still protrude through these notches.

• Aerial perspective. Al Amiri Mosque is small and has opposing entrances in the north and south external walls that lead into open courtyard

• Ground floor plan. Originally there was an open *iwan* connected through three squared portals. The semi-circular *mihrab* opens to the *iwan* with no dividing column

 Prayer hall

 External prayer hall

Courtyard

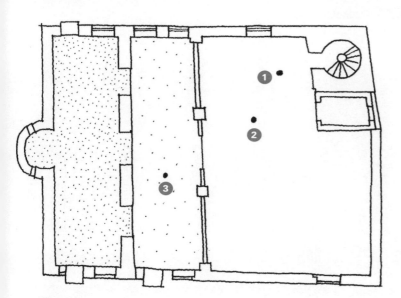

Floor plan

1

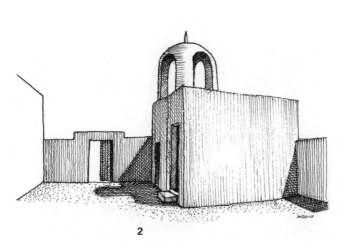

2

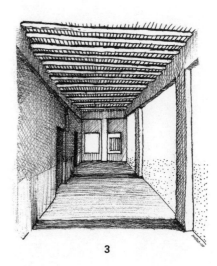

3

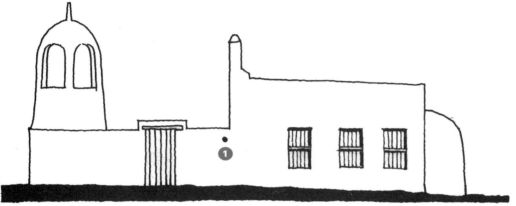

North elevation

South elevation

1

• Prayer hall

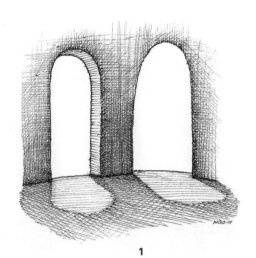

2

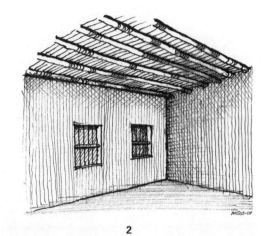

1

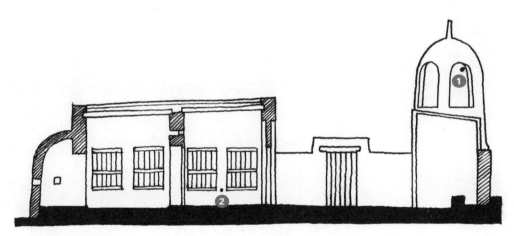

Longitudinal section

265

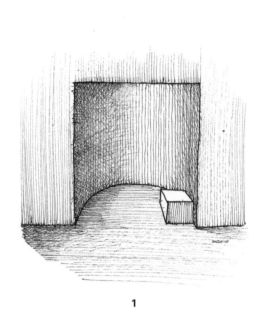

1

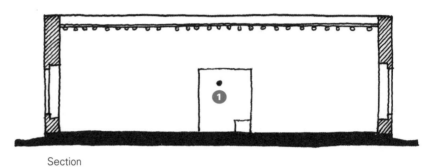

Section

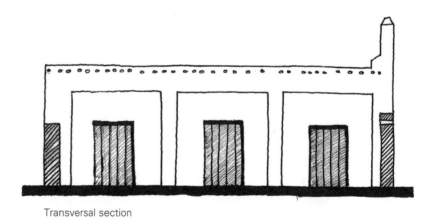

Transversal section

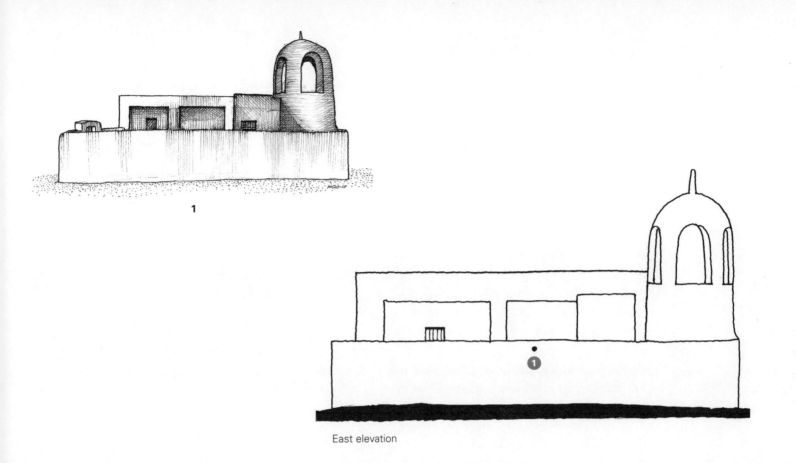

East elevation

West elevation

1

Old Mosque (Al Jumailiyah) (1945)

Brief Description and History

The Old Friday Mosque is one of several old mosques near the village of Al Jumailiyah, approximately 65 kilometres north-west of Doha. It was built in 1945 and still remains in use.

Architectural Description of the Mosque

The mosque has entrances in the north and the south external walls, directly opposite one another. They lead into a concrete surfaced courtyard. The *meda* is located outside the courtyard walls, above a well approximately 5 metres from the south wall. The courtyard entrances have decorative steel double gates.

The Minaret

The minaret stands at the south-east corner of the courtyard and is 6.5 metres high. The base of the minaret is square, and slightly less than 2 metres in height. The middle section is also square but set at an angle of 45 degrees to the base. The top section is also square, slightly less than one metre in height, and set at the same 45 degree angle. It has arched openings for the *muezzin* on either side. The top is a rounded, four-sided pyramid, 1.6 metres high, made of pre-cast concrete. The minaret has a narrow spiral stairway constructed from wood covered with painted mud plaster.

The Open Prayer Area

The open *iwan* is connected to the courtyard through six rectangular portals approximately 2.8 metres in height that have been built in simple post and lintel style. The wood beams of the roof rest on the horizontal front lintel, which in turn rests upon the five square columns and external walls. An ornamental parapet wall was added later to the top edge of the *iwans*, following replacement of the original roof. It is made of decorative brick, using black grout to outline the brick effect in a crenulated design that clashes with the building's original architecture.

The roof over the enclosed and open *iwans* was originally constructed in the traditional manner of *danshal* beams overlain with *basgill* covered with *mangharour*. A thick layer of mud plaster is then laid on top. However, the original roof has been removed, probably due to water leakage, and a new one constructed from wooden beams covered with plywood painted black and dark red. The new roof continues to leak, however.

The Prayer Hall

There are two doors from the outside *iwan* to the inner, enclosed *iwan*. The decorative wood panel doors are in good condition, but probably not original. Inside the enclosed *iwan*, or *mihrab*, is a shallow, five-sided recess in the middle of the west-facing wall marked by a hanging double arch extending approximately to the *mihrab*. The interior walls of the enclosed *iwan*, including the walls of the *mihrab*, are all painted green.

Like some of the other old mosques, most of the windows of the *iwans* have been blocked up. Originally, there were four window openings along both north and south façades of the *iwan* and two other windows in the enclosed *iwan*. The outer *iwan* windows have been blocked up and re-plastered over on the exterior surfaces, so they are no longer visible from the outside. At each end of the inner *iwan*, one window has been blocked up leaving openings for air conditioning units. The one remaining window opening contains an aluminium frame of a fairly recent vintage with a steel mesh covering the outside. Along the rear wall, the four original windows have all been blocked up and the wall re-plastered.

• Aerial perspective.
The mosque has entrances in the north and the south external walls, directly opposite one another.
They lead to open courtyard

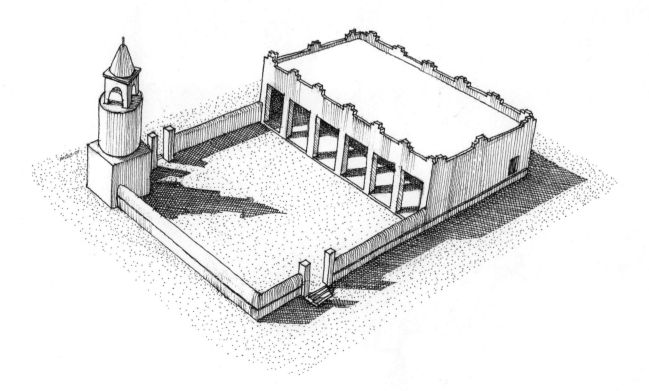

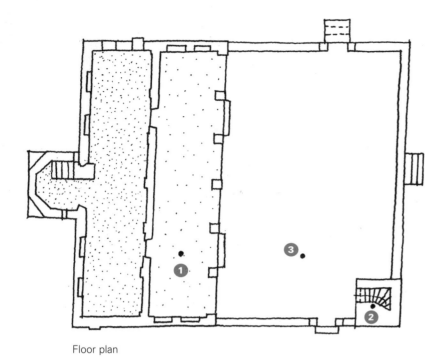

Floor plan

• Ground floor plan.
The open *iwan* connected
to the courtyard through six
rectangular portals.
The enclosed *iwan* and open
iwan are almost the same
size

Prayer hall

External prayer hall

Courtyard

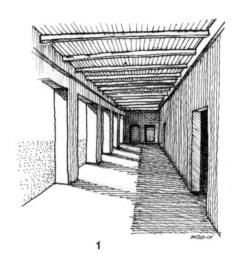

1

• View of the stair

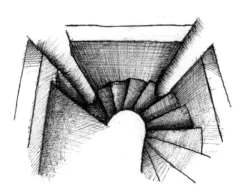

2

• View of stair leading into
the minaret

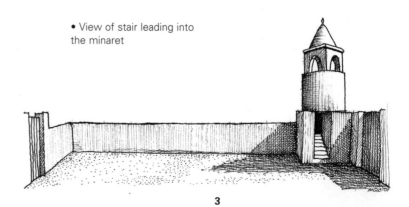

3

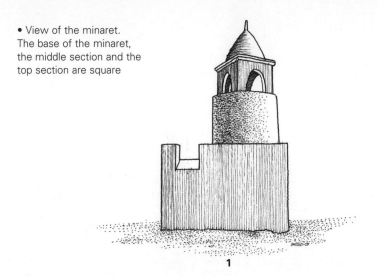

• View of the minaret.
The base of the minaret,
the middle section and the
top section are square

1

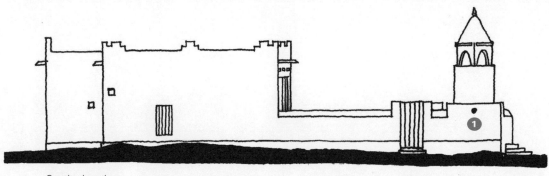

South elevation

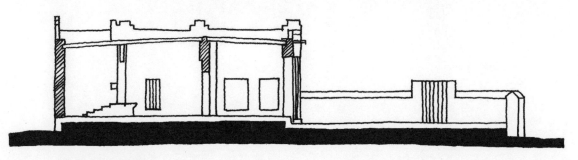

Longitudinal section

Transversal section

• View of the open *iwan*

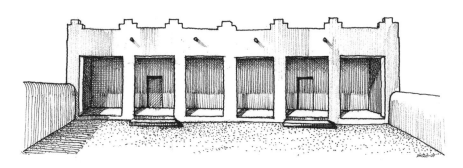

1

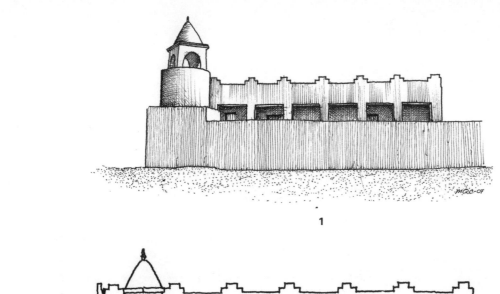

1

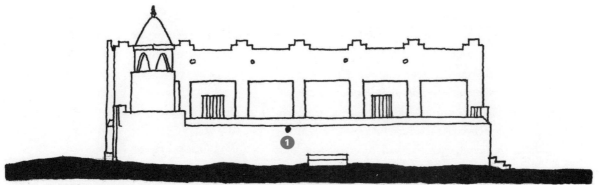

East elevation

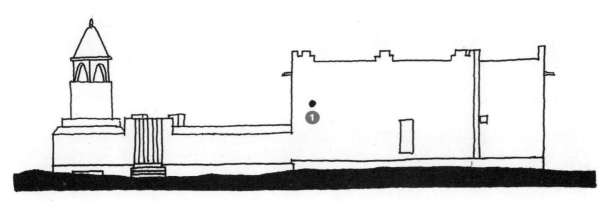

North elevation

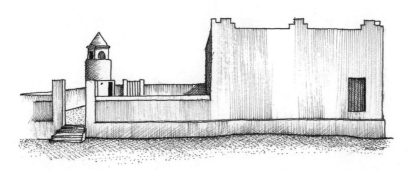

• Entrance to the mosque

1

Old Mosque (Rodat Rashid) (1948)

Brief Description and History

This very isolated mosque is located in the desert approximately 45 kilometres (by road) to the south-west of Doha. It was completed in 1948 in an area that once contained a thriving village, but which today lies abandoned. There are a few small farms about 5 kilometres north of Rodat Rashid, but otherwise the area marks the beginning of the extremely barren, virtually rainless, southern part of Qatar where village life was always precarious. The area is accessible only by unpaved desert road. The mosque at Rodat Rashid is considered one of the most beautiful of the old mosques, most notably for its tall, graceful minaret. The height of the mosque's *iwans* is greater than most of the other old mosques. Consequently, the interior spaces, with their high ceilings, are seen as more spacious and airier.

Architectural Description of the Mosque

There are two exterior entrances to the open courtyard with simple post and lintel portals, one along the east wall and the other on the north wall. The original wooden doors have long since disappeared. The courtyard itself is sandy dirt with clumps of scrubby desert vegetation scattered throughout. The *meda* is at the north-east corner of the courtyard. It stands behind an open wall the same height as the exterior courtyard walls.

The Minaret

The minaret is located at the south-east corner of the courtyard. It is the most distinctive feature of the mosque, perhaps because of its commanding height over the surrounding desert. It sits atop a square base, almost 3 metres high. A cylindrical shaft then rises from the base another 6.3 metres. Finally, the tall rounded cupola rises another 4 metres, so that the total height of the minaret is almost 13 metres. The rounded roof of the minaret cupola sits atop eight square slender columns, conferring grace upon the structure. The minaret's narrow spiral stairway is constructed of *danshal* wood bound together with ropes and *basgill*. The stairs are covered with painted mud plaster.

The Open Prayer Area

The open *iwan* is connected to the courtyard through six tall rectangular portals built in a simple post and lintel style, with decorative *kebla* still intact in all corners. Three doorways spaced evenly apart lead from the open *iwan* into the inner enclosed *iwan* of the *kebla*. The outer *iwan* has two window openings at either end (north and south walls).

The Prayer Hall

The inner *iwan* of the *kebla* has a similar configuration, wide and narrow with a tall ceiling, and two windows at either end. The rear (west) wall of the inner *iwan* has four windows, two on either side of the *mihrab*. The *kebla* itself is square with a rounded roof. There were two small square openings on either side of the *kebla*, which could have contained *badgheers*, but both are now missing. The roof over the *iwans* is made of *danshal* wood that rests on the horizontal lintel on the courtyard side, which in turn rests on the five square columns and the external walls on either side facing the courtyard. *Basgill* is lain perpendicular to the *danshal* beams, which in turn is overlain by *mangharour*. On top of everything is a thick layer of mud plaster mixed with straw.

• Aerial perspective. There are two entrances to the open courtyard with simple post and lintel style portals, one along the east wall and the other on the north wall
• Ground floor plan. The open *iwan* is connected to the courtyard through six tall rectangular portals. The inner *iwan* has a similar configuration. The *mihrab* is square with a rounded roof

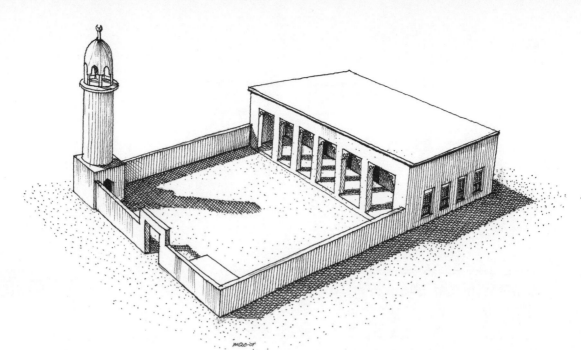

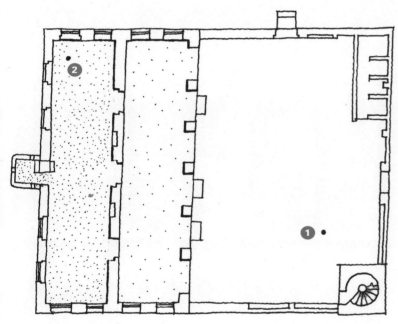

Ground floor plan

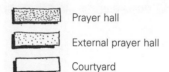

Prayer hall

External prayer hall

Courtyard

2

• View of the inner *iwan*

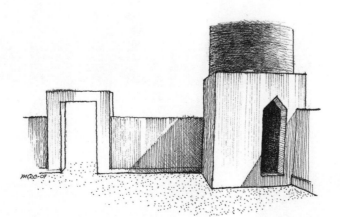

1

• Decorative elements used in the corners of the arches

1

• The minaret is a most distinctive feature because of its height. The rounded roof of the minaret cupola sits atop eight square slender columns

East elevation

2

2

• The minaret is composed of three sections: base, middle and cupola

1

Transversal section

1

South elevation

1

• View of the open *iwan* with a series of decorated arcades

1

• This perspective shows the *mihrab* forming an element on the façade

1

• Entrance to the mosque

2

West elevation

1

• View of the open *iwan*

2

• View of prayer hall

3

• View of the *mihrab*

Longitudinal section

Bin Obaid Mosque (Al Salata, Doha) (1935)

Brief Description and History

In 1935, Doha was a very small city covering only 1.5 square kilometres. Some urban settlements were also found, during this time, on the east coast of Doha around the site of the current Doha Museum. In that area, Bin Obaid mosque was built half a kilometre away from the museum and the sea. With other mosques, Bin Obaid served an area which at that time was far from the centre of Doha. It has survived the immense changes that have occurred during the planning and execution of the current Corniche, hence its importance in the history of Doha.

Architectural Description of the Mosque

The plot on which the mosque is built measures approximately 28 by 20 metres and is cut into two halves: one half is the prayer hall block and the other is the courtyard. The mosque can be accessed through two entrances located on the north and south sides. The entrance gates are wooden and fitted into a slightly bigger arch embellished on the corners with small decorative features.

The original courtyard was defined on its western side by the arcade of the *iwan* and on the other three sides by the boundary wall. Before this wall was replaced, it consisted of a series of concrete block courses that did not exceed 1.5 metres in height.

Some of the bricks were laid on their sides to take advantage of their cavities so as to allow the wind inside the court at low levels and provide a decorative feature. The boundary wall has now been torn down and a new one erected, which takes the two blocks added on the east side of the mosque into consideration. The new parts added are an ablution block and an *imam*'s house.

The Minaret

At the south-east corner of the plot, the minaret still stands untouched. No more than 5 metres in height, it has four distinctive sections; the base, which is round and almost 2 metres high. Above this is the body of the minaret, slightly thinner than the base and cylindrical in shape. The third section is a slab that projects from the body and separates it from the dome. This, in turn, is supported by six arched columns that form the boundary of the space for the *muezzin*. The roof of the dome is pointed and has a small feature at the apex.

The Open Prayer Area

The depth of the outer *iwan* does not exceed 3 metres because of the limitations mandated by the use of the *danshal* beams for the roof. The outer *iwan* has an arcade of ten square arches and eleven columns. The columns have decorations on their corners. There were six windows on the north and south sides of the outer *iwan*, but only five remain, two on the south façade and three on the north. On the top of each window there is a recess filled with a gypsum decoration. The west wall of this *iwan* is fitted with four wooden windows and three doors up to one metre high, the outer and inner *iwans* have wooden panels running along the walls.

The Prayer Hall

The inner *iwan* or prayer hall is approximately 3 metres in depth. By the south and north walls this space has 4 wooden windows, two on each side, while the *kebla* wall has three wooden windows on each side of the *mihrab*. Between the windows, there are wall recesses, previously used as book shelves. Today the two closest to the *mihrab* have been converted into openings for air conditioning units.

The *mihrab* is semicircular in plan; its roof consists of a pointed dome structure decorated at the top with a gypsum crescent. The wall of the *mihrab* is fitted with three small openings that provide ventilation and natural light. The natural ceiling composition is replaced with square wooden beams as a decorative rather than structural feature per se.

• Aerial perspective. The plot of this mosque is divided to prayer section and courtyard section. The size of this mosque is larger than previous mosques

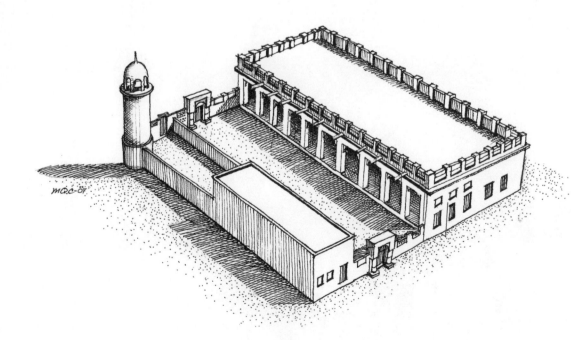

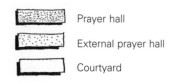

Prayer hall

External prayer hall

Courtyard

• Ground floor plan. The inner
iwan and open *iwan* have
almost the same size.
The outer *iwan* has an arcade
of ten square arches and
eleven columns. The inner
iwan or prayer hall is about
3 metres depth. The *mihrab*
is semicircular in plan

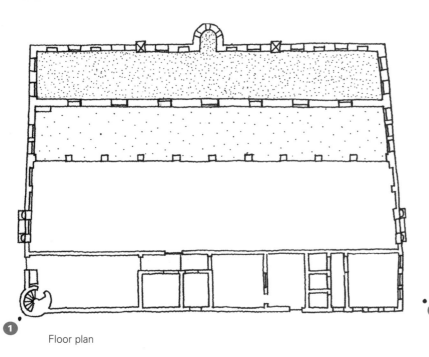

1

Floor plan

• This view indicates the
entrance to the mosque

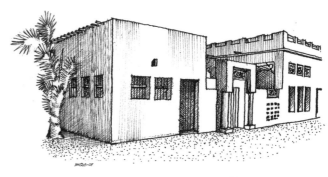

2

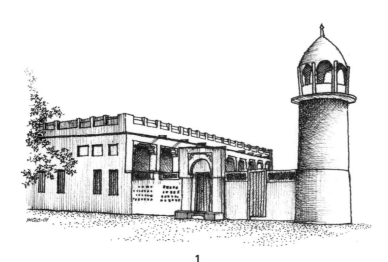

• The minaret stands at the
southeast corner of the
mosque

1

• This mosque is distinctive because of its decorative elements on the walls and arches, and because of its parapets on the top roof

• View of the *mihrab* on external walls

1

2

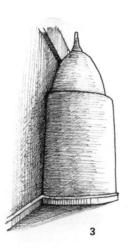

3

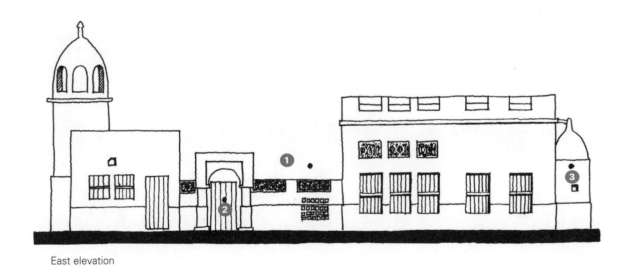

East elevation

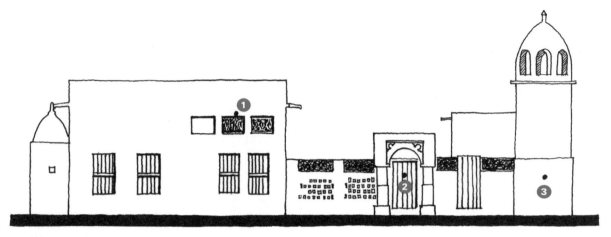

West elevation

1

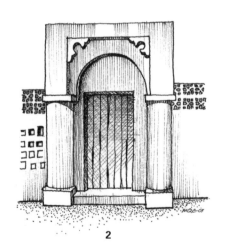

2

3

• Detail of decorative
elements used on the top
of external walls
• Main entrance to the
mosque decorated with
columns and arches

• The minaret has four
distinctive sections, the base,
body of the minaret. The third
section is the slab that
projects from the body and
separates it from the dome.
This in turn is supported by
six arches columns that form
the boundary of the space for
the muezzin

• View of the *mihrab*

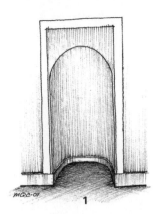

1

2

Section A-A

• This perspective shows decorated arches and parapets

1

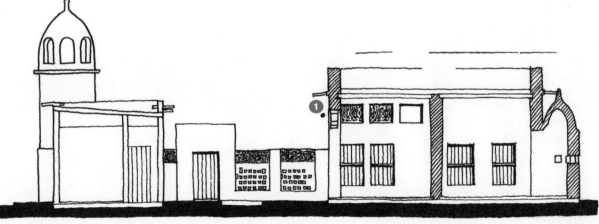

Section C-C

Al Yousef Mosque (Old Salata, Doha) (1940)

Brief Description and History

Al Yousef mosque was constructed in 1940, five years after Bin Obaid (see pp. 278–283), 150 metres south-east of the latter. Al Yousef mosque is pretty small, not measuring more than 15 by 13 metres, nevertheless, it has many features common to all old mosques in Qatar. Its importance lies in the fact that it is still standing today, in defiance of all the harsh hot and humid weather of Qatar. Al Yousef mosque forms part of the urban development that took place in the early 1940s. The mosque remains in use.

Architectural Description of the Mosque

The plan of Al Yousef mosque is a square with an ablution block projecting from its court on the south side. The mosque is elevated above the street level by 50 centimetres and built on a base slightly bigger in plan. The courtyard is entered through a single gate on the west side of the mosque. The east wall of the court is bound from the north by the minaret and from the south by the ablution block.
This section of the fence wall is divided into five parts, the middle section being the gate. To either side of the gate, two equal sections are defined by two columns' and two benches, approximately 85 centimetres high.
The courtyard is rectangular in shape and measures approximately 13 by 6 metres. It has been recently paved with cement tiles. The fence wall is made of concrete bricks laid on their sides to show their cavities as a decorative element and to provide a certain degree of transparency between the interior and exterior. The courtyard provides access to the ablution block through two doors, one to the toilet and water source, and the other to the *imam*'s room. The ablution block seems to have housed an old well.

The Minaret

A conical minaret stands in the north-east corner of the courtyard, not exceeding seven metres in height from the courtyard level. At a height of 4.5 metres, a slab separates the minaret body from the upper part, in which a hexagonal section supports a dome on six round and slender columns. A small, arrow-like feature decorates the top of the dome.

The Open Prayer Area

The open *iwan* is a narrow rectangle, decorated on the courtside with four square columns chamfered at their corners and featuring small decorative details at the tops. The west wall of the open *iwan* used to be fitted with three doors and two windows all made of wood, but today all have been removed. The north and south walls of the open *iwan* are each fitted with two windows, with each window having a small semicircular recess.

The Prayer Hall

The inner, rectangular *iwan* or prayer hall (3 × 12 m) can be accessed from the open *iwan*. The north and south walls of the prayer hall are similar to the respective walls of the external prayer hall. The west wall differs in that it has two windows and two air conditioning unit openings, one of each on either side of the *mihrab*. The *mihrab* is semicircular plan and has a domed roof with no openings. The roof of the two *iwans* is sloped towards the *kebla* wall, this way draining rain water outside of the plot.

• Aerial perspective. Al Yousef mosque is a small structure in size. It has many features in common with all the old mosques in Qatar. The entrance to the mosque is marked by a decorated boundary wall

• Ground floor plan. The plan of Al Yousef Mosque is square with an ablution block projecting from its court. The open *iwan* is a narrow rectangle, decorated on the courtside with four square columns decorated at their corners. The inner *iwan* or prayer hall can be accessed from open *iwan*

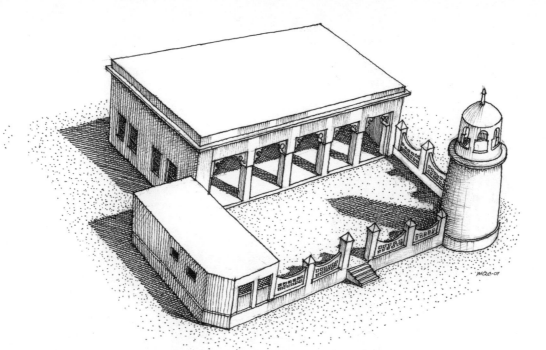

Plan

Prayer hall

External prayer hall

Courtyard

1

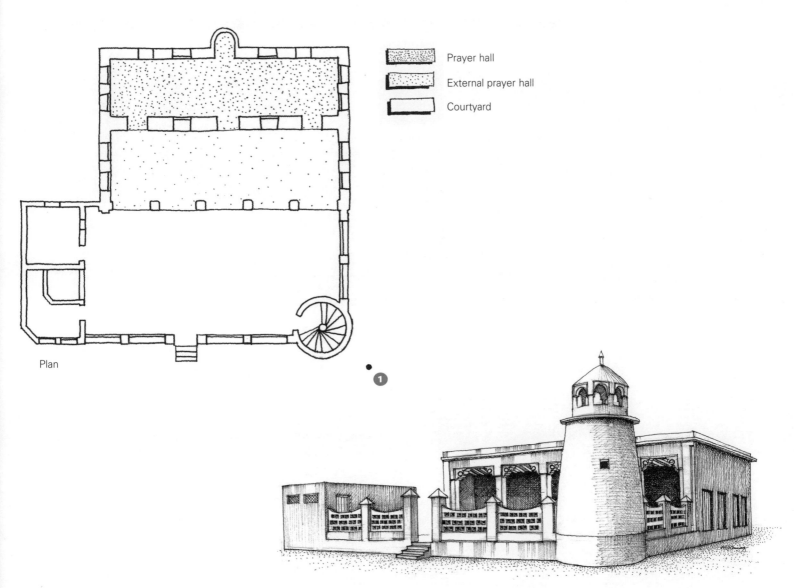

1

1

• The minaret stands in the north east corner of the courtyard, a slab separates the minaret body from the upper part, in which a hexagonal section supports a dome on six round and slender columns

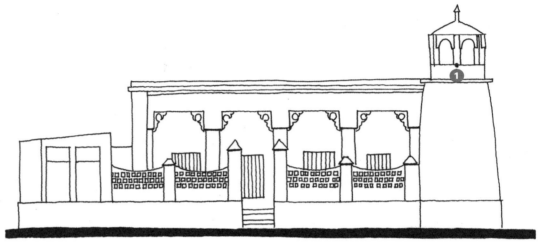

Front elevation

Section A-A

• View of inside the prayer hall

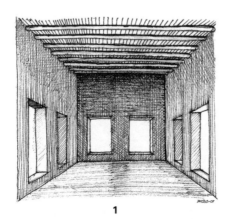

1

2

• Decorative elements used at the corners of the arches

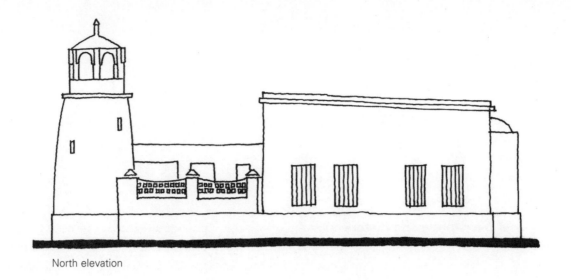

North elevation

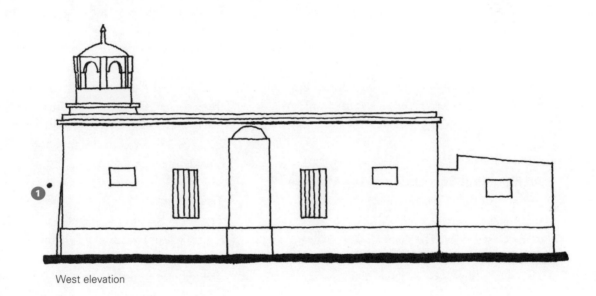

❶

West elevation

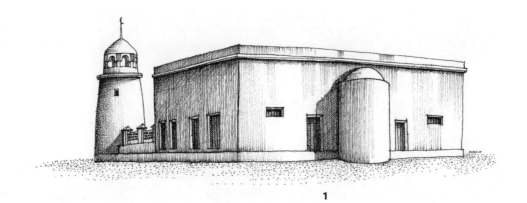

1

Abdullah Bin Soragah Mosque
(Al Rumeila, Doha)
(1940)

Brief Description and History

Abdullah Bin Soragah mosque was built in 1940 on the outskirts of Doha. Even as late as 1959, aerial photographs show evidence that the mosque was still the furthest built structure from the area of the central suq in Doha. At that time, the mosque was located immediately on the shoreline. In consequence of the later development of the new Corniche on reclaimed land, however, the mosque now stands 250 metres from the sea. No buildings were erected further than this mosque in that section of north Doha until that period. Abdullah Bin Soragah mosque has therefore acquired special importance even though it has been altered over the years.

Architectural Description of the Mosque

The area of the plot is 641 square metres. It is considered medium-sized as it has three aisles in the closed *iwan*. The main block contains the accommodation reserved for the *imam*. The plan of the site is a rectangle measuring 28.75 by 22.20 metres.

The mosque can be accessed through two simple gates in the north and south walls. The part of the fence wall between the gate and the prayer hall block is constructed in concrete bricks laid on their sides to provide a decorative element to the wall. The street passes parallel to the south wall of the mosque, a feature that has not altered since the mosque was built. The opposite side of the mosque is not yet paved.

The east side, which used to face the water, now faces the three-lane road that runs parallel to the new Corniche. This side of the fence wall has been turned into a services area for the mosque that can be accessed only from the outside and not through the court. Two doors open to the outside through a curved wall that blocks view from the exterior into these spaces, thus providing them with a degree of privacy. The service block measures approximately 22.20 by 15 metres and is probably built totally outside the main court.

The Minaret

The court is a clear space measuring 21.80 by 8.40 metres and is paved with ceramic tiles. The minaret stands on the south-east corner of the court. It can be divided into four distinct parts separated by balconies. The base of the minaret is a square 2.15 metres high. Next comes an octagon that is transformed, after the first balcony, into a cylinder that ends at the second balcony where the muezzin makes the call for prayer. The muezzin area at the top of the minaret has a circular plan with seven columns arched at the top and roofed with a cone decorated at the top with a small gypsum element consisting of a crescent enclosing a star. The distance to the top of the minaret from the court level is 13.80 metres.

The Open Prayer Area

The main part of the mosque – the prayer area – is a simple rectangle (21.15 × 12.30 m) with a flat roof and gypsum decoration all around its parapet. From inside, this block is subdivided into three spaces or aisles. *Iwan al Kebla* is probably the oldest part of the mosque and the other two *iwans* were probably added as the community grew over the years. This development is suggested by the fact that, contrary to the tradition of having an open space inside the prayer area, this *iwan* (Al Kebla) can be accessed through doors from the adjacent *iwan*; this fact indicates that the second and third *iwan* were an external part, maybe a porch, and afterwards closed to accommodate an increasing number of worshippers.

The Prayer Hall

Three wooden doors provide access to the prayer hall from the courtyard and into the first *iwan*. The *iwan* originally possessed two window openings, one each on the south and north walls, before one of the openings was transformed to fit an air conditioning unit. A set of arches separates the second *iwan* from the first. The former is similar to the latter in size and in the number of openings at the north and south walls, and is approximately 3 metres deep.

The columns separating the first two *iwans* are square and decorated with cement corners at the top. These two *iwans* have recently been paved with mosaic as part of the ongoing restoration process.

A wall filled with three doors separated the *kebla iwan* from the rest of the prayer area. This *iwan* measures 21.15 by 3.80 metres and has a window in each of the north and south walls. The *kebla* wall had some openings that are now closed; instead, the wall has four air conditioner openings and two windows of which one is converted into a door to provide access for the *imam*. The internal façade to the *mihrab* is divided into two arched parts, the left side is the *imam*'s praying area and the other side is the *minbar* area. The projecting *minbar* is decorated with simple gypsum features.

• Aerial perspective. The area plot of this mosque is considered medium sized as it has three aisles in the closed *iwan*. The main block contains immam's accommodation
• Ground floor plan. The main part of the mosque, the prayer hall, is a simple rectangle

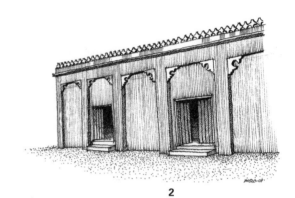

2

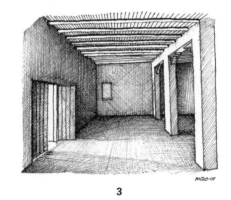

3

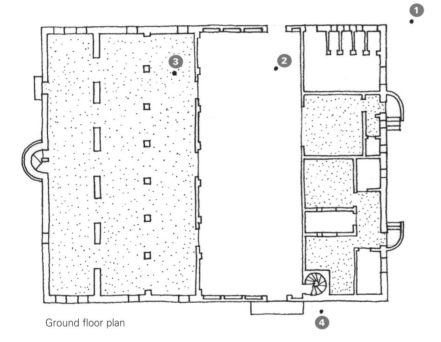

Ground floor plan

   Prayer hall

Courtyard

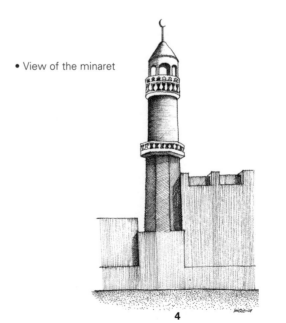

• View of the minaret

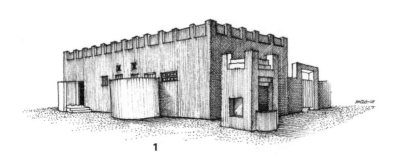

1

4

• The minaret is divided into four different parts, the base, the body in octagon form, first balcony, secondary balcony, and the last part is 'muezzin'

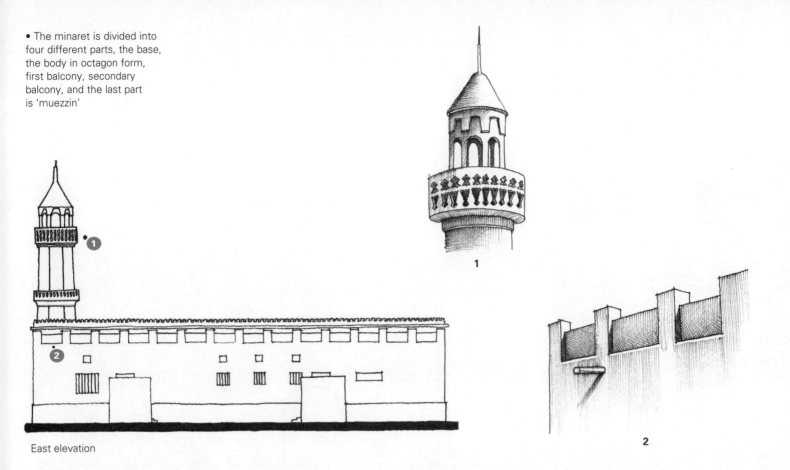

East elevation

1

2

• Entrance to the mosque

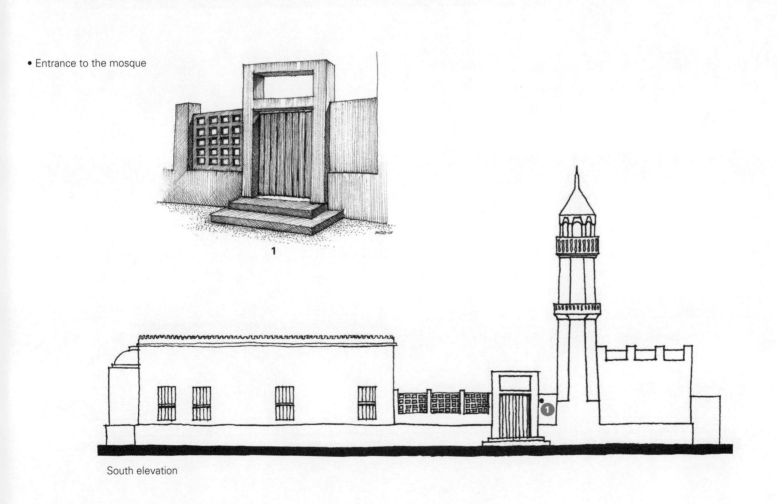

1

South elevation

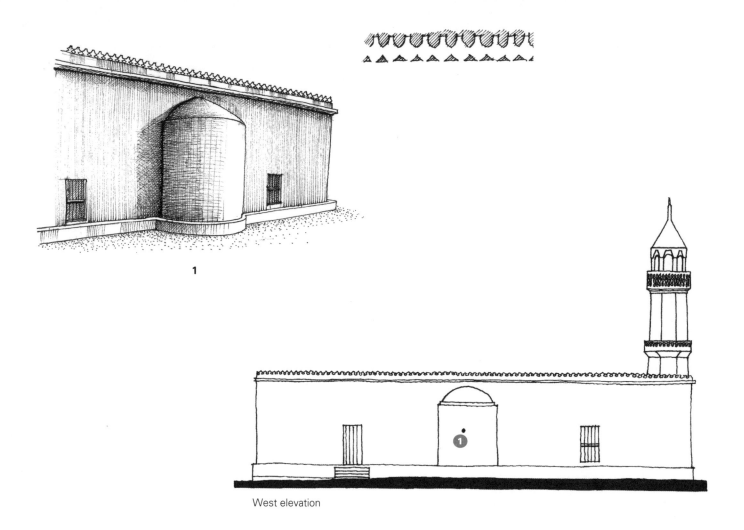

West elevation

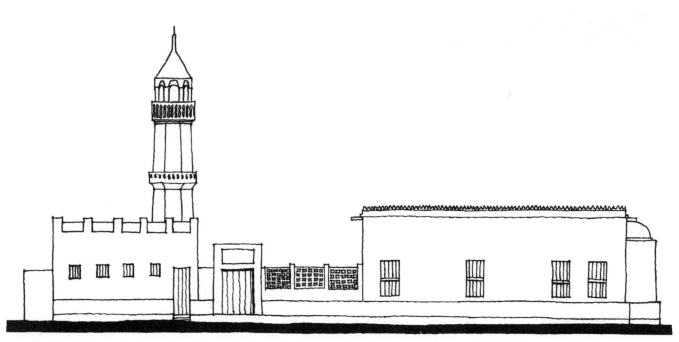

North elevation

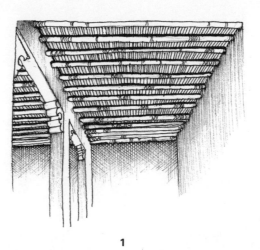

• Traditional roof

1

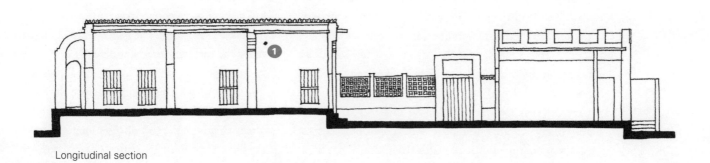

Longitudinal section

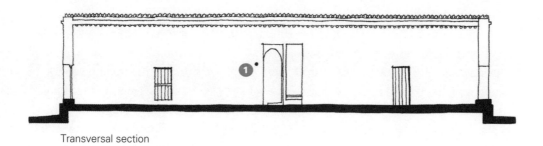

Transversal section

1

Old Mosque (Sumaismah) (1945)

Brief Description and History

The Old Mosque at Sumaismah dates from the year 1945. The Old Mosque (Masjid El-Qadim) is one of the mosques built close to the Arabian Gulf seashore. There is one entrance in the north façade of the mosque that leads to the courtyard. It is sited in the middle of the external wall, with a bench built to the right of the entrance. The minaret is located in the north-east corner of the mosque courtyard.

It is worth noting that the minarets of mosques located close to the sea are often taller than those belonging to mosques built inland. It is legitimate to think that they may have had another role aside from their religious one, namely, keeping a watch on the sea and land.

In fact, the minaret of this mosque looks strikingly like a lighthouse.

The Courtyard

The open arcade of the outer *iwan* is in simple post and lintel construction. There are five squared openings. A sixth opening, next to the courtyard's south wall, has been closed in and converted into a room during a recent restoration. The courtyard has a place for the worshippers to wash in the south-east corner. This area has recently been restored and provided with a water tank. The minaret is situated in the north-east corner of the courtyard. A room has been added along the south wall, probably during the restoration project.

The Minaret

The minaret has a square base on which a tall, cylindrical body stands. It is one of the tallest minarets among the old mosques, standing 10.23 metres high. The minaret is topped by four vertical pillars and a conical dome, which together enclose the space from where the *muezzin* calls the faithful to prayer. A spiral staircase leads to the top of the minaret. The stairs have been built in the traditional way, consisting of pieces of wood tied with ropes then covered with mud. A layer of cement has been recently added.

The Open Prayer Area

The open *iwan* leads to the courtyard through five squared portals. The sixth portal has been converted into a room. The roof of the *iwan* has been covered with pieces of thin painted plywood veneer, thus hiding the traditional roof, but in doing so one of the major elements of traditional Qatari architecture has been lost. Three doors lead into the closed *iwan*, two peripheral ones and a middle one, which face directly toward the *kebla*. The doors are made of wood and have been restored.

The *Kebla Iwan*

The *iwan* is rectangular and has steps leading to the *imam*'s bench to the right of the *kebla*. This *iwan* has been completely renovated. The traditional roof has been covered with thin plywood veneer and painted white. The walls have also been painted, and carpets have been laid to cover the cement-coated floor. All the openings in the wall of the *iwan* have been covered by wall cabinets or fitted with wooden doors. In consequence, they have also been covered over on the external walls, thus the *iwan* has no window openings. The only protrusion is that of the *mihrab*, which also has no windows or openings.

The exterior of the *mihrab* has a half-dome at the top with a few light decorations. There are also six plastic (PVC) drainpipes protruding through the rear wall parapet for rainwater drainage.

• Aerial perspective. There is one entrance in the north façade of the mosque that leads to the courtyard. The minaret is located in the north-east corner of the mosque courtyard

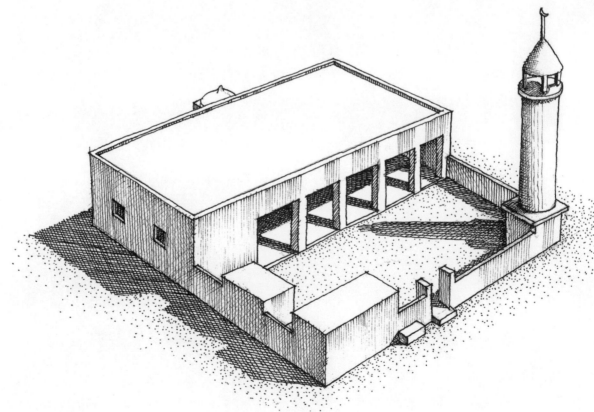

• Ground floor plan. The inner *iwan* and open *iwan* are almost similar in size. The open arcade of the outer *iwan* is a simple post and lintel construction. The open *iwan* leads to the courtyard through five squared portals

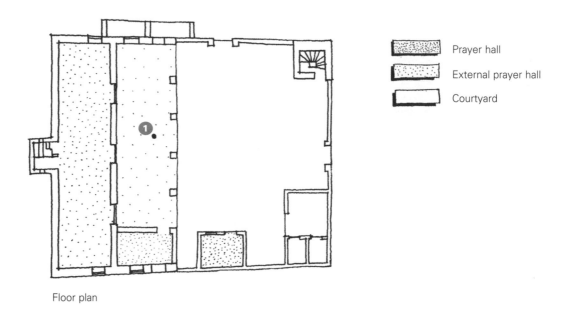

Floor plan

	Prayer hall
	External prayer hall
	Courtyard

• View of the outer *iwan* inside

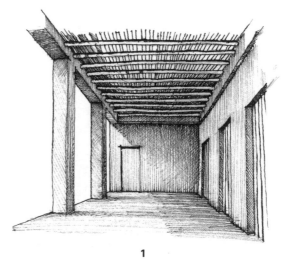

1

• View of the mosque

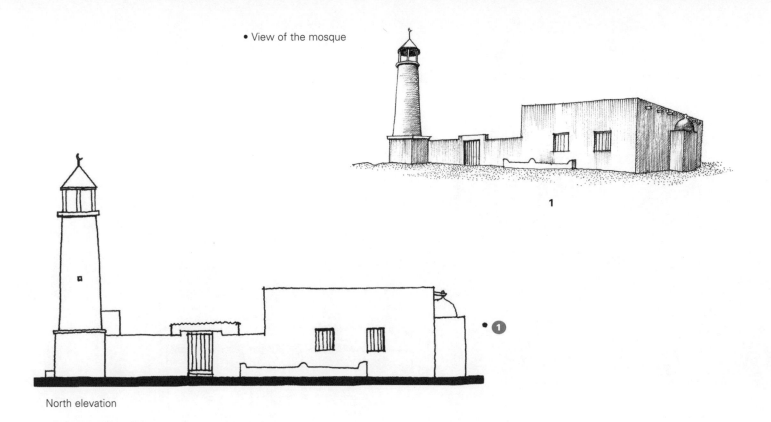

1

1

North elevation

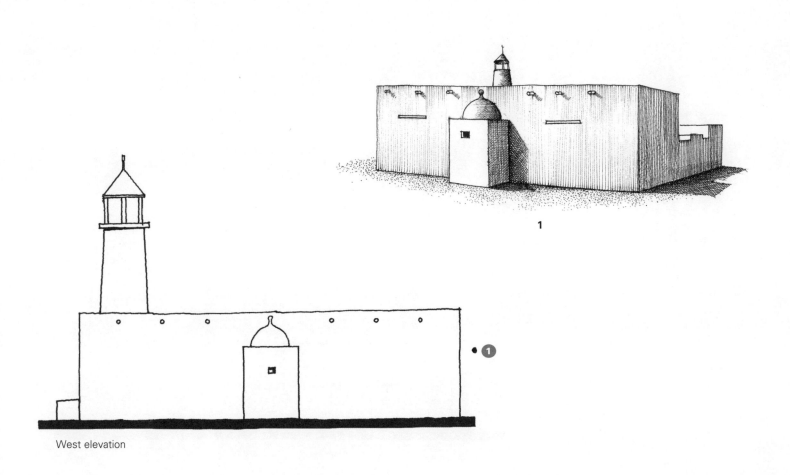

1

1

West elevation

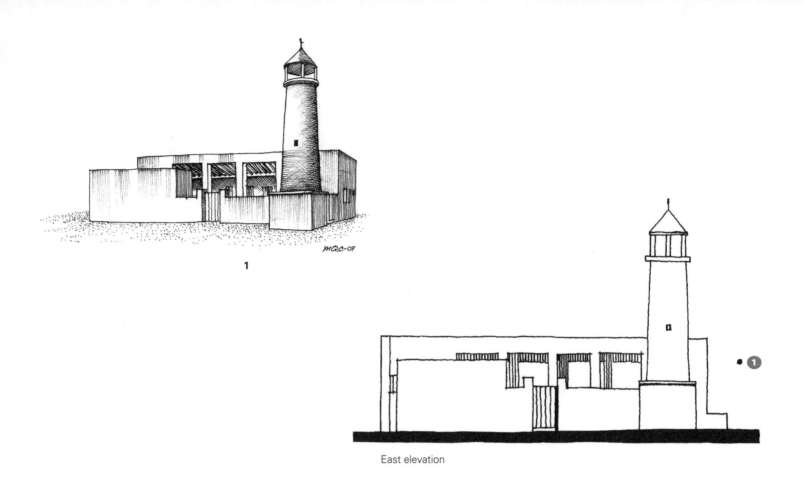

East elevation

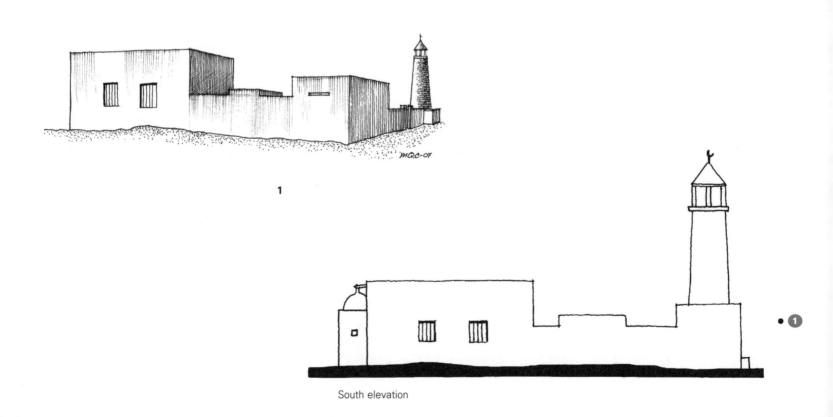

South elevation

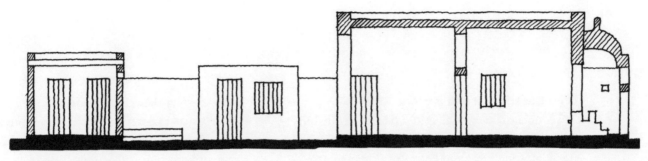

Longitudinal section

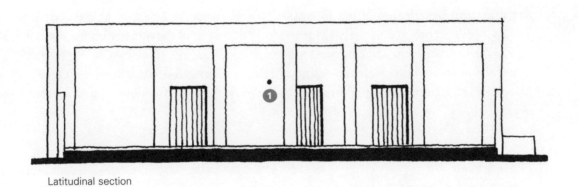

Latitudinal section

• View of the outer *iwan*

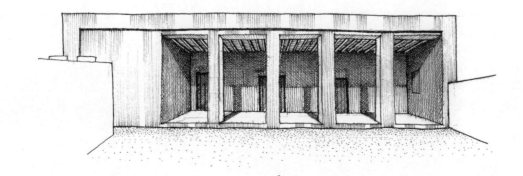

1

Sumaismah Mosque (Sumaismah) (1945)

Brief Description and History

Sumaismah mosque is located on the outskirts of a seaside village. The area surrounding the mosque is flat and there are no remains to indicate that there were ever buildings close by it. The village has the same name as the mosque, Sumaismah, and was inhabited by pearl divers. It is a popular place to catch crabs during the autumn months. There are two other old, small mosques close by.

Architectural Description of the Mosque

The area covered by the mosque is 325 square metres. The entrance into the courtyard is through one of the doors of the mosque. The courtyard has two exterior facing entrances and lies parallel to the mosque's *iwan*. The school, the minaret and the mosque's open *iwan* overlook the courtyard.

El Madrasah

The *madrasah* (the scriptures school) is in a chamber at the north-east corner of the courtyard and occupies approximately 24 square metres (3.79 × 6.75 m). There is a window on each side of the door to the *madrasah*. The side facing the courtyard originally had two openings but these were closed completely during the restoration process.

It is evident that these two openings were *badgheers*, i.e. rectangular recesses built to let air in but keep dust out. It is a solution developed to suit the climate and one of the characteristic elements of classical Qatari architecture. The *badgheers* also create recesses (*aushan*) on the internal side of the room, which can be used either as benches or shelves.

The Minaret

The minaret of the mosque stands above the *madrasah*. The stairs climb from the courtyard to the top of the minaret on the outside of the tower. The tip of the minaret is covered by a small, slightly-rounded, conic dome that rests on four square pillars. The dome resembles those above the *mihrab*.

The *Meda*

The well is a central component of a mosque. The *meda* is essential to Muslim prayer, and ablution a cornerstone of the ritual, therefore, the well and the place for performing one's ablutions is an integral part of the mosque. The *meda*, which is used exclusively for ablutions, lies at the south-east corner of the courtyard. When entering by the south gate of the courtyard, you will find the *meda* on the right.

The Mosque

The mosque consists of the open *iwan* and the *iwan al kebla*. The open *iwan* overlooks the courtyard and has nine arches on eight square pillars. The arches are square and decorated with a *kebla* at each right angle. The façade is just over 19 metres long.

Each side wall of the open *iwan* has two windows. The open *iwan* leads to the *iwan al kebla* through three doors. The middle door is located in the centre of the wall and when opened faces the *iwan al kebla* directly.

The wall where the *kebla* is situated has eight windows, four on each side of the *mihrab*.

The *mihrab* is rectangular with two small, pointed domes on the top exterior. Inside the *mihrab*, there are several steps that lead to the stone bench for the sheikh.

Building Materials

The materials used in the construction of the mosque reflect a close relationship with the environment as well as cultural suitability.

The sea and the desert were the inspiration for the builders, as well as the sources of the building materials.

Coral limestone is used as a construction material for the walls of the mosque. Coral is hard to shape, hence it imposes a certain way of building.

The corals have to be laid horizontally and then held together with a binding material consisting of lime sand. This form of construction allows the erection of thick, insulating walls that help to keep the heat and the cold out.

The placing of the cross beams so that they slope slightly permits rainwater to flow towards the external walls and then down through wooden drains on the outside of the hall where the *kebla* is. This protects the roof from the standing rainwater. Trunks of imported *danshal* wood are used as the main cross beams for the roof. They are covered first with *basgill* and then with *mangharour*. A layer of mortar, consisting mainly of lime sand from the local beach, is then laid above the *mangharour*.

The roof beams of the halls are mainly made from *danshal* wood imported from Zanzibar, on the east coast of Africa. These trees do not grow taller than approximately four metres, consequently, the depth of these halls does not extend more than four metres. This is a good example of how the availability of construction materials influenced the building style.

• Aerial perspective. The mosque is distinctive by its stairs leading to the minaret and the shape of the *mihrab*. The entrance to the courtyard is through one of the doors of the mosque
• Ground floor plan. The mosque consists of open *iwan* and it overlooks the courtyard and has nine arches on eight square pillars. The *mihrab* is rectangular with two small pointed domes on the top

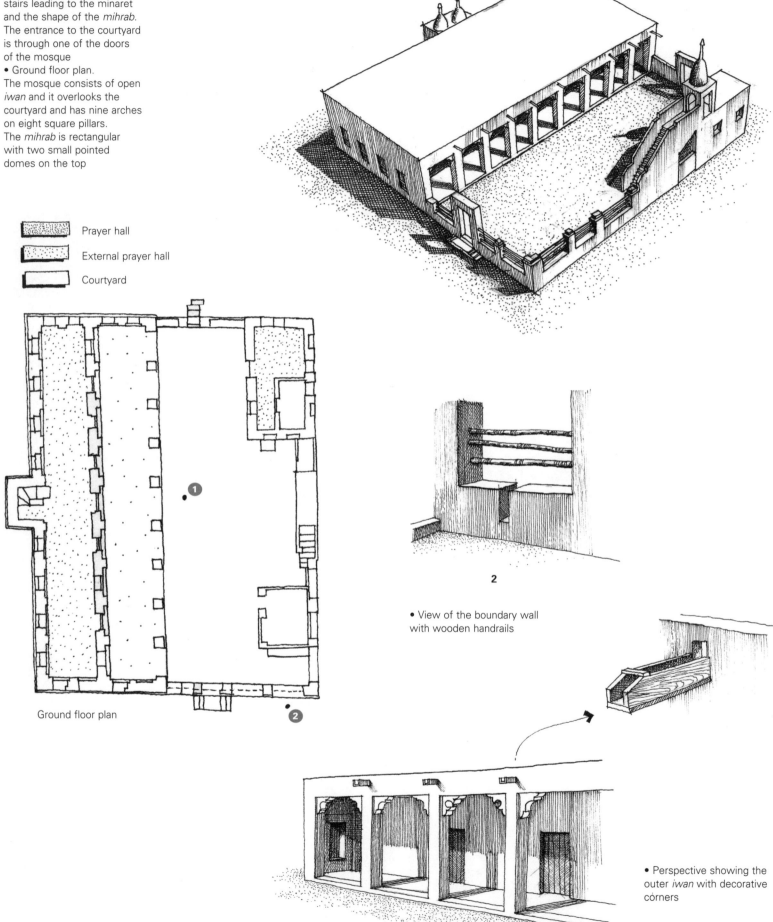

Prayer hall

External prayer hall

Courtyard

Ground floor plan

2

• View of the boundary wall with wooden handrails

• Perspective showing the outer *iwan* with decorative corners

1

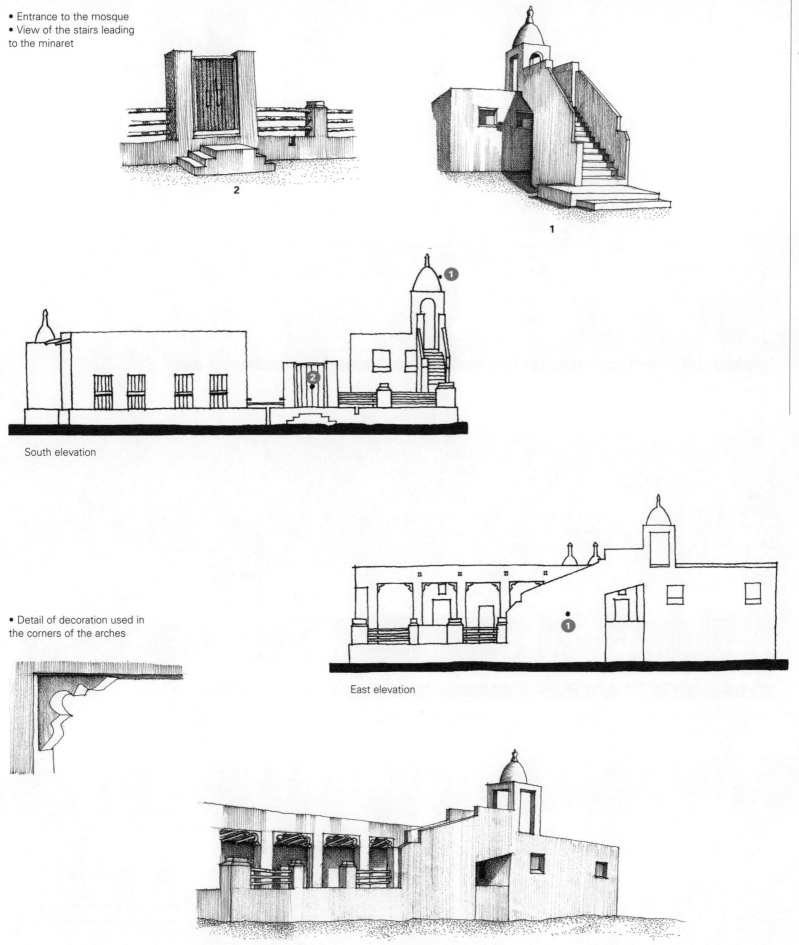

• Entrance to the mosque
• View of the stairs leading
to the minaret

2

1

South elevation

• Detail of decoration used in
the corners of the arches

East elevation

1

• View showing the *mihrab*
with two pointed domes
on the top exterior

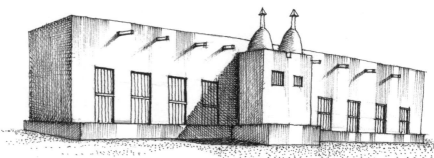

1

West elevation

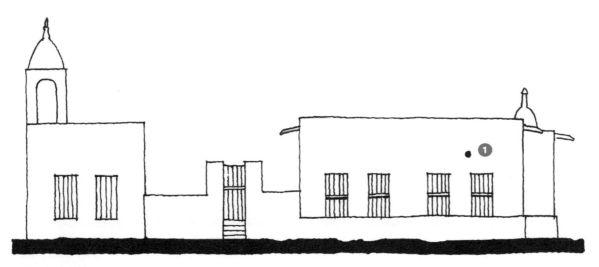

North elevation

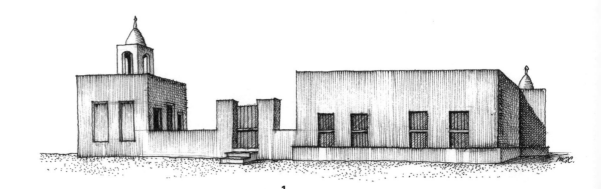

1

304

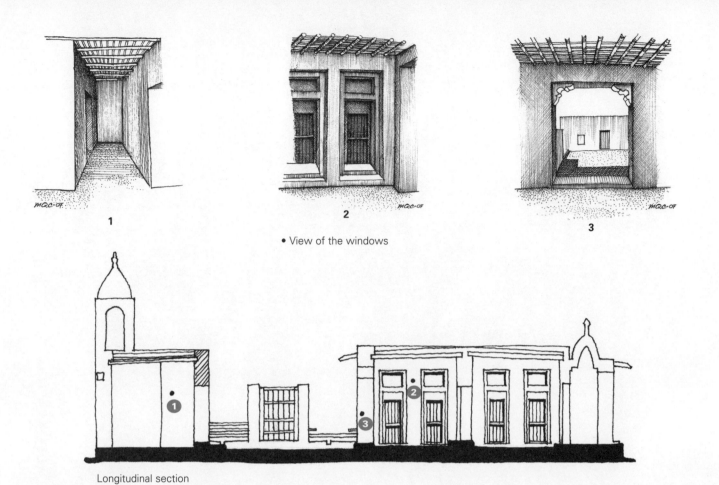

• View of the windows

1   2   3

Longitudinal section

Transversal section

• View of the outer *iwan*

1   2

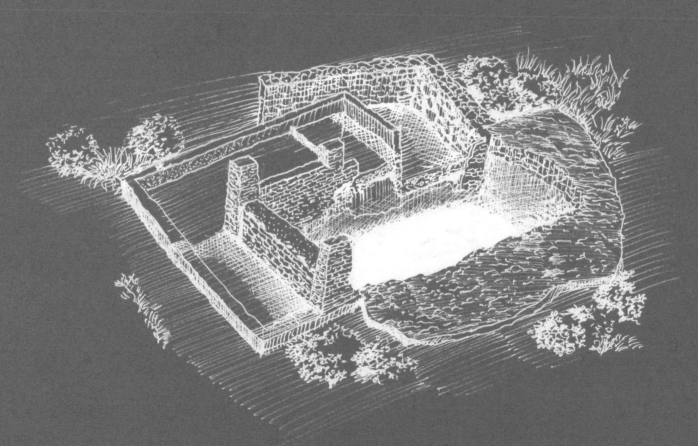

PUBLIC BUILDINGS

Old Al Khor Police Station (Al Khor) (1945)

Brief Description and History

Al Khor is the largest town in Qatar north of Greater Doha. It was once a thriving fishing port and pearling centre. The town extended along the south side of Al Khor Bay and up the low rise that runs inland from the bay. The Old Al Khor Police Station was built in 1945 on the shoreline of what was then the centre of town. Historically, police stations and police posts were often constructed at harbour locations for security purposes, as most traffic entering or leaving town, as in the case of Al Khor, was by sea.

Today, Al Khor is a quiet town best known for its attractive Corniche overlooking the scenic bay. The Old Police Station was completely restored in 1991 and is now the home of the Al Khor Museum. It stands at the east end of the landscaped portion of the Corniche.

Architectural Description of the Building

The original police station consisted of a simple, two-storey, rectangular building measuring 9 by 13.5 metres. There is a small watchtower room, approximately 3.5 metres square, extending to a second floor at the north east corner of the original building, giving that area of the building a total height of approximately 11 metres. This older building forms the south (two-storey) portion of the museum that exists today. It is constructed using traditional materials, mainly layered limestone rock covered with thick layers of limestone mud mortar. The rest of the museum, including the top parapet wall on the older two-storey section, is constructed from hollow concrete blocks, suggesting that it was added later.

Befitting the historical museum which it now houses, the building has been meticulously restored. Particular attention was given to installing wooden windows and heavy wooden doors throughout. Reproductions of the originals were fitted where necessary, however, refinishing of the original wood was completed wherever possible.

The original ceilings have been carefully and meticulously restored as well and add to the historic aura of the museum rooms below. These are constructed of *danshal* wood tree limbs, overlain with *basgiil* and *mangharour*. The roof surface on top of the building was originally covered with a layer of rocks topped with *tanqa al-tiin* mud plaster. During restoration, the roof was rebuilt with more modern materials, including the use of roofing paper covered with a top layer of gravel. Though not historically accurate, this was done to provide better waterproofing to protect the museum. On the south façade of the building, four wooden *marsams* project outward in the original style along the roof tile just below the outer parapet wall, which was added later.

A decorative parapet wall, 1.5 metres high, made of hollow concrete blocks, was added to the top of the building. It runs along all four sides of the building, butting against the tower room at the north-east corner.

The exterior of the building has refurbished traditional style wooden windows throughout. The six windows on the south façade (three on each floor) are very similar to the old-style windows found in most of the old mosques, called *derisha*,[1] with wood frames and vertical metal bar inserts.

The one large window on the west façade, near the main entrance from the outside, has decorative lattice-like wooden shutters, to provide privacy whilst letting in air.

The north façade, which contains open porches on both levels, has *derisha*-style windows and a heavy wooden door on each level. The upper porch, called a *riwaq*,[2] is adorned with decorative, lattice-like wood screens between the support columns. These were a common decorative element that provided privacy and overlooked the interior courtyards of traditional-style houses; they could be made either of wood or cement plaster.

The remainder of the museum consists of later additions added for practical purposes, as the rooms used for the museum's exhibits occupy most of the original two-storey structure. The later additions are single storey and contain museum offices, a kitchen and restrooms. They occupy the north half of the museum site and are separated from the main, older building by an open courtyard. The main exterior entrance is in the middle of the west façade, entering through a short wall that connects the older two-storey building on the right with the newer addition to the left.

[1] A *derisha* is a traditional window, which consisted of a wooden frame divided horizontally in the middle, with vertical bar inserts for security when the window was open to let air in.
[2] A *riwaqi* is an open porch or balcony overlooking an interior courtyard, where people would sit during the hot season because it provides more shade than the open courtyard; it is a common feature of traditional courtyard houses.

• The original police station consisted of a simple two-storey, rectangular building. There is also a small watch tower room

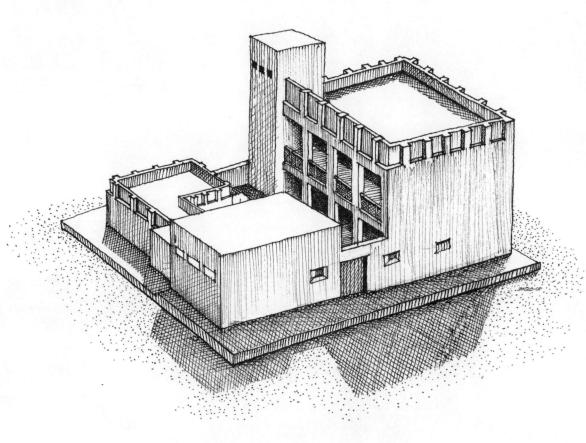

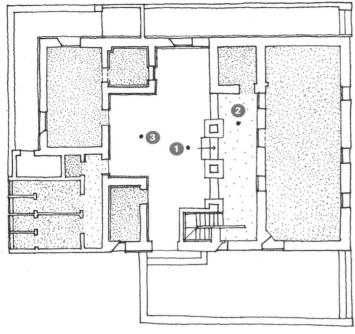

Ground floor plan

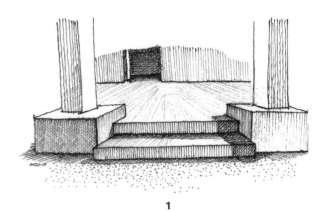

1

• View by entrances to the rooms

• The original ceilings have been restored. These are constructed following the traditional way

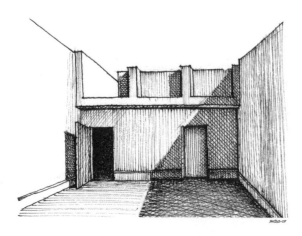

3

2

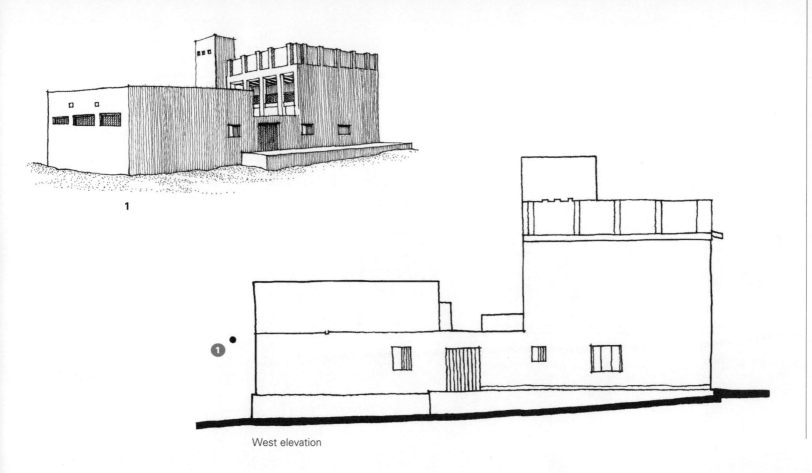

1

West elevation

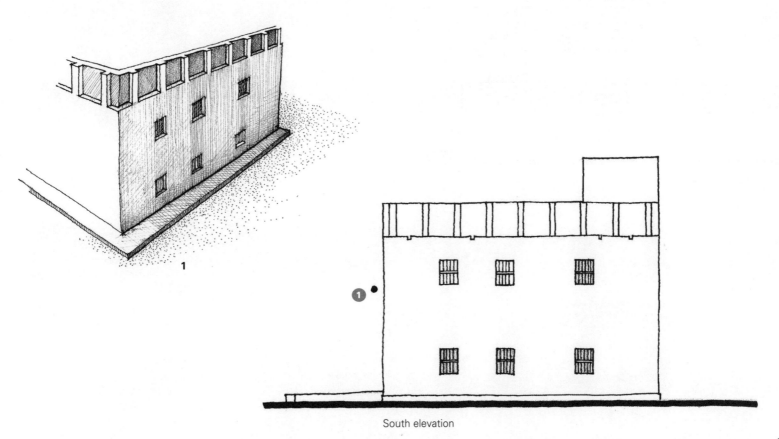

1

South elevation

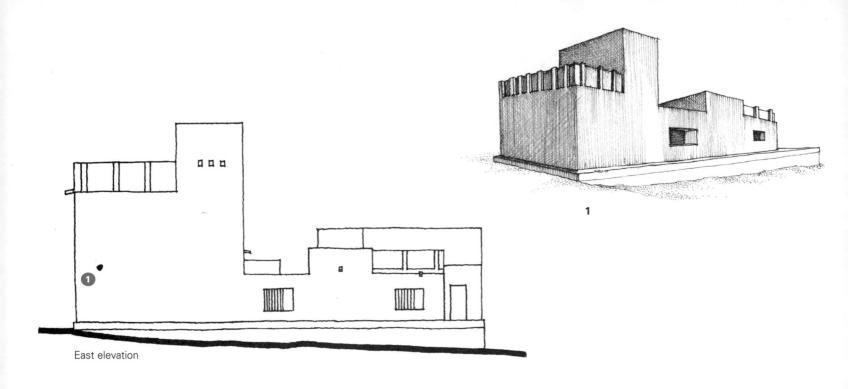

1

East elevation

North elevation

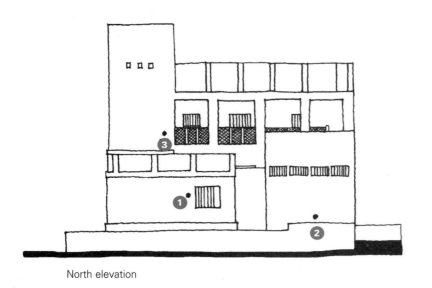

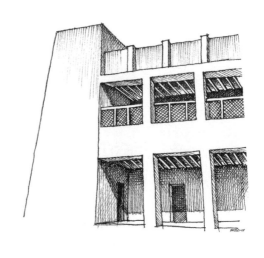

3

• Typical example of window

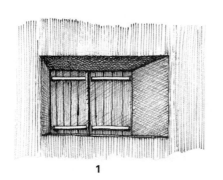

1

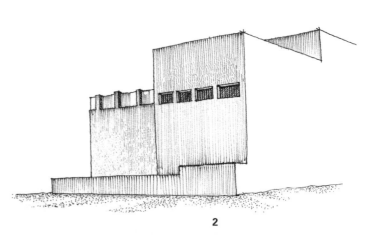

2

312

Head room plan

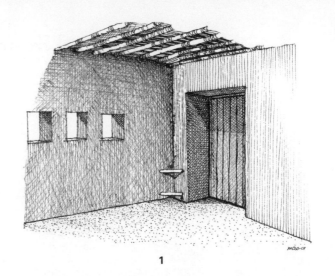

1

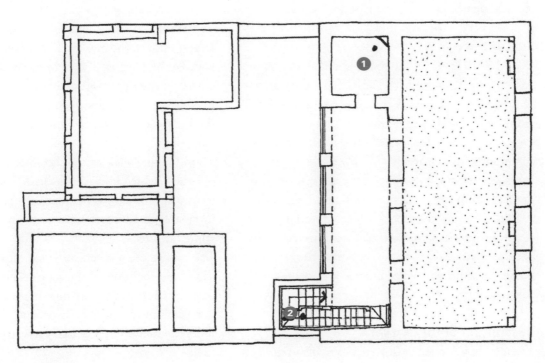

First floor plan

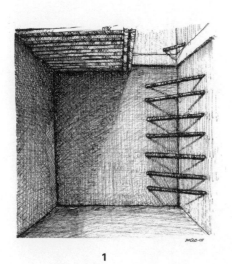

1

2

Old Al Khor Suq (Al Khor)
(1910)

Introduction

Al Khor is a large port to the north of Doha famous for its fish and pearls. The market is named after the town: Suq Al Khor.

Suq Al Khor

Suq Al Khor is one of the few traditional markets still in existence outside of Doha. The market is one of the oldest buildings in the town. Sections of the old urban fabric still surround the market.
The market not only served Al Khor, but other small communities in the area.
A house from the beginning of the last century, the property of the Al-Ansari family, stands behind the market. The suq was probably located in the middle of the residential area and directly connected to the houses adjacent. With the exception of the Ansari house, these have now been replaced by new constructions.

Description of the Market

The market is located close to the mosque, in the centre of the town. Nine shops remain from the original suq. The shops stand in a row, each with a shade in front. The shades rest on large square pillars made of limestone bricks made from *al somy*. The limestone pillars are connected with squared cross bars of imported *danshal* wood. The bars are fixed to the pillars with ropes to form horizontal supports for the courses of the upper parapets, where the drains are fixed. *Danshal* beams are vertically arranged on the lintel of the arches, and then covered with *mangharour*.
The shade rests on several brick courses above the shop walls. Rectangular openings directly beneath the shades in the top of the wall let air flow freely. In this way, a natural air conditioning system is created. The shade also functions as a common meeting place.

Every shop has a large wooden door made of four hinged slabs and a square window that looks onto the backyard. In the middle of the market there is a row of right-angled arches. Here there is a large wooden double door with a *khokha*. This is the largest door in the market, but is now blocked by a wall on the inside. The door opens to a vestibule, where on the right side, another door used to lead to a backyard. The door is narrow, so it is likely that the backyard had another entrance for animals and goods.
The adjoining walls of the shops have some low openings, which now are blocked. They used to connect the shops. Perhaps the opening made it possible to go from one shop to another without going outside.
The roof of the market is divided into two parts; the shade and the roofs of the shops. The shades end near the shop-fronts and contain the drains to carry rainwater away. The shop roofs end close to the rear to let the rainwater flow easily towards the wooden drains.

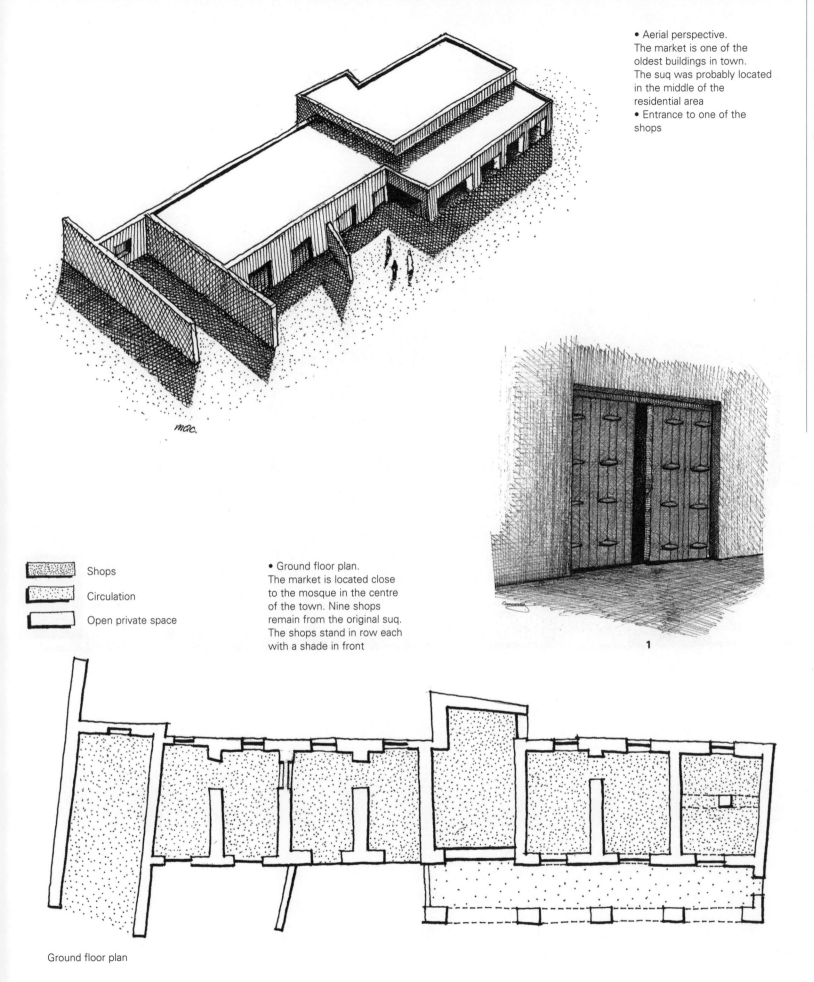

• Aerial perspective.
The market is one of the
oldest buildings in town.
The suq was probably located
in the middle of the
residential area
• Entrance to one of the
shops

Shops

Circulation

Open private space

• Ground floor plan.
The market is located close
to the mosque in the centre
of the town. Nine shops
remain from the original suq.
The shops stand in row each
with a shade in front

1

Ground floor plan

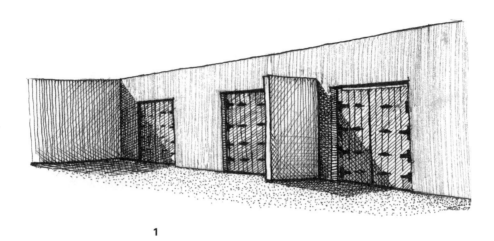

1

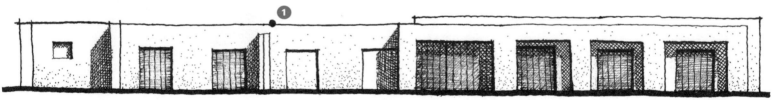

North elevation

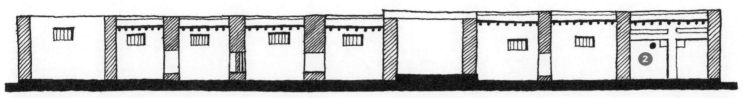

Section A-A

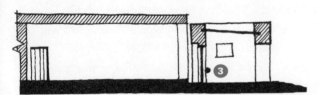

Transversal section

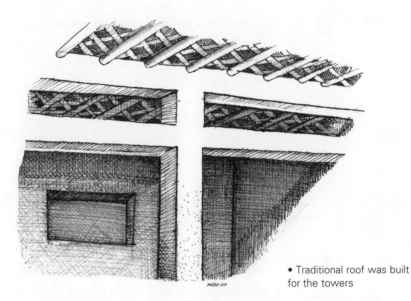

• Traditional roof was built for the towers

2

3

Suq Al Baker (Doha)
(1950)

Introduction

The suqs in Old Doha were among the first facilities to be built. Around the middle of the twentieth century, the suqs area lay adjacent to the sea with some buildings directly on the shoreline, close to the port area for easy unloading of goods. It was a very active part of Doha City. All the trade took place here and Suq Al Baker formed part of the daily routine at the time.

The contemporary building is not very old and most of the buildings that used to constitute the old suqs are now demolished.

In general, all the old suqs in the Arabian Gulf Region were similar in layout and general form. They consisted of a lines of small shops facing other lines of shops. The *sikka* between them was usually covered to shelter people from the sun and the heat.

Suq Al Baker

Suq Al Baker is one of the few traditional markets remaining in Doha. It forms part of Doha's history, as it houses one of the original restaurants and "juice stalls" of the older areas of the city. The building it is sited in, as it stands today, is modern, with two storeys. The upper floor has been added relatively recently. Judging from photographs, the original market was a small, single-storey structure with two rows of shops and a covered walkway between. Other suqs nearby serviced the port.

Description of the Market

The market is located close to the mosque, in the centre of the old town, where the commercial activities usually take place. Suqs like Al Baker were not only places for commercial activities. They also functioned as important meeting places for travelling merchants and were called *wakalat*.

The strong influence of Islamic architecture in other Arab countries is evident in the structure of the market. Nevertheless, the architecture of each country possessed its own characteristics.

The interplay of the architectures in Qatar and other Arab countries lies behind the special structure of the suq.

Unfortunately, little of the original building remains, as the Suq Al Baker has recently been rebuilt. The modern structure, however, still serves as an active market, with many jewellery and multipurpose shops. Its proximity to a large mosque makes it popular with local people. The upstairs area has been converted into accommodation, with many small rooms. This occupies approximately a quarter of the roof area, leaving the rest open. Stairs on the east side of the *sikka* lead to an open hallway and the upstairs rooms. The hallway then has access to the open part of the roof. Less than 12 months ago, another structure was added on the east side of the market.

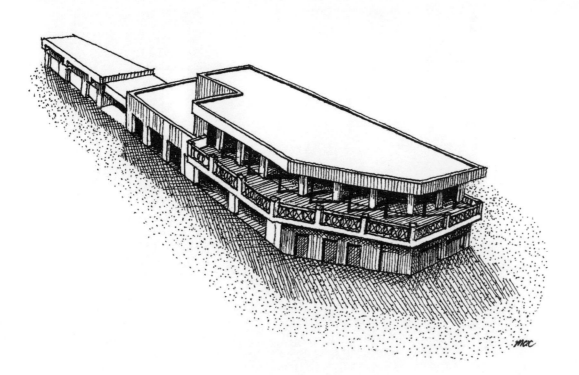

• Aerial perspective.
Suq Al Baker is one of
the few traditional markets
remaining in Doha.
The layout of the suq and
form consisted of a lines of
small shops facing other lines
of shops. The streets (*sikka*)
between them was usually
covered to protect people
fron the sun and the heat

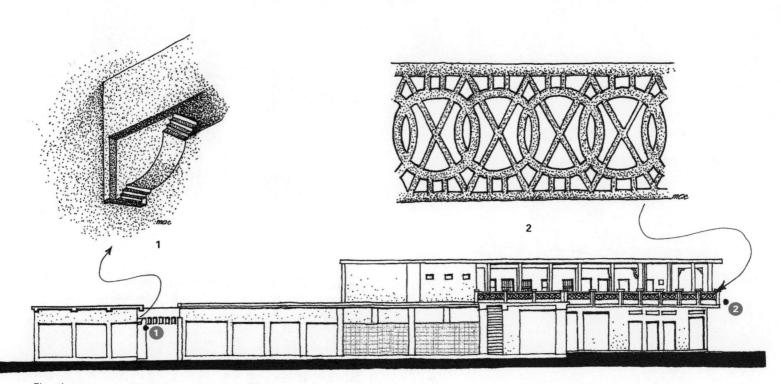

1

2

Elevation

1

2

3

• The perspective indicates shaded area for the shop

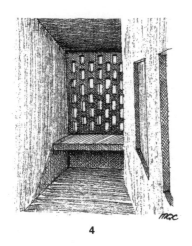

4

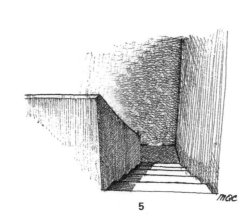

5

• View of the stair

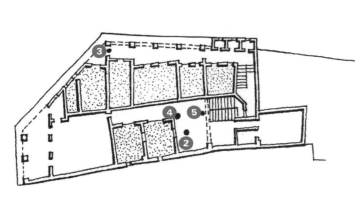

First floor plan

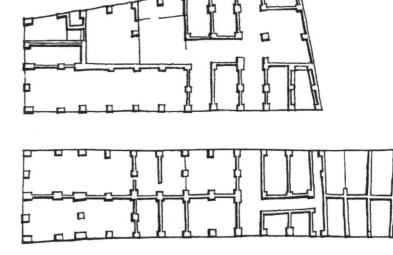

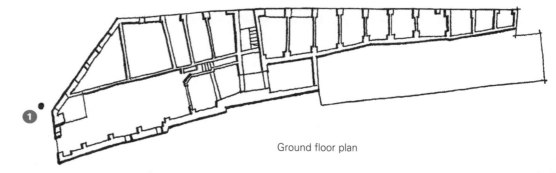

Ground floor plan

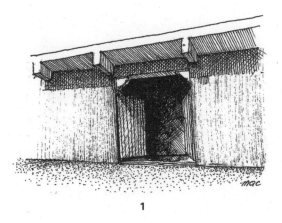

1

• Detail of traditional roof

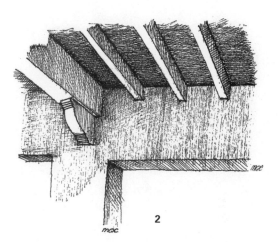

2

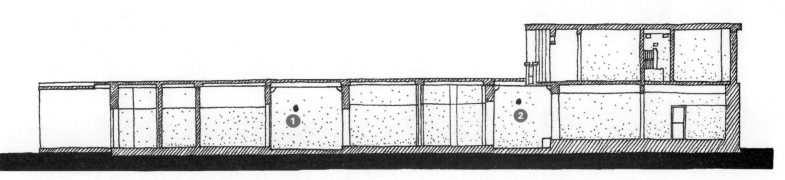

Section

Al Shagab Water Well (Al Rayyan)
(1935)

Introduction

Freshwater wells were very rare in old Qatar. Their scarcity made them so critical that tribes used to fight over them and built forts around them to keep them protected from the enemy. Usually, civilisation developed on the coastline where most activities occurred, such as fishing, pearl diving, and trade. However, farmers needed to go inland to graze their flocks, so the construction of forts around wells was also able to provide shelter for farmers and their flocks.

Wells were of two types: freshwater and saltwater. The former were very scarce. In Doha, for example, only two sources of drinking water were available, in Musheirib and Noueija, while saltwater wells were more widely available, with one in almost every house. The water they provided was used for washing and cleaning purposes.

Architectural Description of the Well

Al Shagab well lasted longer than other wells, probably because it stands as an entity on its own. Dating from 1935, part of the main walls of the well still exist, together with 3 columns of the roof structure that sheltered those who came for water and protected the well from the elements. The main floor of the well no longer exists but some evidence of it is still present. On the north and south facades there are two benches approximately 85 centimetres high.

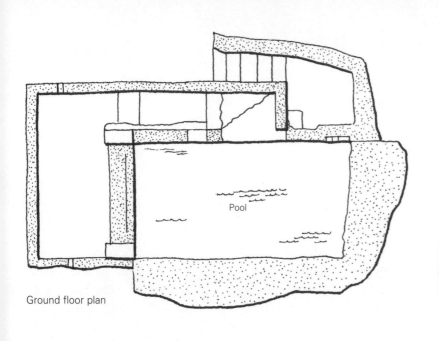

Ground floor plan

• Ground floor plan. Fresh
water were very rare in
Qatar. People in the past built
forts in order to protect the
water well from the enemy

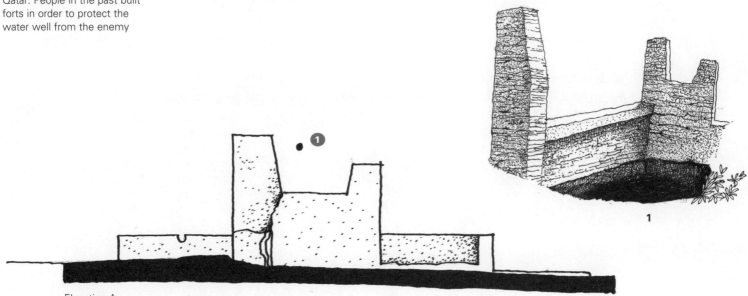

Elevation A

1

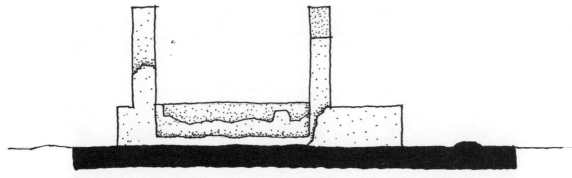

Elevation B

Al Shagab Swimming Pool (Al Rayyan) (1935)

Introduction

A distinctive feature dating from 1935, the swimming pool was unique for its period. Built about nine kilometres from the sea in an area that was then virtually empty of buildings (at that time housing had not reached further than Al Asmakh), this pool was probably part of a larger complex that included a *majlis*.

Architectural Description of the Well

The pool, a rectangle measuring 8 by 6 metres, is built on a base approximately a metre high and can be reached up a flight of six steps on the east side.

The building contains three pools, two of them are inside the structure, the third lies outside. The first indoor one is not very deep and has a bench-like structure inside. This smaller pool opens out onto the main pool outside through a low square opening, while the largest and deepest pool lies adjacent to the east façade of the building. Five columns divide the east façade into four square arches, while the north façade has four columns. The building material is stone that has been plastered and rendered. The roof composition is *danshal* wood beams overlaid with *basgill* and *mangharour*.

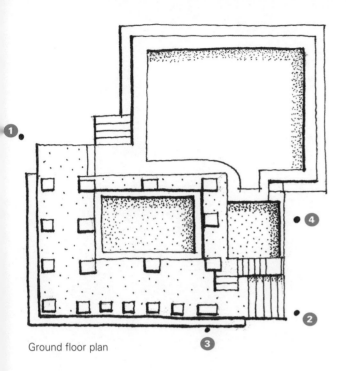

 Ground floor plan

Circulation

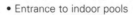

• Ground floor plan. The pool, a rectangle form and contain three pools, two of them are inside the structure, the third lies inside

• Aerial perspective

• Entrance to indoor pools

1

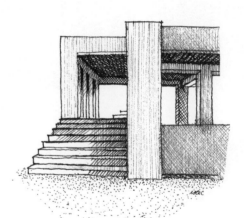

2

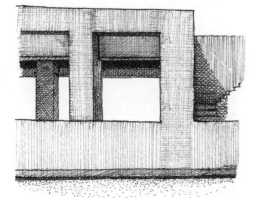

3

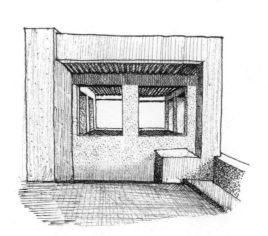

4

• Traditional roof

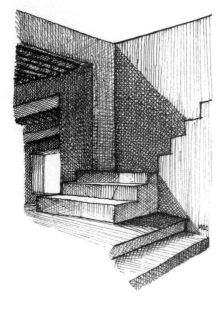

1

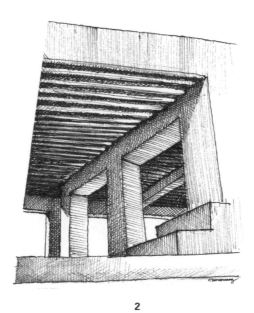

2

3

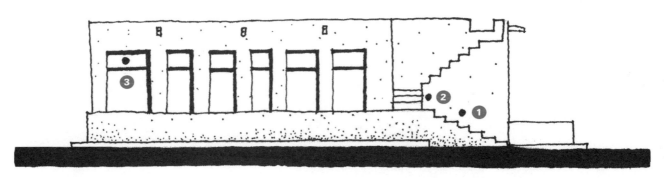

East elevation

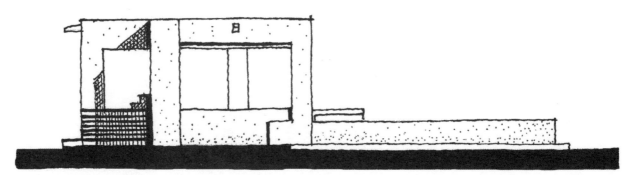

North elevation

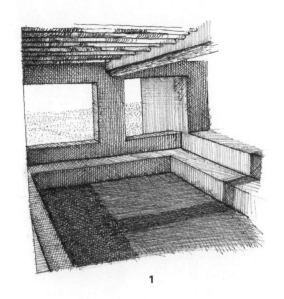

1

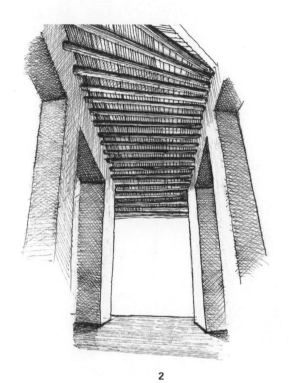

2

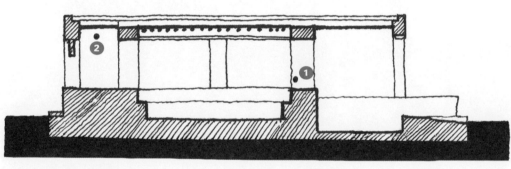

Section A-A

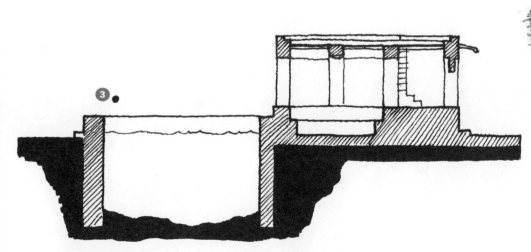

Section B-B

3

Al Shagab *majlis* (Al Rayyan) (1935)

Introduction

Half a kilometre east of Al Shagab horse stables, and a few metres east of Al Shagab swimming pool, stands a detached *majlis* constructed in dates from 1935. Isolated on all sides, the *majlis* is a distinctive feature.

Architectural Description of the majlis

This *majlis* has a rectangular plan 15 metres long by 9 metres wide. It occupies the east corner of the layout and is bounded by an L-shaped porch that provides shelter from the heat of the sun and helps to decrease the heat absorbed by the *majlis*. The façade of the porch is fitted with arcades supported on heavy square columns. The east and south sides of the building are both fitted with recesses above the wooden windows. The windows follow the traditional design of windows in Qatari houses, consisting of wood leafs installed behind a grill of steel bars. The roof is the traditional design of *danshal* wood beams overlaid with *basgill* and *mangharour*.

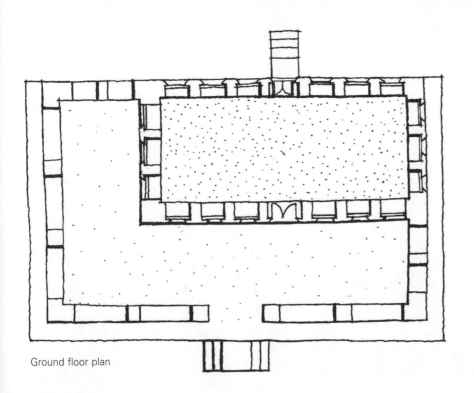

• Ground floor plan.
The *majlis* has a rectangular
plan. It occupies the east
corner of the layout that
provides shelter from the
heat of the sun

Ground floor plan

• Aerial perspective isolated
on all sides. The *majlis* is a
distinctive feature

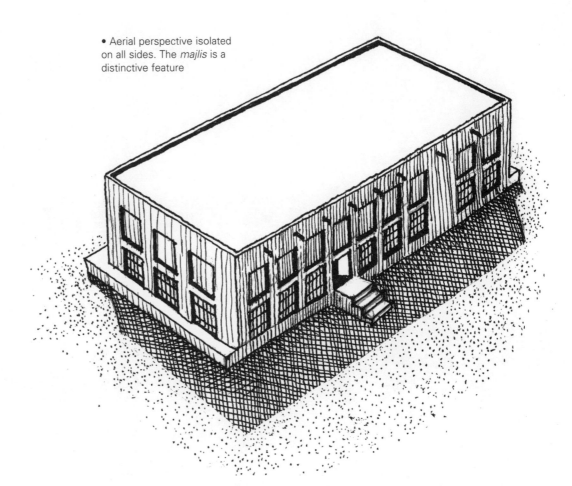

• Detail of the entrance
to the *majlis*

• Perspective showing details
of windows and recesses on
the external walls

• Another view of the
windows and recesses
• The shaded porch
decorated with window and
recesses on the walls

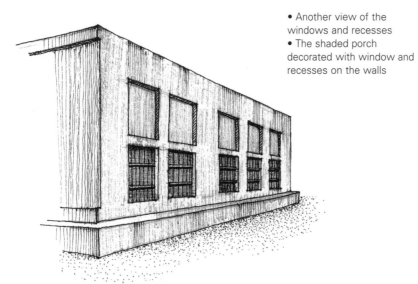

1

2

• South elevation.The façade of the porch is filled with arcades supported on heavy square columns

South elevation

East elevation

The Future of Qatari Architecture

The aim of this book has been to present major trends in Gulf vernacular architecture. Gulf States are marked by the extraordinary expansion and transformation wrought by urbanisation. Furthermore, throughout the Gulf States, rapid urbanisation accompanied by population growth has had a significant impact on local architecture. Economic growth and diversification intended to reduce dependence on oil revenues has resulted in the flow of people, goods and capital into the Gulf States. As a consequence of its ability to attract investors and instantly translate funds into large real estate projects, the Gulf has undergone spectacular urban transformation in just a few years. Therefore, the cities of the Gulf boast many examples of modern architecture. However, this wealth should not be allowed to divert attention from the heritage of traditional building forms. Throughout the Arabian Peninsula varied forms of traditional architecture exist that combine distinctive decorative features with forms that have developed in response to the region's demanding climate.

In his article Elsheshtawy (2008: 4) argues that the Arab/Middle Eastern city is caught between a variety of worlds, ideologies, and struggles. The author means that the Arab/Middle Eastern city struggles with modernity and is trying to secure a place among the twenty first-century cities.

In the case of Qatar the beginning of the oil period signalled the start of the transformation of vernacular architecture. This transformation may in part be explained by a change in how the house expresses the standing of its owner. The introduction of this new architectural language occurred at a high social level, and has extended beyond detail to embrace the overall form of the house. It is argued here that the loss of local, vernacular traditions may have been due to a simultaneous weakening of adherence to old structures and style, which have been freed of their status associations and

thus made possible the spread of the new architecture. Furthermore, the introduction of durable building materials and modern technologies may have encouraged clients to select modern housing designs.

This book has shown that traditional Qatari architecture was influenced by cultural, social, political and economic logic in terms of its physical fabric, layout, and the uses to which space was put, but these characteristics can provide a lesson for modern design and planning practices. Vernacular Qatari architecture can easily be adapted to meet the requirements of modern functionality and high living standards while maintaining congruence with our natural, social, and cultural environments. It remains relevant to and viable in the urban requirements of modern society, as has been confirmed by a number of schemes, such as Hassan Fathi's vernacular architecture projects in Egypt.

Unlike other architectures, Islamic architecture in general and Qatari architecture in particular originated in the Arabian Peninsula. It involved city planning along with its squares, streets and styles of accommodation, and was affected by economic and climatic conditions in addition to social customs. In the traditional model, the mosque is usually situated in the city centre and the minarets are high enough to provide a landmark to arriving travellers. The souk in the city centre defined the major streets, and the physical layout of the neighbourhoods – based on the values of extended family and privacy – together formed the underlying structure of the urban form.

Today, modern and postmodern architecture have gone their own way and disregarded tradition, with the result that architectural identity has been erased: for example, courtyards, narrow streets and architectural styles have disappeared. Then, deconstruction architecture emerged, a philosophy that opposes valuing one's architectural heritage. It can be argued that we need a new approach, one that maintains the principles of vernacular architecture but which takes advantage of some of the modern technologies. This approach is called the *renaissance of vernacular architecture*. In practice, this is simply the desire to revive traditional architectural style whilst including modern techniques and sustainable design practices. At a practical level, the new vernacular architecture will respond to cultural and climatic factors. In today's design, these are important for the preservation of local culture and the minimisation of energy consumption. To respond to Qatar's climate, small windows and shading devices can be used to repel the heat during the summer months while letting sunlight in during the winter period. Buildings can be shaped to catch the light summer wind and the interior space designed to allow that air to circulate. Landscaping elements, such as trees and plants, can protect buildings from solar heat and strong winds. The selection of suitable building materials should take into consideration durability and environmental factors. In addition to these aspects, cultural identity must also be considered in the design process.

Tourism too could benefit by the adoption of the renaissance of vernacular architecture. Architecture, construction and design are all drawing the attention of the public today, but the innovative potential of contemporary architecture to attract the public is still hard-ly used in the tourism industry, though it could simultaneously benefit the process of maintaining the cultural heritage and identity of Qatari architecture. Traditional architecture and the function and design of tourism-related projects in Qatar have not been taken into consideration in the past. What has to be remembered is that hospitality projects such as hotels and resorts shape the cultural heritage, landscapes and living environments of the local population as well as affecting tourists' perception of their surroundings. In the long term, the objective is to bring about sustainable tourism development in addition to raising tourism in Qatar through contemporary architecture and design. Historical buildings are still important signatures as well as highly valued objects; therefore the new research agenda should reconsider the preservation of traditional architecture and integrating it internally within the city. Furthermore, at the city level the new research should focus on forming a new urban cluster based on efficient use of space, house types, livable streets, and public spaces.

In this line of thinking, a new approach to understand the old traditional city is proposed with an aim to contribute at preserving local identity, creating a new shape of city and ensure a sustainable development of this particular architecture and society.

Glossary

Al somy: a kind of limestone which can be easily found anywhere in the desert.

'Ayyin: mud that it is used for construction as a mortar.

Arrish: a small room made of palm leaves.

Aushan: a recess in a wall, sometimes decorative.

Badgheer: a rectangular opening designed to let air in but keep the dust out.

Bait: a house.

Basgill: bamboo lain over *danshal* wood beams in traditional roof construction.

Benna: a mason or builder.

Bi'r: a freshwater or saltwater well.

Burj: a tower.

Buyut: houses (plural of *bait*).

Danshal: a tree that grows in Zanzibar (now part of Tanzania). Its wood was imported and used in the construction of traditional Qatari buildings.

Datcha: Qatari name for a bench.

Derisha: a traditional window, which consisted of a wooden frame divided horizontally in the middle, with vertical bar inserts for security when the window was open to let air in.

Diwaniyah: a formal room for receiving (another word for *majlis*).

Faraush: flat coral stones usually found near the beaches used to construct thinner walls.

Feriq: a neighbourhood (sometimes the word *freedj* is used).

Fet'ha al murakaba: small holes in the walls of defensive buildings that permit protected viewing and some ability to use small arms against attackers.

Hamam: a toilet.

Haramlik: a courtyard reserved for use by women.

Hasa: rubble.

Hasa bahri: sea rubble.

Housh: a courtyard.

Imam: the man who leads the prayers in the mosque.

Iwan: a vaulted hall that opens onto a courtyard on one side.

Iwan al kebla: the iwan lined on one side by the *kebla*.

Jareed: palm ribbing used in roofing.

Jum'a musjid: Friday mosque.

Juss: a white powder used as a mortar and paint after mixing with water.

Kebla: the prayer wall that faces the direction of Al Kaaba in Mecca.

Khazina: a place for storing valuables.

Khokha: a small door inside a bigger door to allow entry without opening the big doors.

Khor: a bay.

Libbin: earth and chaff mixture for building.

Liwan: the space under an arcade.

Madrasah: a Koranic school.

Mahal al galwah: coffee hall.

Majlis: a formal room for receiving guests (also known as *diwaniyah*).

Malqaf: a wind catcher.

Mangharour: a mat of woven cane branches.

Manzil: a settled Bedouin encampment.

Maqbara: graveyard

Marsam: a wooden drain spout that usually protrudes from an opening in the top parapet.

Masbah: light.

Mastaba: a bench.

Mazaghel: openings in fortified buildings that allowed stones and small objects to be thrown.

Meda: the ablution fountain.

Mihrab: a niche in the wall of a mosque that faces towards Mecca (see *kebla*): it indicates the direction of prayer.

Min'a: a port.

Minbar: the pulpit for the sheikh.

Mirzam: a water spout.

Muezzin: the person who calls the faithful to prayer five times a day from the minaret.

Muqarnas: progressively projecting tiers of niche-like geometric elements. In buildings, they often decorated the hoods of portraits.

Musjid: a mosque.

Naqsh: a carver.

Qatiya: a wall up to head height built to give privacy.

Raushan: a square or rectangular lattice work set into a wall to allow air and light to filter in from the outside.

Riwaq: an open porch or balcony overlooking an interior courtyard, where people would sit during the hot season because it provides more shade than the open courtyard; it is a common feature of traditional courtyard houses.

Sahan: a courtyard.

Saqf danche: a pole and lattice ceiling.

Selamlik: the men's courtyard.

Shamal: a wind from the north-west.

Sikka: an alleyway.

Sufra: a round, woven mat.

Suq: a traditional Arab market.

Tanqa al-tiin: a layer of mud, usually mixed with straw, applied to the top of a roof in a traditional construction.

Ustad: a master-mason.

Wakalat: a kind of commercial station existing in many Arab cities such as Cairo and Aleppo. The *wakalat* consists of many small shops and was where the caravans stayed to sell their goods. These markets were also used for storage, e.g., dates, ropes and fishing equipment.

References

Abdel Al Aal, M. *Gulf Architecture: between the Past, Present and Future*. Dar Al Rateb University, 1985.

Al-Khulaifi, M.J. *Folk Building in Qatar*. National Council for Culture Arts and Heritage, 2000.

Al-Khulaifi, M.J. *Architecture of the Old Palace: Qatar National Museum*. The National Museum for Culture, Arts and Heritage. Museums and Antiquities Dept., 2000.

Al Rostomani, A.H. *Gulf and its Architectural Heritage*. Renoda Modern Printing Press, 1993.

Cruickshank, D. *Sir Banister Fletcher's: A History of Architecture*. S.K.Jain for CBS Publishers & Distributors, 1999.

ElSheshtawy, Y. "The Great Divide: Struggling and Emerging Cities in the Arab World". In ElSheshtawy Yasser (ed.): *The Evolving Arab City: Tradition, Modernity & Urban Environment*. Routledge, 2008.

Hawker, R. *Traditional Architecture of the Arabian Gulf*. WIT Press, 2008.

Kazerooni, F. *Gulf Islamic Architecture*. Oriental Press, 2002.

La Mission Archéologique a Qatar. *Qatar Architectures*, 1984-85.

Mortada, H. *Traditional Islamic Principles of the Built Environment*. RoutledgeCurzon, 2003.

National Council for Culture, Arts and Heritage, Management Engineering Environment (GHD), and Building Engineering Department. *Survey of Old Buildings in Qatar*.

National Council for Culture, Arts and Heritage, Management Engineering Environment (GHD), and Building Engineering Department. *Old Amiri Palace*.

Ragette, F. *Traditional Domestic Architecture of the Arab Region*. Menges, 2006.

Taha, M.Y. *Qatar in Pre-Historic Periods*. National Council for Culture Arts and Heritage, 2003.

Tixier, J. Mission Archéologique française a Qatar: Tome 1. Ministry of Information. Department of Tourism and Antiquities. Dar Al-Uloom, Doha, 1980.

Yarwood, J. & El-Masri, S. *Al Muharraq: Architectural Heritage of a Bahraini City*. Miracle Publishing, 2006.